Winning Converts

Winning Converts

A Symposium on Methods of Convert Making for Priests and Lay People

Edited by Rev. John A. O'Brien

Catholic Answers
SAN DIEGO

Contents

Foreword

WHEN I FIRST read this book, I marveled. Could the Church in America have been *that* successful? Did parishes really produce one hundred or more converts a year, sometimes as many as four hundred a year? Apparently so. Success like that was common enough to be a commonplace.

Part of it, of course, was that in the 1940s there was a sense that being Catholic *mattered*. Nowadays even many Catholics take a "So what?" attitude, having forgotten or never having been told that our Lord established the Church to ease our way to heaven—and implying, by his doing so, that apart from the Church the passage would be rough, if it could be made at all. A lively appreciation of the *necessity* of the Church is something *Winning Converts* may help revive, as it may help revive the conviction that convert making is a praiseworthy activity inseparable from true evangelization.

Reading his words five decades later, we see unintended irony in Fr. John A. O'Brien's remark that this book tells of "the common impression of our laity that they have no duty to help in the winning of souls for Christ, that such is exclusively the business and concern of the clergy." How different today! Most evangelization work is conducted not from the pulpit, not from the rectory, but in the work place, at the university, on the sidewalk, and it is conducted mainly by laymen, not by priests. This is not to say priests no longer participate, but evangelization now has a lay stamp.

Fr. John T. McGinn opened his contribution with an especially poignant sentence: "The writer takes the view that the American clergy are vividly aware of the necessity of a more systematic and energetic apostolate to the non-Catholics of our country." In light of the near absence from most pulpits, for thirty years or more, of any mention of the need to seek converts, this line throws into relief the extent to which evangelization has become a lay enterprise.

Five decades ago there were high hopes. Fr. O'Brien expected Catholics "to transform the meagre number of converts now trickling into our parishes into torrential streams," but the torrential steams did not materialize. In the decades that followed the publication of *Winning Converts*, conversions dipped, then plummeted, and the Church grew not so much because the unchurched or Protestants were being brought into it, but because of the baby boom and immigration. Still, Fr. O'Brien was right to sense the power of "the good will and latent zeal of our laity."

That power finally is beginning to manifest itself, as lay Catholics begin to appreciate the necessity of evangelization. They are coming to see that the task of the lay convert maker is not to win a debate, but to lay bare the facts. As Fr. O'Brien put it, "The only defense which truth needs is exposition." It is sufficient that we explain the faith—no need to browbeat anyone into accepting it.

Of the original contributors, only one survives at this writing. Fr. William J. Quinlan, ordained in 1938 for the Archdiocese of Chicago, has been in active retirement since 1984. "I always have been a street man, knocking on doors, searching for fallen-away Catholics," he told me. As the title to his chapter suggests, true evangelization involves going "into the highways and byways," looking for people who have been waiting for a reason to investigate the Church for the first time or for an invitation to come home after years of not practicing their faith.

Understandably, getting out is no longer easy for a man in his ninth decade. "Often I don't feel like going door to door," admitted Fr. Quinlan. "Maybe I'm tired or it's dark. But I know there's someone waiting for me, so I go. After all, I'm a priest." That is the spirit in which each of the contributors to *Winning Converts* wrote.

The ninth chapter, "Winning Negro Converts," is credited to anonymous "priests engaged in the work in Chicago." Fr. Quinlan has identified the unnamed priests as Fr. Martin "Doc" Farrell and Fr. Joseph Richards, whose success at making converts bordered on the legendary. We are pleased that Fr. Quinlan's memory allows us to give posthumous credit to such indefatigable fishers of men.

A few words about the text. Except for minor changes in punctuation and capitalization, for the most part the text appears as in the original edition. Chapter-and-verse citations have been added to scriptural quotations.

Most of the apostolic organizations mentioned in these pages are defunct. Of the few that still exist, some have changed their names, while others have changed their purposes. We have omitted street addresses that were printed in the 1948 edition—no sense in trying to fill the dead letter box at the post office.

Population statistics have not been updated. When this book first appeared, there were 25 million Catholics in the U.S. Today there are 60 million. Other figures also need to be read in light of changing demographics.

Readers will note now-dated terminology, such as "colored" and "Negro." Fifty years ago these were the terms preferred by all races. We presume readers will not impute improper sentiments to any of the contributors but will take into account that connotations and usage change over time.

Yes, in some ways *Winning Converts* is a period piece, but it is also a reminder that what once was can be again. More than that, it is a manual of techniques that are as practicable today as they were at mid-century. After all, if a parish in Harlem—an area not known for a high concentration of Catholics—could grow from 318 members to 6,500 in just fourteen years, and if other parishes could report yearly conversions in triple digits, then there is room for hope today.

Karl Keating
President
Catholic Answers

1

The Contemporary Scene in America

Rev. JOHN A. O'BRIEN, Ph.D.
University of Notre Dame

THE STATEMENT OF THE PROBLEM

THE OUTSTANDING PROBLEM facing the Church in America to-day is the winning of the 80,000,000 churchless men and women of our land. In comparison with this, all other problems are secondary. Its achievement will require concerted action on the part of both clergy and laity. It will demand training, discipline, vision, and organization.

No nation can endure half Christian and half pagan. Either one or the other will ultimately become the American way of life. It is like being in a boat in midstream with a fast current. There is no such thing as remaining stationary through inactivity. You either row up stream or you are carried down stream by the current.

The purpose of this volume is to present the most effective methods of winning that vast multitude for Christ. It is designed for the use of priest and people. It shows how, through joint action, the number of converts can be multiplied manifold—how the total of 100,000 converts can be lifted to the several million mark.

The methods have been tried and tested and have proven their effectiveness in all types of parishes and with all kinds of people.

1

They represent a cross-section of the techniques developed by the foremost convert makers of America.

A TIMELY SUGGESTION

In the spring of 1946 we received a letter from Father Albert A. Murray, C.S.P., editor of *Information*, a monthly magazine devoted to the spread of the convert movement, saying in substance: "Interest in convert work is growing among priests and the laity.

Pastors have derived both inspiration and practical guidance from your symposium, *The White Harvest*, which did more than any other work to make them convert-minded. Since that was published, however, there have occurred, as you know, certain developments which it would be well to bring before them. Why not bring out another symposium, say, *The White Harvest Twenty Years Later*? It would do a world of good."

These gracious words from Father Murray, reflecting his wide knowledge of the convert movement, to the spread of which he has devoted his life, strengthened a growing conviction in us that sufficient progress in the working out of new techniques had occurred in the twenty-year interim to warrant a new symposium. His words touched off the springs of action. To his suggestion we owe then the inspiration for this volume.

In order to mirror the significant developments, we again conducted a survey of convert work throughout the nation. Through the kindness of chancery offices from coast to coast, and through appeals to priests in the three leading clergy magazines, we received reports concerning the parishes wherein unusually large numbers of converts were being won. When the returns from the chancery offices poured in, we were startled and thrilled to discover that some parishes were averaging over 200 converts a year!

Topping all was the report from Monsignor William R. McCann, pastor of St. Charles Borromeo and the subsidiary church of St. Aloysius in New York, listing 450 converts for 1946 and a total of 7,000 converts for the past 13 years! That, we decided then and there, warranted a personal visit so that we might glimpse at first hand one of the truly remarkable pieces of convert work being done in America. And it was well worth traveling the 2,000 miles to see.

A MARKED IMPROVEMENT

Chancery offices reported hundreds of parishes wherein the annual total of converts ranged from 25 in small parishes to 100 and more in larger ones. Recalling our survey of some twenty-odd years ago, wherein the parishes passing the fifty mark could be counted virtually on the fingers of two hands, the contrast was both gratifying and encouraging. The priests who had taken time out of their crowded days to detail their methods of winning converts in *The White Harvest* had not labored in vain.

Their spirit, their methods, and their enthusiasm had proved contagious, especially among the young priests and seminarians. Some of the latter, studying and discussing that volume in their clubs and classrooms, flung themselves immediately after ordination into the search for converts. They made it an integral part of their day's routine. Within a dozen years after ordination some of them, like Monsignor Charles Helmsing, have gathered in over 500 converts, and they are still going strong. They trace their inspiration, enthusiasm, and success largely to that symposium.

Since we played but the humble role of bringing together in *The White Harvest* the methods of recruiting and of instructing prospects, employed by the outstanding pioneers in convert work, we think we can with becoming modesty say a brief word—never mentioned before—about that volume.

When we discovered that the publishers had priced the book at $3.75—a high price for a book twenty years ago—we realized at once that it would not reach in any appreciable degree the young priests and seminarians for whom it was chiefly intended. Accordingly, after a few months of languid sale, we purchased the stock and the plates from the publishers and, reducing the price drastically, quickly disposed of the entire stock.

Several editions in paper cover retailing at $1.00 were quickly disposed of. Other editions in cloth cover retailing at half the original price were likewise issued and completely exhausted. Repeated orders for large quantities poured in from the major seminaries of our country and from the American colleges in Louvain and Rome. In the seminaries and among the younger clergy the volume rendered yeoman service, and letters have come to the editor from priests in all parts of the nation, testifying to its helpfulness and asking for more copies.

It is now being brought out in revised form to continue its distinctive service in laying the solid foundation for convert work. The methods of those great pioneers, bringing in totals of converts ranging from 1,000 to 6,000, have not been outmoded. They embody the fundamental principles upon which effective convert work is based. This new volume is designed therefore not to replace it but to supplement it with the account of new techniques and new developments. Both should be read by priests, seminarians, and lay people who wish to have their apostolate crowned with the largest measure of success.

JOINT EFFORTS

To return to our present symposium. We have endeavored to select our contributors from among those priests ministering in parishes reporting unusually high totals of converts. Those totals are generally achieved through the joint efforts of all the priests. We share the solicitude of each contributor to acknowledge the work of his associates, whose voice in telling the story the contributor becomes.

Furthermore we wish to make it clear that our spokesmen in this book are but a slender cross-section of the multitude of zealous and eminently successful convert makers. On the desk before us, as we write, is a long list of convert makers in virtually all the dioceses of the country. We wish that space would permit us to record their individual achievements, made known to us by their ordinaries, chancellors, and brother priests.

The volume has already grown larger than planned, and limitations of space compel us to forgo the detailed mentioning of many parishes wherein flourishing inquiry classes are annually turning out large numbers of converts. We pay tribute here to the hundreds of such unnamed levites. Though too numerous to be mentioned here, their names are not unknown to the Recording Angel.

THE ONE CONVERT MAKER

Another point: God is the only convert maker. Priests and people, even the most zealous and holy, are but his instruments. Many priests are understandably shy about speaking of their convert work. They do not wish to appear to be infringing upon the role that only God can play. Faith is a gift of God. He alone can give the grace which brings the mind of man to an unhesitating espousal of divine truth.

This is the premise underlying our whole discussion, the unwritten paragraph at the beginning of every chapter. Having stated this, we hasten to point out that such a clear recognition of the role which God plays in every conversion is entirely consistent with the effort to develop the most efficient technique of recruiting prospects, of instructing them, and of winning them to an espousal of the gospel of Christ. Ours is the task of developing suitable channels through which God's grace will flow to the inquiring soul.

God uses weak human beings as his agents. His grace does not ordinarily flow through a vacuum but through a human agency. "For Christ therefore we are ambassadors," said St. Paul, "God as it were exhorting by us" (2 Cor. 5:20). Are we better ambassadors of Christ, better spokesmen for the divine Redeemer, when we ignore the art of human persuasion and make no effort to acquit ourselves creditably?

St. Paul answers with a thundering "No!" Listen to his stern admonition to Timothy: "Carefully study to present thyself approved unto God, a workman that needeth not to be ashamed, rightly handling the word of truth" (2 Tim. 2:15).

If there is a serious obligation to prepare ourselves properly to proclaim the gospel of Christ, there is an equally serious obligation incumbent upon us to prepare ourselves as effective "salesmen" of

Christ, capable fishers of men, successful searchers for the sheep that have strayed from the Master's fold.

Since the winning of souls for whom Christ died is a divinely appointed obligation upon all his followers, clerical and lay, there is an obligation upon us to study the methods by which we can most effectively discharge that duty of discipleship. There are few actions more virtuous or more pleasing to God than the action of a convert worker in sharing with his brothers in the sacred ministry the methods which he has found most effective in winning souls.

Holiness and a genuine zeal for souls do not imply a clam-like reticence in regard to a technique for recruiting prospects which a priest has perfected after years of experience. They demand that he proclaim it to his brother priests and people—yes, proclaim it from the housetops. The highest peaks of holiness are being scaled by the individual who wades, through reams and reams of publicity flowing from the press and the radio, to win one soul for Christ.

St. Paul, the greatest convert maker of the ancient world, was willing to become all things to all men that he might win them for Christ. "We are made a spectacle to the world, and to angels, and to men," he tells the Corinthians. "We are fools for Christ's sake" (1 Cor. 4:10). If the great Apostle of the Gentiles was willing to play that humble role for Christ, why should we fear to let our light shine from the mountain top, even though it entails publicity which we fain would escape?

REMOVING A FALSE NOTION

We have developed this point because here and there we have encountered the utterly false notion that reticence concerning convert work is the only appropriate attitude. If this attitude were to become prevalent or widespread, it would do great damage to the efforts to equip priests and people with the most effective methods.

If this attitude were to obtain in regard to preaching, it would erase every course in sacred oratory in every seminary in Christendom and would end by heaping praise upon the individual who with no preparation would mount the pulpit and bring shame upon the gospel of Christ by his inept and boring attempt to preach it.

No! Away with such sham and pretense! Away with an attitude that is in clear violation of the inspired words of St. Paul! Let there be reticence about claiming credit for oneself. But let there be the greatest frankness in sharing with others techniques, methods, hints, and suggestions which will increase the effectiveness of all our efforts in winning souls for Christ. The unspoken sentiment that throbs in the heart of every Catholic in disclosing how he was instrumental in leading souls to the feet of Christ is this: "Not to me, O Lord, but to thy name be praise and honor and glory for ever and ever. Amen." No contributor to this study is "tooting his own horn," but every one of them is trumpeting the power of God.

That is the spirit in which this entire volume is projected and in which every chapter is written. Whenever we speak of convert making, then, it is always in the sense of being the humble instruments which God uses—the mere channels through which his grace flows. We shall strive to be such effective tools, however, as to open wide the channels of grace—even to the bankrupting of the Redemption to win souls for Christ.

ENLIST LAITY

In *The White Harvest* we repeatedly sounded an appeal for the enlistment of the laity. We sound that appeal again, only more loudly and more urgently. With so many millions of unchurched people in our midst, a scant battalion of levites will be laboring until doomsday without penetrating much beyond the fringes of that mighty army. The Church needs the active help of all her lay men and women . . . and she needs it desperately. Scarcely one in a thousand makes any earnest effort to win a soul for Christ.

We must change their whole attitude from one of mere passive attendance at Mass into one of vigorous aggressive action. They must tear a page from the Witnesses of Jehovah's handbook and emulate their zeal. In the colloquial language of students, we won't get to "first base" in our divinely appointed task until we have mobilized all our laity into earnest, persuasive "salesmen" for Christ.

With a view of achieving this end, we have addressed the volume not only to priests and to religious but to all our laity as well.

The contributors to this volume are all busy people. In accordance with our request they undertook the job—not too easy for people geared day in and day out to action—to describe their methods of procedure and to pass on to others the benefits of their experience and insights. This they did. While some editing was done, no effort was made to mould each contribution into a uniform style or pattern. A brief foreword for each chapter serves as a unifying thread and weaves the entire narrative into a reasonably unified story as to what is taking place in the field of convert work in America today.

We have supplemented the information provided in the numerous reports from chancery offices and letters from priests with personal conferences with some of the outstanding convert makers, as well as with the leaders who are promoting this movement. While such conferences have entailed thousands of miles of traveling, we believe they have enabled us to glimpse at first hand the methods used and to catch the spirit of enthusiasm and determination which always pervades successful convert work. We have endeavored to reflect faithfully both the method and the spirit in the symposium and to make both stand out clearly in the brief editorial foreword preceding each chapter.

In the ear of all who read this book will be echoing the words addressed by our divine Master at Jacob's Well to his disciples, as he saw the Samaritans thronging towards him: "Behold, I say to you, lift up your eyes and see the countries, for they are white already to harvest. And he that reapeth receiveth wages and gathereth fruit unto life everlasting." Those are the words which the divine Master is addressing to the 25,000,000 Catholic people in America today. God grant that they may hear his cry and answer it. Such is the prayer of the contributors, the editor, and, we feel sure, of all who read this book.

2

How You Can Win Converts

Rev. JOHN A. O'BRIEN, Ph.D.
University of Notre Dame

EDITOR'S FOREWORD: The enlistment of the laity in the apostolate of winning souls is the most important and urgently needed step in the development of the convert movement in America. In our country there are approximately 80,000,000 people without any definite religious affiliation and about 100,000,000 who rarely darken the door of any church or temple on Sunday. To bring the complete deposit of Christian truth to these millions, the efforts of the 40,000 priests must be supplemented by the cooperative missionary zeal of our 25,000,000 lay Catholics.

The harnessing of the good will, zeal, and latent power for missionary effort of all our laity is absolutely necessary to raise the annual total of converts from 100,000 to the million mark. The failure to harness that mighty reservoir of potential energy is the greatest loss which the Church in America is experiencing. It is of such a magnitude as to approach the nature of a disaster.

The Witnesses of Jehovah increased their membership in America from 44,000 in 1940 to 500,000 by the end of 1946—an increase of more than 1,000 per cent! What is the secret of their almost incredible growth? The flaming missionary zeal of their members. If our Catholic lay men and women display similar zeal, we shall win for Christ the churchless in our land within a few decades.

In this chapter we show how laymen and laywomen can participate actively in this crusade for Christ and souls. This appeal for greater lay cooperation in the convert movement in America is the refrain which runs through virtually every contribution to this symposium. God grant that it be not sounded in vain!

∽ᴓ

HEEDING A DIVINE INVITATION

CONGRATULATIONS, Mr. Pierce!" said Father Cronin, as he shook hands with his new parishioner. "May every day of your life be as happy as today—the day of your First Holy Communion."

"Thanks, Father," replied Mr. Pierce. "That wish of yours is a generous one, but too good to be realized. For this is the happiest day of my life . . . and they can't all be filled with such joy."

"Let me congratulate you too, Dad," said his son, Father Pierce, who had just enjoyed the rare privilege of baptizing his own father and of giving him First Holy Communion.

Others—grown children, relatives, and friends—came forward to shower their felicitations upon the elderly man who had just been elevated from the status of a creature of God to that of a son of God by the sacrament of regeneration. While young in the sonship of God, Mr. Pierce was no youngster in age. He was pushing on toward the seventy mark, a grandfather many times over with a son in the priesthood for twenty years.

"Our joy would be complete," said his married daughter, Mary, "if only Mother were here to witness the scene."

"Yes," replied the dad, "that's the one sad note in the music today: 'I'm sorry now that I waited so long.'"

"BECAUSE NO ONE . . ."

"Why *did* you wait so long?" inquired Mr. Spencer, a business friend of Mr. Pierce for forty years.

"Chiefly, I suppose," he said slowly and with some hesitancy, not wishing to offend, "because no one ever *asked* me."

In those words spoken on the steps of a church in a western city, in the presence of twenty witnesses, is contained a story fraught with meaning for all interested in the growth of the Church in America and particularly in the winning of converts for Christ. It is the story of the strange reticence of Catholics about their faith, of the common impression of our laity that they have no duty to help in the winning of souls for Christ, that such is exclusively the business and the concern of the clergy. The purpose of this discussion is to correct that false impression, to remove that reticence, and to enlist the wholehearted cooperation of all our people in the divinely appointed task of carrying the saving truths of Jesus Christ to every man, woman, and child on this globe.

THE BOTTLENECK

After relating the incident previously mentioned, the priest who had witnessed it added: "You've been interested, Father O'Brien, in convert work for many years. There's some grist for your mill. In fact, I would say there's the bottleneck of the whole movement. You'll have to break that bottleneck if you hope to speed up production."

He hit the nail on the head. More than thirty years of study of the convert movement, along with detailed investigation of the methods used by outstanding leaders in all parts of the country, have engendered in me the profound conviction that the success of this movement hinges upon the degree to which the 25,000,000 lay men and women bestir themselves to interest friends in the religion of Christ.

We shall be able to transform the meagre number of converts now trickling into our parishes into torrential streams only when we have found a way of harnessing the good will and latent zeal of our laity to the divine task of extending Christ's kingdom on earth. The failure thus far to tap that mighty reservoir of lay energy and power and to channel it into every city, town, and hamlet in our land represents the greatest loss to the Church in America today. An army of 40,000 priests is struggling to accomplish what only an army of 25,000,000 can achieve—the winning of the 80,000,000 churchless people of our country.

If our laity remain reticent, rarely lift a finger to help an outsider find his way into the household of the faith, and manifest no awareness of a divine obligation to share their saving truths with others, priests will be able to recruit but few prospects for their instruction classes and will reap a correspondingly meagre harvest. The key to the solution of the problem of winning the 80,000,000 churchless people in America is in the hands of the laity. Thus far they have made but little use of that key.

HOW TO CHANGE THE PICTURE?

How can we change that picture? How can we give them a vision of the great white harvest of America—a harvest that is waiting for reapers to gather into the Master's granary? By preaching a sermon every few months upon the duty which Christ placed upon all his followers to continue his work, to spread his teachings, and to win souls for him. "Go ye into the whole world," said Christ, "and preach the gospel to every creature" (Mark 16:15). Again: "Teach ye all nations . . . all things whatsoever I have commanded you: and behold I am with you all days, even to the consummation of the world" (Matt. 28:19, 20). These words were addressed not only to the apostles but also to all his followers.

In this land whitening with a harvest of nearly a hundred million souls, ungathered by any reapers, there is a crying need for the lay disciples of Christ to supplement the work of the bishops and priests who are able to gather but a small fragment of the vast harvest. To the lay Catholics of America, Christ is now addressing the words first uttered at Jacob's Well in Samaria: "Do not you say, there are yet four months, and then the harvest cometh? Behold, I say to you, lift up your eyes, and see the countries; for they are white already to harvest. And he that reapeth receiveth wages, and gathereth fruit unto life everlasting" (John 4:35–36).

This is the message which needs to be preached from every Catholic pulpit in America until every one of our millions of lay men and women is kindled with a consuming zeal to share the legacy of divine truth with their countrymen and thus win America for Christ. Frequent and urgent have been the appeals of our pontiffs to our laity, calling them to Catholic Action, to participate with the clergy in the apostolate under the direction of the hierarchy. We must continue to echo the appeal of our Holy Father until every man, woman, and child in America is galvanized into action in the noblest crusade in which a human being may participate—the crusade of winning souls for Jesus Christ.

A NEW CRUSADE

If we could devise a suitable hypodermic needle by which we could inject the zeal virus of the Christian Scientist, of the Seventh-Day Adventist, to say nothing of Jehovah's Witnesses, into our lay Catholics, we would win the unchurched multitude of Americans for Christ within a decade or two. With a zeal worthy of a better cause, these sectaries are spreading leaflets and pamphlets like snow flakes across our land. They are ringing our doorbells and seeking to edge their way into our homes to play their phonograph records. They are on our street corners, holding their magazines before our eyes and dinning their wares into our ears. They are aflame with zeal.

On the very day I write these lines, a letter arrives from the Catholic Action Committee of Brazil, organized for the defense of the faith and morals of their country. It reported the feverish missionary activities of Jehovah's Witnesses, Adventists, and Pentecostals in spreading their bizarre creeds in that country. Backed by American money, the men and women of these sects are flooding Brazil with propaganda, seeking to win adherents in that Catholic country.

The Committee is alarmed at the inroads being made by these zealots who have descended upon the natives like a swarm of locusts. The Committee reports that the Seventh-Day Adventists registered a seventy-per-cent increase in eight years. During the same period, the Pentecostals achieved the staggering gain of two hundred fifteen per cent. No wonder that a note of alarm and dismay is sounded by the Committee as they view the feverish pace at which these lay men and women are working to win converts to their man-made creeds.

Catholic men and women of America! Christ is calling you to proclaim him and his teachings from the housetops. He is calling you to go out into the highways and the byways to announce his gospel of mercy, forgiveness, and love. He is asking you to open your eyes and see the fields of America whitening with a harvest for the reaping of which the clergy are all too few. Christ is hungering for the souls of our churchless countrymen—pleading with you to hand them not a stone but the nourishing bread of divine truth.

In the ears of all our lay men and women are sounding again the pleading words of the Good Shepherd: "And other sheep I have, that are not of this fold: them also I must bring, and they shall hear my voice, and there shall be one fold and one shepherd" (John 10:16). Catholic men and women, will you respond to this plea of Jesus Christ? Will you set yourselves like flint to the fulfillment of the divinely appointed plea of Jesus Christ? Will you set yourselves like adamant to the task of winning the other souls for the Good Shepherd?

If you answer this call of the divine Master with zeal and courage, the success of the convert movement is assured. The number of converts will increase by leaps and bounds. We shall lift the annual number of converts from the hundred thousand to the million mark. We shall win America for Christ.

The reward to all who respond to his plea was promised by the divine Master when he said: "And he that reapeth, receiveth wages, and gathereth fruit unto life everlasting" (John 4:36). And again he promised: "Everyone therefore that shall confess me before men, I will also confess him before my Father who is in heaven" (Matt. 10:32).

With their eyes open to the vision of the whitening harvest of souls in America and with the divine promises echoing in their minds and hearts, the Catholic lay men and women of America will throw themselves into the greatest crusade of the twentieth century—the crusade of winning America for Christ.

WINNING 100 CONVERTS

"Say, Hank, were you at church yesterday?"

"No, Chuck. I rarely go to any and am a member of none."

"You're making a mistake there, Hank."

"How so? I don't see any need to go."

"Well, you're more than an animal that eats and sleeps and dies, aren't you?"

"Suppose I am. What has that got to do with it?"

"Lots. You're different from animals chiefly because you possess a spiritual nature, a soul that will live long after your body has passed into dust. That's the important part of you, and that's what needs attention, care, and nourishment."

"You got something there, Chuck. But how do you care for your soul—nourish it, as you say?"

"You care for your spiritual nature by exercising it. You do this by worshiping God. Prayer is food for the soul. Religion is the business of keeping you spiritually alive, healthy, and strong. That's why Christ founded a church, the Catholic Church: to care for your spiritual needs, to enable you to be a man instead of just an animal."

"ALL LOOK ALIKE"

"I don't know much about churches, Chuck. They all look alike to me. Where would a guy like me start?"

"I'll take you over to see Father Flynn. He's a fine priest. He'll show you how the Church can help you to come to life spiritually and to grow, how you can keep close to God and save your soul. That's what we're here for—to save our souls and to gain eternal life with God in heaven."

"I'll take you up on that, Chuck," hesitating a trifle, "if it won't cost anything or tie me up before I'm sold on it."

"I'll guarantee you, Hank, on both those points. Expect me to call for you at eight tonight."

"O.K., Chuck, it's a date."

A ONE-ARMED FISHERMAN

The above conversation took place in the Round House of the Illinois Central Railroad. It took place not once but many times. It was the simple, human appeal that Charles Fisher, a one-armed laborer, made to his fellow workers over a period of twenty-five years. It had enabled him to bring nineteen men to his pastor for instruction and occasioned him the unusual joy of seeing every one of them embrace the Catholic faith.

Most of them subsequently brought their families into the fold. Thus about one hundred people owed their Catholic faith, under God's grace, to Mr. Fisher's missionary zeal—to his willingness to ask his fellow laborers to investigate. He was a Fisher not only in name but also in deed.

In contrast to the university students to whom I was ministering, Mr. Fisher had not completed the elementary school course. Yet I am safe in saying that he had been instrumental in bringing more converts into the Church than my entire congregation of a thousand students. Though God had taken his wife, he gave his only daughter to the Dominican Order.

When I inquired how he managed to bring so many recruits around for instruction, he related to me the conversation previously mentioned. Though that was more than thirty years ago, it is as vivid in my memory as though it were related only yesterday. More than any other individual, this one-armed fisher of men, untutored in the things of this world but wise in the things of the spirit, opened my eyes to hitherto unsuspected possibilities in lay convert work.

A PATTERN FOR MILLIONS

What Mr. Fisher did, millions of other Catholics can do if they would but try. What he did, millions of others must do if we are to fulfill the command of Christ: "Preach the Gospel to every creature." What Mr. Fisher accomplished, millions of Catholic men and women must accomplish if we are to win the churchless people of America for Christ.

What is needed is to unleash the pent-up energy and zeal of Catholic men and women upon the mission fields whitening at our very door. This development will take place, however, only after we have given our laity the vision of this mighty harvest and the encouragement to undertake its reaping.

This is the note sounded by Father Lester J. Fallon, C.M., director of the Confraternity Home Study Service, St. Louis, Missouri. From his strategic post of duty, with inquiries coming to him from all parts of America and from many foreign countries, Father Fallon is in a position to appreciate the need for the cooperative assistance of Catholic lay men and women. "Why did not Catholics whom I knew at home introduce me to their religion?" Such is the question often raised, he reports, by the persons whom he is instructing by mail.

HUNGER FOR TRUTH

The hunger of people to learn the teachings of the Catholic religion is evidenced by the enrollment of 8,487 persons in his correspondence course in 1946. While the vast majority are from the United States and Canada, not a few come from the Philippines, Nigeria, Palestine, Brazil, India, Korea, and New Zealand. It is interesting to note that the number enrolling from rural districts, where there is little opportunity to hear Mass and no chance to receive personal instruction, is just about equal to the number of city people who enroll because circumstances prevent them from consulting a parish priest.

On the basis of the thousands of inquiries pouring in upon him from all the states of the Union, Father Fallon sounds this clarion call to the lay Catholics of America: "The mission field to which you are called is all around you—the druggist on the corner, the boy you met last week at a dance, the woman who shared a table with you at lunch, the man waiting with you in the barber shop, that new family next door. Won't you sow the seeds of faith and let us cultivate them?"

The seed will be sown in millions of places when Catholics lay aside their traditional reticence and invite their neighbors to Mass, to a Benediction service, to a Catholic lecture. It will be planted when Catholics offer a word of explanation about their faith, when they loan a Catholic book or donate a Catholic magazine or pamphlet to their friends outside the fold. If we turn to the right or to the left of us, we are rubbing shoulders with people who never have been given the opportunity of securing a true insight into the Catholic faith.

USING CASUAL CONTACTS

The most casual contacts can be utilized for a divine purpose. Let me cite an example. Some years ago I drove into a filling station. Noticing a stranger standing by the gas pump, I said to myself: "I'm going to see if I can land this soul for Christ." I remembered that Christ in a vivid phrase had styled the priestly ministry a fishing for souls when he said to the apostles: "Come ye after me, and I will make you to be fishers of men" (Matt. 4:19).

I greeted him cordially. He responded in a friendly manner. After a few minutes' conversation, I inquired if he would be interested in seeing a new altar which we had recently erected. He was glad to accept the invitation. In a few minutes I was showing him not only the altar but also the whole church, with its stations, paintings, statues, and stained glass windows.

Coming down the aisle. I called his attention to the confessionals, opining that he had probably heard many a tale about them. He smiled an affirmation.

"Plenty," be added.

I opened the doors and invited him to take a look inside, calling his attention to the grating, covered by an opaque white cloth, and also to the crucifix hanging on the partition before which the penitent would be kneeling. This afforded me an opportunity to explain the sacrament briefly. On passing through the vestibule, I invited him to take along a few of the many pamphlets on display; he gladly did so.

I invited him to an inquiry class which had just gotten under way. Though he was to be in the city for only a couple of weeks, he agreed to come. When those two weeks expired, he thanked me and bade me good-bye. I gave him a note of introduction to a pastor in Evanston, to which city he was returning, and advised him to complete his course. The incident had just about faded from my mind when some three months later a telegram arrived. It read: "Just received my First Holy Communion. Am the happiest man in the world. Many thanks."

THE MIDAS TOUCH

I mention the incident as typical of the thousands of casual contacts which can be utilized for a divine purpose if we but try. I mention it with no thought of vainglory. In all probability, I have allowed many opportunities to escape for a few utilized. If we shall but avail ourselves of the opportunities placed in our way, we all shall find that never a week goes by without bringing us a contact with a non-Catholic which with a little zeal may be turned to a holy cause.

We who are in possession of the full legacy of divine truth have a power like Midas, who was able with a touch to turn anything into gold. By exposing a bit of the shining pearl of divine truth to the eyes of the passing stranger, we have the power of arresting his attention and, with the aid of divine grace, the prospect of winning him for Christ and for his Church. Catholics have the Midas touch because they have the truth, the whole truth, and nothing but the truth.

The appeal of the Church to all her members and particularly to her laity is to bestir themselves to utilize the missionary contacts which they make every day of their lives. Catholic men and women of America, the future of the Church is in your hands. Strive every month to bring at least one recruit to your pastor for instruction. Be a fisher of souls for Christ! Enjoy the divine thrill and rapture of bringing a soul into the net of Peter. To those who recruit converts not less than to those who instruct them will be bestowed the reward promised in Holy Writ: "They that instruct many unto justice shall shine as the stars for all eternity" (Dan. 12:3).

USING CASUAL CONTACTS FOR CHRIST

"Hi there, Jane! Any fresh peach sundae today? And I mean *fresh.*"

"If it were half as fresh as you are, big boy, it would be plenty fresh."

"Oh yeah? Just for that I'll keep on saying you're a peach, not a lemon, but a . . ."

"I've heard that line before. Why not think up something new?"

"I will, when you give me that date I've been asking for. And I'm going to stop asking and . . ."

"And what?" challenged Jane defiantly.

"Start *demanding*," replied Herb with a disarming smile of entreaty that was in sharp contrast to his belligerent word, "a date for tonight. How about it, Jane? Can't you give a fellow a break?"

"Well, if you called this evening, you'd find yourself taking me to a place . . . where you wouldn't feel at home."

"WHERE?"

"Where . . . for instance?"

"At church. We have devotions in honor of the Blessed Sacrament every Thursday. And that's where I'm headed tonight."

"I'm a vet, and if I could take Iwo Jima and Okinawa, I guess I could take your church service. Anyway," hurrying to get in before the slightly opened door might close, "I'm taking you up on that date. So I'll be ringing the doorbell. At what time?"

"At 7:15 on the nose. But remember this is no romantic affair. My heart's mortgaged, as I've told you, but it won't do you any harm to say some prayers and learn something about the Catholic religion."

"I'm not backing out, even with all the cold water that you've thrown on me. I'll be there. It's a date."

WINNING A GREATER PRIZE

Such was the manner in which Jane McFarland detoured the romantic interest which Herb Brown had for her into another channel. Already engaged to a boy not yet out of the armed service, Jane turned Herb's sentimental interest to a Being more worthy of it than even her lovely self.

That evening was the turning point in Herb's life. Without any religious affiliation, Herb felt in the atmosphere of reverence, in the fervor of the Eucharistic prayers, and in the heartiness of the congregational singing a warmth and a devotion which promised to fill the spiritual void within him.

He wanted to learn more about a religion which could inspire such reverence and devotion—and incidentally which kept Jane so wholesome and lovely. It was an easy step for Jane to take now, bringing him to her pastor for instruction. This she speedily did. Herb Brown never won Jane's hand. But he won a greater prize. He won the intimate friendship and love of Jesus Christ and the pearl that passeth all price—membership in the Church established by the divine Master to guide all men safely to their eternal home.

OPPORTUNITY IS KNOCKING

This incident, related to me by the priest who received Herb into the fold, is an excellent illustration of the manner in which Catholic men and women may utilize the most casual contacts for a divine purpose.

The friend seated at your side in a bus, the barber cutting your hair (if his loquacity permits you to get a word in edgewise), the beautician giving you a permanent wave, the man playing golf with you, and the man delivering your mail—all these may be made the recipients of your solicitude for their spiritual welfare and eternal salvation.

All these are souls meant by divine Providence to be aided by your kindliness and zeal. Don't ever say that you don't know anyone who might be interested in a course of instruction in the religion of Christ, unless you live alone on a desert island.

Catholic men and women of America! Opportunity is knocking at your door. It is knocking every day and many times a day. It is the golden opportunity to lead souls to Jesus Christ and thus to enrich their lives for time and for eternity.

ALCHEMY OF ZEAL

Even the most unpromising contacts can be utilized for the good of souls. Father James B. McGoldrick, S.J., who, in addition to teaching college students and writing a notable book on psychiatry, finds time to instruct about twenty-five converts each year, has given all of us good illustration of this truth. A woman called upon Father McGoldrick to register a protest.

"I've just learned," she said, "that you have received my sister into the Catholic Church. I was furious when I heard of it, and I'm here to protest against your scheming tactics. We were all brought up to despise the Catholic Church. You couldn't ever have got Betty into the Church of Rome unless you outsmarted her, outmaneuvered her with your wily tactics. It's not fair, open, or aboveboard."

"That's most interesting," replied Father McGoldrick in a calm friendly manner, "if true," he added with a smile. "You're making a charge here against the intelligence of your sister as well as against the Catholic Church. You imply that Betty could not discern truth from error, could not weigh the logic of evidence and reason. You're drawing conclusions without having looked at the premises. Is that fair or reasonable, Mrs. Hill?"

PLAYING FAIR

"Well, I know in advance that the Roman Catholic religion abounds in priestcraft, superstition, intolerance, and error. I'm certain that an investigation wouldn't alter that conclusion."

"No? Well, the honest thing to do now is to play fair with yourself as well as Betty and investigate the teachings of the Catholic faith. You are warring against caricatures of her doctrines, caricatures you imbibed from the writings of her enemies. You are an intelligent woman, and all that the Catholic Church asks is that a person look at the evidence of her divine origin and teachings with an open mind."

"I'm not afraid to look into them, nor am I afraid of the result."

"Splendid. We shall start right now."

When the three months of instruction ended, Mrs. Hill took the same path which her sister had taken and which millions of truth seekers had taken before her. The only defense which truth needs is exposition. Light, not heat, is needed to win souls. Like the wise psychiatrist that he is, Father McGoldrick knows that the best method of removing the prejudice and the antagonism of the adversaries of the faith is large and frequent doses of the unadulterated truth. The above incident, narrated to me by a former colleague of Father McGoldrick, shows how even points of friction may be converted into channels of light and grace.

Just as an oyster transforms an irritating grain of sand lodged in its shell into a shining pearl, so a Christian can convert the antagonism of the Church's enemy into the precious opportunity of flooding his soul with God's light and love.

WHAT YOU CAN DO

Father Joseph T. Eckert, S.V.D., for many years pastor of St. Elizabeth's in Chicago, tells of a colored[1] man in his parish who has brought at least forty converts into the Church through his personal efforts. His secret? Unflagging zeal and tireless effort. He has no

---

1. As mentioned in the foreword, in this reprinting we have preserved the terminology of the original writing. A few words that have fallen into disuse since the 1940s carry different connotations today. We think the reader will be able to take into account changes in usage and will not attribute improper sentiments to the original writers.

greater knowledge of the faith than that of millions of Catholics. He has less education than most. But he surpasses them in zeal. Therein is the motive power for convert work. What is needed by most of our Catholic men and women is a realization of their duty to win souls for Christ and zeal and courage to fulfill that divinely appointed duty.

To offer help and guidance to individuals desirous of winning souls for Christ, there has been established an organization, Convert Makers of America, of which Rev. John E. Odou, S.J., is director. Members bring religion into their conversation with at least one new person each month, invite persons to Mass, and write a weekly letter to the director. In return, they receive a weekly bulletin carrying timely tips, a pep-letter each month from the director, a personal priest adviser who answers their questions, and a set of convert instructions. There are no dues. Each reader is urged to send his application for membership to Father Odou to receive the personal guidance that will greatly enhance the effectiveness of his missionary labors.

INQUIRY CLASS

In a parish of mostly Negroes, where conversions averaged only about three a year, we have recently launched an inquiry class and have appealed to the lay men and women to bring prospects. Delighted to be taken into partnership in such a divine enterprise, they responded valiantly. More than twenty prospects were brought to the class. It is the opening wedge through which the light of Christ's truth will be brought to constantly increasing numbers of colored people in our community.

In another inquiry class launched a year ago at St. Joseph's, Mishawaka, Indiana, the parishioners invited about forty people having no religious affiliation.

It was the first time the laity had ever been called upon to do such missionary work. At the end of the class, we were able to receive into the Church twenty-five men and women in a public ceremony at the Sunday Mass. Not only was it an inspiring sight for the laity, but it was also an eye-opener as to the possibilities in this field. One lady who had brought her husband, father, and a neighbor lady to the class had the great joy of seeing the three of them receive their First Holy Communion.

Perhaps the greatest convert service which lay men and women can render is to recruit prospects for instruction by their pastor. Through the quarterly establishment of inquiry classes in every parish and the recruiting of people for such classes by our laity, we can lift the present annual total from the hundred thousand neighborhood to the million mark.

WIN THE WORLD FOR CHRIST

This means the harnessing of the vast missionary power of Catholic men and women to the winning of the churchless people in America for Christ. It means work and plenty of it. But with enlightened zeal and unflagging effort, aided by God's grace, it is a goal which can be achieved within our generation.

Thus fortified, we can win not only America but we can win the whole world for Christ. If there were only 25,000,000 Catholics in the world, and if every Catholic would win each year a single convert, we would win the whole human race for Christ in less than seven years! Our appeal is for the establishment of inquiry classes in every parish and mission in America. We ask every Catholic man and woman to bring at least one prospect to such a class. The power of divine truth will make itself felt in the minds and in the hearts of men, and within our lifetime will be realized the prayer uttered by Christ shortly before his death: "Other sheep I have, that are not of this fold; them also I must bring, and they shall hear my voice, and there shall be one fold and one shepherd" (John 10:16).

LAYMEN TOO CAN WIN CONVERTS

"You just referred to your pope as 'Holy Father,' " interrupted a heckler. "But the Bible says, 'Call no man your father upon the earth, for one is your Father which is in heaven' [Matt. 23:9, King

James Version]. Why don't you Catholics do what the Bible commands?"

"But don't you use the term 'father' in referring to your own earthly father?" asked the speaker.

The heckler was silent, stumped for the moment by the unexpected query. Then he said slowly:

"Why, come to think of it, I do. But I never thought I was disobeying the Bible in doing so."

"You aren't violating the Scriptures in doing so. That passage means simply that we must recognize God as our *heavenly* Father and give supreme honor and homage to him alone. When we Catholics refer to the pope as 'Holy Father,' we give to him a title of honor and respect, just as you do in referring to your own father, but we never bestow upon him any of the exalted homage and honor which belong to God alone."

The heckler was fair enough to recognize that his question was satisfactorily answered.

THE SCENE

The scene took place on a Sunday afternoon in Hyde Park, London. The speaker, mounted on a soap box, was a young man of twenty-five and a representative of the Catholic Evidence Guild. A crowd of about a hundred people, men and women, had been listening intently to him for forty-five minutes with occasional interruptions by hecklers. At the conclusion of his talk, questions were fired at him, thick and fast.

It was a moving spectacle for myself and my priest companion from America, where such sights rarely, if ever, are seen. All afternoon long and well into the evening, at intervals of about an hour, a young man or woman would mount the box to carry on the street preaching.

This work has been going on for more than twenty years and has afforded excellent opportunity to Catholic laymen to explain the teachings of the Catholic faith to their fellow Britishers.

As we listened to the young man speak with great earnestness

BELIEVE IT
OR NOT
but the
Catholic Church
has the
Truth, Satisfaction. and Happiness
you desire in life

You Owe It to Yourself to Investigate
at the
CATHEDRAL INQUIRY CLASS

**A Series of Twenty-two Lectures on the
Catholic Faith**

**MONDAY & WEDNESDAY EVENINGS
7:30 P. M.**

APRIL 7th — TO — JUNE 18th

**CATHEDRAL GRADE SCHOOL
SIXTH STREET, AND CASS AVENUE**

Admission Free

FACTS ABOUT THE CLASS

1 These classes are especially for non-Catholics Kindly dismiss therefore any thought of uneasiness or embarrassment at being all alone among a crowd of Catholics. Almost all of those who attended our last class were non-Catholics We assure you that after the first class any feeling of hesitancy will disappear

2 Mere curiosity inquisitiveness, mild interest or avid interest — even an tagonism. If you will any reason at all for coming is acceptable

3 By attending this class you are not making any commitments on joining the Church This is an "Inquiry" class, not a "Convert" class Whether you will enter the Church at the conclusion of the course God alone knows. We are anxious only to have you hear the true teachings of the Church the rest is leave in the hands of God for the gift of faith is from Him alone

4 Tolerance charity respect for other religious opinions will be the predominant note of the lectures We realize every one must follow his own conscience

5 The lectures will appeal to reason, not emotions Religion must have intellectual foundations We desire to foster convictions not prejudices

6 Questions may be submitted either from the floor or through the Question Box that will be provided

7 Lectures will begin promptly at 7 30 P M If however you happen to be late, don't hesitate to come in

8 Classes unavoidably missed can be made up privately

9 There is no fee for any lecture literature or service

10 The instructions necessary for a non-Catholic contemplating marriage with a Catholic. can be fulfilled by attending these lectures

11 You may bring anyone you wish with you either Catholic or Non-Catholic

12 For further information or registration call The Cathedral 7 7382

Lectures Conducted By

REV FRANK J O'HARA   REV FRANCIS E CUNNINGHAM

Catholic lay men and women can help win converts by recruiting prospects for such Inquiry Classes.

and vigor, expressing himself simply and driving his points home with apt illustrations, we found a lump forming in our throats and our hearts burning within us.

SYMBOLIZES NEED

If that scene could be reenacted in every city, town, and village in America, what a tremendous force would be exerted by our Catholic laity for the spreading among our countrymen of an accurate knowledge of the teachings and practices of the Catholic faith. That scene in Hyde Park symbolizes the outstanding need in America today—the need for the enlistment of Catholic men, women, and children in the divinely appointed task of spreading the religion of Jesus Christ among our churchless fellow countrymen.

Not all need to become street preachers, but all should seek to carry the knowledge of their holy faith to their non-Catholic acquaintances and friends. They should invite their friends, especially those having no religious affiliation, to attend Mass with them. They should avail themselves of every favorable opportunity to interest them in the Catholic religion. They should pass on to them Catholic papers, pamphlets, and books which would enlighten them concerning Catholic belief and practice.

We have a splendid body of Catholic laity in America. They are earnest, loyal, and devoted to the Church. They attend Mass with edifying regularity and receive the sacraments frequently. But thus far we have not worked out a suitable means of harnessing their good will, devotion, and tremendous latent power for missionary efforts, for convert work, and for the winning of our beloved America for Christ.

GREATEST LOSS

Our failure to harness that Niagara of potential energy constitutes the greatest loss of the Church in America—a loss that approaches the proportion of a catastrophe, as I said before. Instead of sitting idly by, bemoaning the loss, it is high time that we do something about it. To stop that loss by harnessing the power and latent zeal of Catholics in America to the task of winning souls is the purpose for which these lines are written.

Thus far, our laity have played, on the whole, a passive role. Their lethargy in winning converts for Christ is in sharp contrast with the feverish zeal of the communists in winning disciples for the gospel of Karl Marx. If in some way we could infuse into our laity the crusading zeal of the communist, we could win America for Christ within a generation or two.

The dominant note sounded by our recent pontiffs has been the plea for Catholic Action, the summons to our laity to participate intimately in the apostolate of the priesthood under the direction of the hierarchy. One of the noblest expressions of Catholic Action is in winning converts for Christ.

Nothing is dearer to the heart of Christ than the winning of the people that have strayed from the fold. The repeated appeals of our pontiffs to our laity to throw themselves wholeheartedly into the divinely appointed task of winning souls echoes the plea and the summons of Christ himself.

The reader, however, may ask: "But how can we manage to win converts? Isn't that beyond our capacity and training?"

OUR ANSWER

All can do something toward the winning of converts. You can pray daily for that intention. You can bring prospects to Mass and supply them with Catholic literature. You can interest them in the Catholic religion and bring them to a priest for systematic instruction. There are others, however—and many of them—who are capable of instructing prospects in the Catholic faith. Certainly every graduate of a Catholic college should be able to do this. What a commentary it would be on sixteen years of instruction in the Catholic religion—in the elementary school, high school, and college—if after all that training a graduate would be unable to give a reason for the faith that is in him.

All that is needed is a little courage, effort, and determination.

As an ounce of fact is worth a ton of theory, we cite an example of what one Catholic college graduate accomplished in this matter and what thousands could likewise do if they would only try.

George M. Reichle was teaching public speaking at Notre Dame when suddenly be was called into the Army. He proceeded to utilize his new contacts for a divine purpose. Finding many officers and enlisted men with no definite religious faith going into battle, from which they might never emerge alive, George *personally* instructed forty-one of them and saw all of them received into the fold!

Amidst the raucous blasts of war, George rendered a far more precious service than he ever could have made in the class room. We wrote to George for some details concerning his missionary work in the Army and received an intensely interesting letter in reply. Because it offers so many helpful hints and suggestions for similar work by men and women in all walks of life, we reproduce it here in its entirety.

A UNIQUE LETTER

Milwaukee, Wisconsin

Reverend and Dear Father:

Your special delivery caught up with me just this evening as I returned from work. The work done with converts in the service was so simple that I never thought it worthy of publication of any kind. What little I give you in this briefly stated and rough account is not submitted with the thought of personal publicity, but only with the thought that those who might read will be inspired, even if only one, to undertake similar fascinating work, and surely the field is ripe for a rich harvest.

Suddenly finding myself an enlisted man in the field artillery, Camp Shelby, Mississippi, in late May 1942, after having been told by three ex-World War I doctors in South Bend that no examining board would take me for anything, I missed Mass the first Sunday in camp for the simple reason that no one knew where the chapel was. I resolved then and there that, war or no war, that sort of thing would not continue. So I located the chapel, found the time when Mass would be held, got the commanding officer to announce it to the entire outfit, and found that only four of us were present.

Meanwhile, I learned that about two-thirds of the men in our battery were Catholics from Pennsylvania, many of whom had not been to the sacraments in twenty or more years. That week was spent in contacting each Catholic to urge him to get to confession the next Saturday. All except about six agreed it was the sensible thing to do. So off I went to Father Murphy, our zealous Catholic chaplain, told him to be ready for the catch, and off we went in a group to confession that Saturday night. I am sure that for many of the men it was a mighty fine thing. Father Murphy announced at Mass the next morning his tremendous satisfaction.

NOT TOO HAPPY

But I was not too happy. Those six who refused to go were on my mind. I finally succeeded in getting them in line.

Naturally, the word got around. One day a non-Catholic asked me to teach him to say the rosary, which I did. He then told me of his desire to take instructions, but insisted that I would have to give them to him. Back I went to Father Murphy, who gladly gave me permission to give the instructions, outlined the successive instructions, and told me he would have to question the man on the given instructions before baptism. So I started the instructions, soon finding I had four prospective converts.

Instructions were given mostly at night after a rough day, usually in what I call an ordinary "bull session" out under some tree in the dark or off some place where no one knew what was taking place. Before leaving for officer candidate school in March 1943, I had given instructions via that method to nineteen men, from various parts of Camp Shelby, who entered the Church. Officer candidate school followed, and I found myself, several assignments intervening, at Luke Field, Arizona, in December 1943. There we had another wonderful Catholic chaplain, a certain Father John

Brew. Learning of the work done at Camp Shelby, he announced one Sunday at Mass that weekly instruction class would be held and had his sergeant stop me after Mass. He took me to Father Brew's office, where I learned he wanted me to conduct the instructions. We argued that out in detail. He agreed to outline for me from week to week what he thought would be pertinent. Instructions were held right in the chapel every Monday night. Father Brew's office was right in the chapel, so he kept out of view, with his door open so that he could come to the rescue, if and when necessary.

IDEAL SET-UP

It was an ideal set-up. Many of the enlisted men and women and commissioned officers, I know, would never have attended had Father Brew been giving the instructions. Many lay people feel, as you know, a barrier between themselves and a priest. Not so between them and a layman. The instructions went on with as many as seventy frequently in attendance.

A similar set-up was had at Hobbs, New Mexico, where I was later stationed, and at SAACC, San Antonio, Texas, and Ellington Field, Texas. By the time I was discharged in April 1946, forty-one enlisted men and officers to whom I had given instructions entered the Church.

In every case I gave the instructions, but the priest, whether it was the Catholic chaplain in the service or some neighboring priest, always assured himself the men had been properly indoctrinated for baptism and formal entrance into the Church by having at least a one- or two-hour interview with the prospective convert before the actual conferring of the sacraments.

Before telling you of two interesting cases, permit me to say that in every case the one big problem facing these converts was the matter of confession. It was the roughest of all difficulties.

CAME TO SCOFF, BUT . . .

Mr. Smith was an enlisted man, about thirty years of age, holding a master's degree, a widely read man, well educated, and extremely proud of his talents. He came to me out of what he called mere curiosity, found fault with most everything said, challenged me to accompany him to his Baptist minister. This I did. The three of us had four most interesting discussions on confession, the Virgin Mary, why priests do not marry, and purgatory. These discussions, though I had never told the Catholic chaplain that I was holding them, were less heated and more rational than one can imagine. I still hear from the Baptist minister.

But Mr. Smith still had his difficulties. I got several enlisted men to begin with me a novena for a special intention. Three days following the completion thereof, Mr. Smith, who knew nothing of our novena, told me that he believed he had the faith. The possibility of his ever being attracted to Catholicism, he declared, had been the one danger which he feared most since he finished high school. He had come to scoff but remained to pray. From there on in, as you know, Mr. Smith was no problem. What happened in his case was typical of each of the forty-one mentioned. If forty-one men entered the Church, it was prayer, not my human efforts, which brought them in.

ALARM CLOCK STARTS IT

Perhaps a more interesting case was Captain Brown, a young Air Corps pilot instructor with the cadets for more than a year. He roomed next to me in the officers' quarters. We discussed men, women, drink, religion, politics, the Army, the Air Corps, and most everything men speak about while in uniform. Captain Brown was a clean-cut man. My alarm clock used to grate upon him when it would ring at an early hour to assure my attendance at the first Mass on Sunday.

One Sunday, hearing the alarm, he got up, dressed, and said he wanted to go with me to see what foolishness inspired me. We went to Mass. Nothing much was said about it all. Then on Christmas Eve, he informed me that he would like to see what midnight Mass was. We attended. He seemed impressed. That following week two of his cadets crashed up and died. As was usual, he and I held a post-mortem on the crash. There were many such crashes.

During that particular session he asked me where I thought those two cadets were at that particular time, now that they had died. I forget just what the answer was. He called for several Catholic books. Within three weeks he began instructions, insisting that such action on his part was only to qualify him for more intelligent discussion. I knew better. Within three months he was thoroughly prepared for baptism and asked what his next step was. I suggested we go to the Catholic chaplain to tell him and to let him make the necessary inquiries.

"No, we don't," was his reply.

NONE TOO SOON

I finally sensed that he would find it quite trying for him to be baptized there at the Air Corps station chapel. He and I caught a bus to the nearest Catholic parish priest, who, in due time, administered the necessary sacraments. The first Sunday following his conversion, he and I attended Mass and received Holy Communion.

On the next day, Monday, he was due at the flight line for some early instruction. We shaved, showered, and ate breakfast together. He went to the flight line, and I to the ground school where I was instructing the cadets. Within less than an hour the crash alarm sounded. Ambulances, medics, and chaplains took off for the scene of the accident. Captain Brown was pulled from the wreckage. His death was a fact. So, too, was his conversion, thank God, and none too soon.

I later found his rosary at the scene of the crash. And my alarm clock, which seemed so instrumental in getting him interested, is among my prized possessions. But there was far more behind it all, as you know, than this old alarm clock, and that something again was prayer and God's good graces beginning to work.

This account has been hurriedly written, Father O'Brien, so excuse the off-hand expressions and the absence of all effort at literary elegance. I know full well you can revamp any or as much of this *information as you want in an interesting fashion.*

With continued good wishes for God's choicest blessing on the great work you are doing, I remain,

Respectfully yours,
George M. Reichle

WILL YOU RESPOND?

Have you ever read, dear friend, a more interesting letter? Does it not open your eyes as to what millions of Catholic men and women could do in winning souls for Christ if they would only try? If an Army officer, under the pressure of manifold war duties, could personally instruct forty-one men within a couple of years, how many could the lawyer, the physician, the teacher, the merchant, the office worker, the salesman, the beautician, the clerk, the laborer, the housewife, and the student win if the same effort were put forth?

The progress of the Church in the mission fields is largely in proportion to the zeal and effectiveness of the work of the lay instructors. America, with its 80,000,000 unaffiliated with any religion, is the mission field *par excellence* in the world today. It is white for the harvest.

Priests are calling. Bishops are calling. The Pope is calling. Christ himself is calling every Catholic in America to gather that harvest. "He that reapeth," promises the divine Master, "receiveth wages, and gathereth fruit unto life everlasting" (John 4:36). When you stand before the judgment seat of God, dear friend, will you stand with empty hands or with the record of many souls won for Christ? No bridge unto life eternal is so firm or so safe as that living bridge composed of those who have been won for Christ by your zeal and holiness.

PRACTICAL RESOLUTION

It is well, dear friend, to end the reading of these lines with a definite resolution, a clear commitment, a specific promise to try each day to win a convert. Otherwise, your good intention someday to do something about this matter is apt to evaporate into thin air. What is needed is *action*, not tomorrow but today—right now.

Accordingly, it is suggested that, kneeling before a crucifix— the crucifix on your rosary will do—you promise, not under pain of sin but simply on your word of honor, the following: "Dear Jesus, my crucified Lord and Saviour, I promise that I shall heed your invitation to seek and to win for you the precious souls for whom you died on Calvary's cross. I shall try earnestly and zealously to win souls for you through a life of virtue and holiness, by setting an example of charity toward all men, by bringing non-Catholics to holy Mass, by loaning them Catholic literature, by explaining to them points of doctrine, and by bringing them to a priest for further instruction. I shall do my utmost to win at least one convert for you, dear Jesus, every year of my life. So help me, God."

Then kiss the crucifix and seal your promise with the sign of the cross, saying: "In the name of the Father and of the Son and of the Holy Ghost. Amen."

3

The Convert Makers of America

Rev. JOHN. E. ODOU, S.J., Director
Glendale, California

EDITOR'S FOREWORD: What has been needed for years is an organization of zealous lay men and women to win converts for Christ. The Convert Makers of America, under the direction of its founder, Father John E. Odou, S.J., is the answer to that need. It is the first step in providing for the Church in America a trained and zealous members who will carry the teachings of Christ to the churchless people of our land.

If we are to win the bulk of this constantly increasing multitude, we must utilize more and more of our laity in that apostolate. Only when they put their shoulders to the wheel will the proper momentum and power be secured.

CMOA is a young organization that already has accomplished much, but its potentialities are truly great. It seeks to incorporate a somewhat new idea into the lay apostolate, namely, that a lay person can present the teachings of the faith to an inquirer. Instead of simply bringing the non-Catholic to a rectory, CMOA encourages its members to undertake a good share of the work of instruction.

Who would deny them the privilege of making the attempt? Perhaps the instruction would not be couched in the same language as that used by a priest. But that may have its advantages. It is almost certain to be simple, direct, down-to-earth. The experience of the

Catholic Evidence Guild in England and elsewhere shows that, with training, our laity can acquit themselves creditably as salesmen of Christ. Priests and people will find many valuable suggestions in this meaty article. Our advice to all lay readers is simple and direct: Join the Convert Makers of America today.

∽

CMOA

EFFECTIVE CONVERT MAKING requires systematized action. To gain converts on a large scale requires the cooperation of the laity. The purpose of CMOA (Convert Makers of America) is to make converts for Christ through lay action.

We know from experience that the laity have the contacts. We know from theology that the laity have the spiritual qualifications. But we have somehow forgotten to enlist their active support.

It is true that men and women who are rank-and-file Catholics do not often understand the faith with the thoroughness of a trained theologian, but they possess the supernatural requisites for spreading the faith. We find the first apostles, who were the original convert makers, huddled together in the Upper Room, afraid to meet the people and convert them. It was only when the Holy Spirit came down upon them that they were filled with courage and zeal and went out immediately to convert the world. It is confirmation and not ordination that makes one qualified to spread the faith. And it is in confirmation that the Holy Spirit comes down upon the heart and soul of the lay Catholic.

But does the average lay person know enough about the faith to discuss it intelligently? Is he enough of a technical theologian to be accurate in his opinions and arguments?

Most of the laity have had an excellent Catholic education in our parochial school system. Many have gone through a Catholic high school and some even through a Catholic college. No other way of worship provides its rank-and-file membership with such a thorough religious instructional program. Though some courses and some religion teachers may be poor, by and large we can be proud of the magnificent religious training the Church gives her members.

Is it absolutely necessary to know technical theology today in order to spread the faith? The more one does know, the better qualified he is for the work. But strictly speaking, convert making today is almost like going up to a man and in simple language telling him what he already wants to know. The work of making a convert today is largely a matter of personality, kindness, and a genuine interest in him personally. It is less and less a matter of producing the right argument at the right moment.

HOW DOES CMOA OPERATE?

It operates on a very simple basis. There are no officers, no dues, no fixed fees, no meetings, no dunning letters. Catholics who wish to be members must write one letter a week to a priest-advisor who will be provided by CMOA. In the letter the member reports on the past week's work and in turn receives from the priest-advisor help and personal instructions on convert-making for the coming week.

For every lay person there is one priest-advisor and vice-versa. The lay person and the priest-advisor form a team; each team is expected to make one convert a year.

The purpose of the weekly letter is to guarantee sustained interest and work in convert-making. It is a weekly obligation like weekly Mass on Sunday and weekly abstinence on Friday, only it does not bind under pain of sin. We have found that convert work is dull at times and often meets with little or no results at all. Those who fail to write are eliminated from active membership by the automatic filter system which divides members into preferred, deferred, defunct.

In return for the weekly letter, members get a weekly bulletin which is produced by volunteer editors and contains excerpts from all the letters received from eight hundred active CMOA members. It is by reading the inspiring work done by fellow members that active members are constantly remotivated, and it is in the bulletin that members find a remedy for their personal problems in convert work.

CMOA WORKS ON TWO FRONTS SIMULTANEOUSLY

All members are expected to do personal and project work. The difference between the two is simple. Personal work is whatever one can do in daily life through personal contacts, casual meetings, and planned interviews to spread the faith. If one has the attitude of a convert-maker, he is ever on the alert for opportunities to spread the faith. Trains, hotels, depots, beauty parlors are all crowded with potential converts. Occasions for making a convert are found in business life, at school, at home, in the neighborhood —almost anywhere.

That is why the slogan used by every CMOA is: "Never let an opportunity slip."

Project work is the work on a systematic basis done by each individual member. CMOA has but three projects. These three are being chain-stored across America. Members are asked to select one of the three projects and start it in their locality. Then, they enlist the help of local existing Catholic organizations to make the work successful. Progress being made on the three CMOA projects is reported monthly in a special release to members only.

THE PURPOSE BEHIND THE THREE CMOA PROJECTS

Today more than ever before, Americans are looking for peace, security, beauty, truth. These values are found in the Catholic Church. But we lack salesmen to bring the faith to the waiting public. Today the average non-Catholic is not hostile or antagonistic toward the Church. It is not apathy or indifference that keeps him out of the Church. It is simply a lack of information.

Where can a non-Catholic find out about the Church? He is afraid to go to the rectory and call on a priest. He does not know the location of the rectory, and, if he does, he probably does not know the priest or even his name. His next opportunity is to ask a Catholic lay person. The average Catholic is often afraid to discuss religion and will usually turn the conversation into other topics or direct the inquirer immediately to a priest. Information about the Church should be made easily accessible. It is often difficult to find out about the Catholic Church from professional sources, and that is one reason why many are not Catholics.

CMOA attempts to bring information about the Church to the waiting non-Catholic are made in the hope that it will remove some of the misinformation prevalent and simultaneously provide practical helps for making a thorough investigation of the Church. If information is to be effective, it must be placed at the disposal of the public. In other words, it must be given in a downtown area or through public forms of communication.

FIRST PROJECT: INFORMATION CENTERS

CMOA tries to bring the Church downtown. The purpose is to make it easy for non-Catholics to drop in and inquire about the faith without obligation. This is done through information centers for non-Catholics.

A center is usually situated in a downtown locality where the traffic is leisurely. In many respects it resembles a Christian Science reading room. An attractive window display appeals to the non-Catholic mentality. Through the window the pedestrian can see into a comfortable, home-like reading room where he is welcome to browse about and read the Catholic magazine s, books, and pamphlets. He can direct his questions to a trained receptionist—and all this without obligation.

We believe the evidence is so good that anyone who will take time to examine it will eventually be converted. The information center for non-Catholics presents the evidence for Catholicism in a most stimulating and inviting setting.

CMOA operates information centers through the sponsorship and work of the laity. The laity find the location, pay the rent, provide the furniture, and supply the receptionists. In general it can be said that the laity take complete charge of the project. A priest is not on duty at all times, but there is usually one who can be consulted by non-Catholics at stated times or by special appointment.

The center is a wonderful feeder for the parish convert class or inquiry forum. CMOA supplies each of its fifteen centers with professional window displays that are changed once a month. A special staff to service the growing chain of CMOA information centers stands ready to give expert aid on the establishment of new centers.

SECOND PROJECT: INFORMATION RACKS

Wherever a non-Catholic rack is already in existence, it is the aim of CMOA to put in a Catholic rack. Racks are being installed at the rate of five a week. The official CMOA rack is unique in as much as it is designed by Mr. Ed Ellwanger and contains a beautiful picture of the Sacred Heart. It is believed that the Sacred Heart will bless both the place where the rack is located and the person who takes the literature.

In Chicago alone over 10,000 pieces of literature for non-Catholics are distributed free each week. The project is being replicated across America, and it is hoped that racks soon will be found in all hotels, bus depots, hospitals, waiting rooms, beauty parlors, and the like. It is usually easy to get permission to install a rack wherever a non-Catholic rack already exists, because not to do so would imply unfair discrimination against Catholics.

The racks cost $3.50, and it is customary to get one before asking permission to install it. The rack often sells the idea to a hotel manager or depot manager if it is displayed at the time the permission is asked. Literature for the rack is provided by the rack-sponsor, which is usually a Catholic organization like the Knights of Columbus, Daughters of Isabella, St. Vincent de Paul Society, Holy Name Society, or Sodality of the Blessed Virgin. A rack-tender keeps the rack filled. The leaflets are offered free to non-Catholics. Mr. Ellwanger and his qualified staff have a folder to explain the details of this project.

THIRD PROJECT: INFORMATION TALKS IN PRIVATE HOMES

The information talk is a series of six talks in a private home, in order to break down misinformation about the Church. These talks are given not by cradle-Catholics but by converts because they usually understand the non-Catholic mind better and avoid a Catholic terminology that might be meaningless or misunderstood by non-Catholics.

The speaker follows a very brief plan: Each talk lasts usually fifteen minutes, with five minutes for each point to be developed. The first point is: "What is the doctrine we are to discuss tonight?" Five minutes are used to define and limit the subject matter of the evening. The second point is: "How do you prove this doctrine to be true?" The third and last point is: "How does this fact or doctrine enter into my daily life and habits?" In other words, the last point is a tie-in with personal life and morals.

The audience, after the talk is over, is permitted to ask questions. Only questions pertaining to the subject of the evening are answered. All others are written and placed in a box, to be answered the following week.

About fifteen non-Catholics attend the meeting. It is conducted in a very informal atmosphere, always in a private home. No refreshments are served. The meeting is officially over in one hour, but non-Catholics usually remain another hour to continue discussions.

Catholics are not allowed to attend unless they bring a non-Catholic. It is difficult to keep Catholics out, because they seem to be interested in knowing more about their own faith. However, this is the danger that faces information talks. It can easily become a Catholic group and be transformed into a study club. To avoid this mistake, it is wise to keep the number of non-Catholics proportionately greater than the number of Catholics.

The final talk is always a tour of the church. The non-Catholics under the guidance of the parish priest see the inside of the church, the vessels, vestments, altar stone, and everything that pertains to Catholic worship. On the following Sunday they are brought to

Mass by the Catholics who invited them to the information talks. It is practically impossible to take a non-Catholic to Mass on three consecutive Sundays without producing a convert.

But the information talks do not always produce converts. At least they take away misinformation. They plant a seed. They feed the parish convert class, because many find the talks so interesting and the Church's doctrines so comforting and beautiful that they continue by joining the parish convert class. A free folder with full details on how to organize information talks in private homes can be obtained from CMOA.

LOOK TO THE FUTURE

The Church needs more lay convert makers. It needs a systematized method that is easily adapted to local conditions. All these are provided with CMOA.

Though there be a million methods for spreading the faith and a hundred gates by which individuals enter the Church, no two ever enter at precisely the same angle. CMOA is therefore *specialized* convert-making. It offers the parish a method for eliminating mixed marriages by converting the non-Catholic partner (through information talks). CMOA brings recruits to the parish convert class (through information centers). And CMOA gives parish organizations a vital project for Catholic Action (the sponsorship of information racks). You can help the professional convert-makers who are our priests, brothers, and sisters by joining CMOA, by selecting one of its projects, or by bringing its work to the attention of others.

4

Getting Them to the Rectory Porch

Rev. LESTER J. FALLON, C.M., S.T.D., Director
Confraternity Home Study Service, St. Louis, Missouri

EDITOR'S FOREWORD: One of the most significant developments in convert work in recent years is the establishment of Catholic bureaus which send religious instruction by mail to interested inquirers. The outstanding one is the Confraternity Home Study Service, under the direction of its founder, Rev. Dr. Lester J. Fallon, C.M. No less than 38,000 servicemen were enrolled, bringing the total enrollment over the 50,000 mark.

Father Fallon is likewise directing a Catholic advertising campaign in public newspapers, under the sponsorship of the Knights of Columbus in Missouri. These short articles, which explain various Catholic beliefs and practices, especially those often misunderstood, elicit many inquiries. In the course of three years, 28,639 letters were written to inquirers and 39,861 pamphlets were distributed, prompting 710 persons to apply for instruction by mail.

Here is a work in which every Catholic can participate. While the ideal is, of course, to have the inquirer call upon a priest for instruction, that is not always practical or possible. If circumstances prevent your bringing a prospect to the rectory for instruction, have such a person enroll in the Confraternity Home Study Service, which is offered free of charge. It is to be hoped also that the Catholic advertising campaign in the public press will extend to every paper and to every state in the Union. In the enlargement of these two services—the correspondence course and the exposition of Catholic belief in featured advertisements—one sees providential means for the winning of millions of converts each year.

∾

RELIGIOUS INSTRUCTION BY MAIL & ADVERTISING

I N THE BOOK *Slow Dawning*, a convert's story by Jane Howes, there appears this significant sentence: "Perhaps no born Catholic can ever understand how much it takes to get a non-Catholic up there on the rectory porch with his finger on the doorbell."

Perhaps cradle-Catholics cannot appreciate how much it takes, but the average priest who has had considerable experience with converts knows how many non-Catholics are struggling to muster up the necessary courage. After having given instruction by mail to many thousands of non-Catholics, I can testify that this is one widespread reason why so many non-Catholics first turn to religious instruction by mail before approaching a priest in person.

I have before me a letter, recently received, which begins as follows:

"I read in the May issue of *St. Anthony's Messenger* about your course of instruction by mail for non-Catholics. I am very much interested and would like to have it. I am especially glad that I am able to get this information through the mail because I am afraid of going to a priest. I know this is a foolish notion, but if I learn a little first, it won't be so hard to talk it over with a priest.

"I have often wanted to express myself to someone on the subject of religion, but it doesn't come easy for me to talk to strangers, so if I tell you my story, perhaps you will take a special interest and send me the necessary religious instruction."

This letter is typical of many along the same vein. The number of non-Catholics who hesitate to approach a Catholic priest, even though Catholic friends will accompany them, is far greater than most people suspect.

Call it foolish pride, human respect, or downright stupidity, it is there, and it is strong—strong enough to keep them from fulfilling what is really a deep-seated desire. Advertising puts us in touch with them, and a course of religious instruction by mail in the privacy of the home often serves to offset these fears and creates the mental attitude of self-assurance in which the promptings of God's grace are heeded and translated into action.

But wait a moment! Very likely there are those who are not familiar with religious instruction by mail, the form it takes, and the way it originated.

It came into existence as a result of street preaching campaigns throughout rural Missouri. Individuals had been interested in the Catholic Church, and no practical follow-up was available to sustain that interest. Regular mailings of Catholic pamphlets and literature provoked little or no response. Something was needed which would insure sustained contact. A correspondence course covering Catholic faith and practice seemed to be the only answer.

This course could not be long or complicated, and it must not involve too much writing on the part of the person who would receive it. Such a course was drawn up with *Father Smith Instructs Jackson*, by Bishop Noll, as the textbook. Since this book is written in conversational form and covers the *Baltimore Catechism* thoroughly, six objective tests were devised, each covering a section of the book. These tests need only be checked and the correct words supplied.

The course of instruction was tried out on prospective converts, who were already under instruction, with the cooperation of priests who reported on the results. These results seemed favorable, and the next summer's street preaching campaign found the street preachers offering applications for a course of religious instruction by mail.

When these applications were received at Kenrick Seminary in St. Louis, the book and the first two tests were sent out, and, when the tests were returned during the fall and winter months, they were returned corrected and accompanied by letters giving additional explanation where this seemed necessary. On the completion of the course, the person was urged to see the nearest priest, and, when it was thought advisable, the nearest priest was informed.

PRESS NOTICES

Notices in the Catholic press caused the idea to spread. Not only did other seminaries take up the work of giving instruction by mail, but non-Catholics in other parts of the country began to make application in ever increasing numbers. But it was the war that gave real impetus to the work, since such a form of instruction was tailor-made for both chaplains and servicemen. More than 38,000 servicemen were enrolled. The armed forces provided a proving ground, on which it was demonstrated even to the skeptic that, given average intelligence and, most of all, good will, a thorough job of instruction can be done by mail. Let the priests who were chaplains testify!

Since the beginning, over 50,000 people have been enrolled, but not all of these have been non-Catholics or prospective converts. A fair number have been poorly instructed Catholics, who had not the advantage of a Catholic education. Likewise, converts seeking more instruction than they received before baptism, are among the applicants.

There are always the merely curious, usually Bible Christians with their minds immovably fixed on a few pet Scripture texts, who take the course and quarrel with the Church's teaching throughout. There are Protestant ministers, and especially young men preparing for the Protestant ministry, who take the course merely for their own information. But by far the majority are non-Catholics who are sincerely investigating the teachings of the Church.

What prompts them to desire instruction by mail? The reasons are many and various. In fact, each day's mail brings to light some new and unforeseen reason making it necessary that the applicant receive religious instruction by mail. But some reasons occur much more frequently than others.

The most common reason is the one already mentioned. There seems to be an increasingly large number of non-Catholics who are interested in the Church, but who hesitate to visit a priest in person. Perhaps they have heard that priests are educated men, and they are fearful of appearing stupid in asking for instruction in Catholic teaching. Their ignorance of Catholic teaching is what holds them back, coupled with a feeling of awkwardness and pride, lest they seem to ask for something about which they know nothing. The average American doesn't want to even appear to be a "sucker." So they turn to religious instruction by mail in order to know something about the religion which the priest represents, before they venture up on the rectory porch with their finger on the bell.

THEY HESITATE

There are many non-Catholics who are interested in the Church in a vague sort of way and have no idea of what to do about it. It is easy for Catholics to think that it would occur to them to visit a priest. But we must remember that there are many millions in this country who have no idea of elementary Catholic practice, of how the Church is constituted and how it functions. They read about it in the press, they hear it discussed in conversation, they hear Catholic programs over the air. The tug of divine grace asserts itself, but they do not know what to do. They hesitate to ask a Catholic, and many do not have Catholic friends whom they could as k. Often the chief worry of a religiously marooned non-Catholic, after a course of instruction by mail, is what to do next and how to find a sponsor for baptism.

There are reasons for religious instruction by mail rising out of the individual circumstances of people's lives that are too numerous to mention: people handicapped by deafness, and mothers tied down to the home by a family of small children who cannot go for regular instruction; men whose hours of work will not permit regular instruction; traveling salesmen, the inmates of reformatories, penitentiaries, sanatoriums, and the like. There are those who live at a great distance from the priest and those who may live across the street from a church but fear of or dislike for a particular priest moves them to apply for instruction by mail.

Thus it is easily apparent that religious instruction by mail does not compete with oral instructions given by a priest in person, nor is it a substitute, except in relatively few emergency cases. Most often it is a preparation for personal instruction and sometimes a thorough review.

There are many ways in which such individuals learn that instruction by mail is available. Priests throughout the country who are familiar with this system of instruction refer many prospective converts to us when, for some reason, their prospective converts cannot receive instruction from them in person. Applications are distributed to many pastors of far-flung flocks, so that they can be distributed whenever the need arises. These applications are likewise provided to apostolic laymen and laywomen.

In many instances non-Catholics in whom they are interested refuse to visit the priest at once, and in such cases an application for a course of religious instruction by mail is indeed an "ace in the hole." An interested non-Catholic, who has what seems to him a valid reason for not approaching a priest, may find it difficult to refuse an opportunity to investigate the teachings of the Church in the privacy of his home.

But by far the greatest number of interested non-Catholics are prompted to apply for our course of instruction through advertisements inserted in Catholic newspapers and magazines. This is the most fruitful source of prospects. It stands to reason that non-Catholics who are interested in the Church often read Catholic literature. They obtain this literature themselves or Catholic friends and relatives provide it for them. If their interest is such that they are willing to read Catholic literature regularly, an offer of religious instruction by mail in such periodicals is bound to interest them.

We have noticed that such non-Catholics are especially interested in the question box appearing in Catholic newspapers and magazines, and a dummy question offering religious instruction by mail will bring in applications by the hundreds.

Another remarkable fact is the number of non-Catholic partners in mixed marriages who apply for religious instruction as a result of Catholic literature brought into the home by the Catholic

IS RELIGION A RACKET?

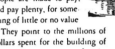

Every now and then, you hear someone say that religion is just another "business."

Some of its harsher critics call it a "racket" people are made to pay, and pay plenty, for something of little or no value

They point to the millions of dollars spent for the building of religious institutions   for the publishing of religious literature for the training and maintenance of ministers, priests and nuns

Certainly, the institutions of the Church represent a vast investment of cash Its activities require the time and talents of large numbers of people who might, if there were no Church, devote themselves to the occupations of the world's trades and professions Unquestionably, the Church requires of its members a certain amount of time and attention that might be devoted to sports and amusements and other occupations of leisure hours

And the critics would be completely right — but for one truth

Religion would be all pretense, all fraud   truly a racket   if there were no God

Priests and preachers, nuns and militant Christians would indeed be charlatans if the lives with which they are concerned actually had no future beyond the grave Theirs would surely be a racket if God were only a fantasy and not a fact.

And yet, how many of those who call religion a racket would trade their own way of life, their own profession or income for that of the average person who serves the Church and has devoted his or her life to Christ and His work? How many would assume the obligations of the priest or nun in exchange for their own?

Even some, who don't mean it, like to jest about the size of the "take" at the Sunday morning collection   or to comment that the pastor with the flourishing parish has a good deal "

But who can say with all honesty that the average priest who has the responsibility of serving his people, no matter where he may be sent, and to support himself on a maximum of $75 a month   or the average nun whose waking hours are devoted to the classroom and prayer has an easy job, much less a racket? How many of us possess such a spirit of sacrifice that we would willingly accept the lives of prayer and service that they impose upon themselves?

Is religion a racket? Even if the faintest suspicion has entered your mind on this question, you should read a pamphlet which we shall be happy to send you free of charge Ask for Pamphlet No. 175-P.

RELIGIOUS INFORMATION BUREAU
Knights of Columbus
4422 Lindell Blvd.   •   St. Louis 8, Mo.
•

This advertisement is one of a series explaining the teachings of the Catholic Church. It is to acquaint our fellow-Americans with the doctrines ;of the Church established by Christ for the salvation of all men that these advertisements are published in paid space in many newspapers.

Sample advertisement run in newspapers by the Religious Information Bureau, sponsored by the Missouri K. of C.

partner or by the children who are being raised Catholics. Mixed marriages are a fruitful source of religious instruction by mail.

It may be asked why advertising is restricted to Catholic periodicals. It isn't. Notices that religious instruction by mail is available have been inserted in the personal columns of classified advertisements in many secular newspapers, large and small, with fair results. In local newspapers pastors have published advertisements offering Catholic information by mail, sometimes referring the applicants to us, sometimes taking care of the course of instruction themselves, but such advertising has not been sufficiently widespread to evaluate the results properly.

KNIGHTS OF COLUMBUS CAMPAIGN

Apart from advertisements which merely make known the availability of religious instruction by mail, doctrinal advertising warrants special mention. In June 1944 the state council of the Knights of Columbus of Missouri began a weekly program of doctrinal advertising in secular newspapers. This advertising campaign has two important and unique features.

First, space in the newspapers was uniformly bought at prevailing rates for religious advertising. Paid space not only insured our freedom to present Catholic teaching in a forthright manner, but also protected the newspaper from a deluge of requests for an equal share of donated space.

Second, each advertisement briefly presented some phase of Catholic teaching or practice followed by an offer of a free pamphlet explaining the subject at greater length. Thus each advertisement was not merely expository, but was designed to provoke a response from the readers.

A religious information bureau, sponsored by the Knights of Columbus, was set up in connection with our office, so we might service the campaign by taking care of all inquiries and requests. It was agreed from the beginning that an important feature was the personal attention that would be given to each inquiry. Each pamphlet sent out was accompanied by a typewritten letter expressing our desire to give correct information concerning teachings of the Catholic Church. A person who would apply for pamphlets one, two, or three times would get a different letter each time, and, upon the third application for literature, a free course of religious instruction was offered.

Since writing the above, the Supreme Council and the local councils of the Knights of Columbus have begun sponsoring advertisements in national and local publications. The results are most gratifying. In the past two months we have had some 41,239 requests for information and pamphlets, and we have enrolled 2,818 persons in our course of religious instruction by mail.

In the course of three years these weekly advertisements have covered practically the whole field of Catholic apologetics, dogma, and morals and were provocative in form and content. Advertisements were published beginning with such titles as: "Is Religion a Racket?"; "Why Waste Money on God?"; "Without God, Nothing Makes Sense"; "No Miracles Today?—What About Lourdes?" "Only a Miracle Could Heal Him and a Miracle Did"; "The 'Open' Bible Was Never Closed"; "Millions Died and None Saw the Bible"; "Do Catholics Want to Rule America?"; "I Want a Religion That Goes Beyond the Grave"; "American or Communist, You Can't Be Both"; "More Husbands Than Babies—Our National Headache"; "Confession—Ask the Man Who Goes There."

The results of such a campaign of Catholic advertising fall into two classifications—intangible and tangible.

INTANGIBLE RESULTS

The intangible results cannot be determined with figures or statistics, but nonetheless can be fairly accurately estimated. First and foremost is the large number of regular readers which these advertisements have every Sunday. Over a period of years, they run into the millions. Advertising agencies have made scientific surveys, testing the readership of these religious advertisements and have definitely proved how widely read they are and how favorably received.

Granting the great number of non-Catholics who would never

read a Catholic book or paper, who would never visit a priest, discuss religion with Catholic friends, or enter a Catholic Church, it is easily seen how many external graces are presented to them Sunday after Sunday with the regular appearance of these advertisements. The general effect cannot but be the removal of prejudice and misunderstanding and the wiping out of bigotry—not to mention the generation of sympathetic interest in the Catholic Church. Priests report converts who were moved to request instruction as a result of reading the advertisements. Non-Catholics have visited Catholic churches with the advertisements in their hands.

There is no way of accurately determining the number of non-Catholics that have been interested in the Church through the medium of such advertisements, but existing indications prove that the number is far greater than we know, and we never shall know the number of fallen-away Catholics who, having been prompted by the regular presentation of Catholic teaching through the press, quietly resume the practice of their religion.

TANGIBLE RESULTS

The tangible results of this campaign of Catholic advertising are highly encouraging. Over the course of three years, 28,639 letters have been written to inquirers and 39,861 pamphlets have been distributed. One must bear in mind that this is not the indiscriminate dissemination of Catholic pamphlets. In this case, each pamphlet was sent to a person who took the trouble to sit down and write a request for it, thus manifesting an initial interest from which we can reasonably conclude the pamphlet was read.

A card file of all inquiries was carefully kept so that those who were requesting pamphlets for the first or second times could be written accordingly. When the third request was received, the pamphlet was sent with a special letter offering our course of religious instruction by mail. There was no attempt to high-pressure anyone into taking instruction and, nonetheless, 710 persons applied for instruction.

It is obvious that such Catholic advertisements appearing in the public press are a public gesture on the part of the Church toward our separated and unchurched brethren, many of whom are persuaded that Catholics are smug, exclusive, and uninterested in those outside the fold. The longer such a campaign of advertising continues, the more impressed are they by the interest of the Catholic Church in their behalf.

Since the advertisements are concerned merely with the presentation of Catholic teaching and never mention other religions, much less attack them in any way, non-Catholics are quick to see that the advertisements are published with the sole purpose of making known what Catholics believe.

The public presentation of Catholic doctrine seldom will go unchallenged by those whose religious faith is based upon a protest against the Church's teaching. In many localities where Catholic advertisements appeared, rival Protestant advertisements were published. No notice whatsoever of these advertisements was taken. In most instances, the competing advertisements were a direct attack or an evident effort to answer the Catholic advertisements. But when these rival advertisements failed to provoke the controversy which they were seeking, they soon disappeared. The overall result was favorable to the Church, because any fair-minded reader could easily discern the absence of hostility in the Catholic advertisements as contrasted with their short-lived competitors.

As this advertising campaign continues, more requests for religious instruction by mail are being received from non-Catholics. The Knights of Columbus in Missouri have definitely proved that it pays to advertise the Catholic Church. They have had to pay. Advertising space in widely circulated newspapers is costly, but not too costly for those who realize that spreading the seeds of faith is as important as multiplying the sales of canned goods or lipsticks— who realize that publicizing the teachings of Christ as they are presented by his Church must be done for all the people, not merely for the few that come within the range of a priest's voice.

There are wealthy Catholic businessmen aplenty in this country who know the value of advertising and realize its costs. Can't they be sold on advertising Catholic truth? They can and will be, when their pastors are sold. The cost of such a campaign in small-town newspapers is not beyond the purse, or at least the money-raising ability, of the average small-town parish. The building of churches and schools is important, but so also is the building of the good will that will some day bring America's unchurched millions up on the rectory porch with their finger on the bell in numbers far exceeding 100,000 per year.

5

How to Interest Prospects

Rt. Rev. Msgr. JOHN A. GABRIELS, D.D.
Resurrection Church, Lansing, Mich.

EDITOR'S FOREWORD: Monsignor John A. Gabriels has been working tirelessly at the task of winning converts during his long priestly ministry. Weekly talks over the radio, frequent talks to after-dinner clubs and civic groups, items in the newspaper, and mingling freely among his fellow citizens are the methods used to recruit prospects. Universally honored and esteemed in Lansing for his leadership in every worthy civic movement, with his assistants he has averaged fifty converts a year for the past twenty-five years and twenty a year for the preceding fifteen years, achieving the magnificent total of 1,550 converts. This indefatigable searcher for the sheep that have strayed gives us a sample of reasoning he uses to interest a prospect. It will repay reading and re-reading, for its logic is bullet-proof.

∽

A TWOFOLD TASK

CONVERT WORK entails a twofold task, namely, the recruiting of prospects and the instruction of the same. In this brief paper we shall confine ourselves to suggesting a few methods of interesting people in the systematic study of the Catholic faith.

We shall present a line of reasoning which we have often used in discussing the matter with individuals. We hope that it may offer a few suggestions to our brothers who are engaged in the work of winning converts for the divine Master.

We have had 63 converts so far this year. We have three classes three times a week from 9 to 10 P.M. all the year round. At other times we have class by appointment. We try to get away from private instructions if we can. We announce it every Sunday and put it in the bulletin (why announce parties and bingo when preaching the Word of God is so much more important?).

I have been on the air every Sunday for over ten years except when I have been on vacation. About once a month I make this announcement over the radio about our classes. They are designed for five groups of people:

1. Those mildly interested in the Church but who do not wish to become Catholics.

2. Those about to marry, or who have married, a Catholic.

3. Those married out of the Church and afraid to visit a priest.

4. Those baptized Catholics who have never made their first confession or First Holy Communion.

5. Those Catholics who want to brush up on the faith that they have.

Our classes run a full hour, sometimes ten or fifteen minutes over, and then we ask if there are any questions. We don't allow any questions on topics that will be discussed in a subsequent session. We don't visit with the people or talk about the weather. We divide our course into ten sections. If they want more, we take them privately. As a rule they have no questions because all their difficulties are touched upon during the class. We don't ask their names, and we insist on their keeping a record of the classes they attend.

THE IMPORTANCE OF PRAYER

My assistants divide their classes as I do, so that if someone calls and says, "When can I get lesson four, as I was out of the city when you had that class?" we can easily tell them when to come. Of course during the summer, the classes are smaller. They average eight to ten an evening in the summer and as high as thirty in the winter. We have had as high as forty people a night. We insist, of course, that the important part of the course is not the attending the classes, but the grace of God which comes by prayer. We make them promise to say some prayers every day, prayers they learned at a good mother's knees or in Sunday School, and we ask them to add four Catholic prayers, the Lord's Prayer, Hail Mary, Apostles' Creed, and the Act of Contrition.

Besides this, they must promise to go to Mass every Sunday and do what the rest do while at Mass, whether standing, sitting, or kneeling. The Catholic who is interested must promise to say the same prayers and go to Holy Communion every Sunday for his non-Catholic friend. This is all-important. I predict that if they say the prayers each day and go to Mass every Sunday, some thing is going to happen. They will get the urge to join the Church even if they refuse to do so. One individual publicly refused to say the prayers or go to Mass. "I know," he said, "if I say those prayers I would be a Catholic, and I don't want to be a Catholic."

We give them some booklets, the *Baltimore Catechism*, *How to Find Christ's Church*, *Catholic Religion Proved by Protestant Bible*, *Pray the Mass with the Priest*, and *The Truth About Catholics*. We have non-Catholics who come out of curiosity. Some finish; others do not. Some join the Church; others do not.

"MAY I ENROLL?"

A non-Catholic Sunday school teacher called and said:

"I hear that you have a course in religion. May I enroll? I have taken two courses, one at my church and the other at the 'Y.' I want to make a better Protestant Sunday school teacher out of myself. What are your fees?"

I told her the course was free and that I would give her a free text book, namely, the catechism. She was pleased and proved to be an outstanding pupil, asking questions which indicated her familiarity with the Bible. When the course ended, she came to me with the remark: "I am sorry I ever came to this class. I intended to be a better Protestant Sunday school teacher, and now my conscience tells me I should be a Catholic. I just can't be a Catholic. Look at my two big girls, Protestants, and my husband who is a strong church worker."

She has not joined the Church yet, but she has a Catholic catechism and a *Question Box* with her while teaching her class in church so that if a pupil asks, "Why do Catholics have incense at funerals?" she can give them the correct answer.

"AUTOCRATIC AND DICTATORIAL"

I always stand during the classes and try to make them peppy and interesting. I use lots of illustrations, give them a laugh from time to time, and sometimes I give them a preview of the next class (like the movies) to induce them to come again. Here is a story that I start out with:

A man came and told me he was interested in a Catholic girl.

"Is it true," he asked, "that I must sign a document promising that I shall allow her to be a Catholic?"

I answered in the affirmative.

"I am broadminded enough for that," he said. "She can go her way, and I will go mine. But must I promise that, if I have any children, all will be Catholics?"

"Yes," I replied.

"Well, to be frank with you," he said, "I don't like the idea at all. I think it very autocratic and dictatorial on your part."

"I don't blame you for that remark," I observed, "because if half the things you have heard about the Church are true, you should not even allow your wife to belong to such an organization."

Apparently he expected me to put up an argument. Finally he asked:

"May I marry the girl without signing the agreement?" I answered, "Yes, if you can induce her to give up her religion. Nobody is keeping her in the Church except herself. This is a free country."

He was silent for a while, and then he said, "I wouldn't trust her if she quit her church. Her religion means too much to her. A girl that isn't true to her God will not be true to her husband."

I agreed heartily with his last statement. After a while he asked, "Have you got time to answer some questions?"

"Yes," I replied, "but it won't do any good."

He wanted to know why. I told him that he had asked those questions before and he was never satisfied with the answers. He agreed that I was right. He said that the girl he was interested in was a graduate from a Catholic college. "I would ask her a question," he continued, "and she would give me an answer. It seemed to satisfy her, but it didn't make sense to me."

PREMATURE QUESTIONS

"Do you know why?" I asked. "It is because you are asking questions out of the back of the book."

When he didn't quite understand what I was driving at. I asked him his business. He had been a teacher at a Normal School. I asked him if he had ever taught mathematics. He said that it was one of his subjects.

"Now," I continued, "suppose in September you have a new class and a new textbook. One of the pupils wants to know how to work out a problem on page 478. What would you do? Would you try to explain it or tell him to wait until you reach that portion of the textbook?"

He agreed that I was right. Then I said, "Religion is a science, the same as mathematics. The reason you haven't been satisfied with the answers to your questions is that you have asked questions before you were ready for the answers."

I guaranteed him that if he would come for a course of instructions, every question that he had would be reasonably answered.

He asked, "Does that mean I have to come more than once?" When I told him "about ten times," he said: "I don't want you to waste your breath on me. I am not going to be a Catholic. You won't get me to sign on the dotted line."

I said, "I am not asking you to join the Catholic Church. The

Catholic Church got along without you for nineteen hundred years and will get along whether you join or not. Moreover, if you want to become a Catholic only because you are interested in a Catholic girl, no priest in the world would receive you."

"Well," he said, "I couldn't be a Catholic if I wanted to because I am a Mason. Why can't Catholics be Masons?"

"I can't answer that tonight, but if you come to my classes, I'll give you an understandable answer at the end of the second lecture." So we started.

"I AM GOING TO JOIN"

He became very interested, did a lot of reading, and came twice as often as most people did. When he finished, he said, "I am going to join the Catholic Church."

I said, "No, you are not. Do you remember when I told you that you couldn't be a Catholic just to marry a Catholic girl?"

"I am going to be a Catholic," was his reply, "even if I never marry her."

As a matter of fact, he never did marry her. He joined the Church, however, and one year later, he introduced me to a young lady.

"This is not the girl I had in mind when I came to your classes. I have known this girl for six months. We want to get married. She is not a Catholic, but she should be one. Her mother was married out of the Church. Most of her relatives are Catholics. The only church she ever went to was a Catholic Church." After she joined the Church, I married the couple.

They are a prominent Catholic couple today with a nice large family. The last time I saw him, he said, "That first night I called on you, if you had told me that I was ever going to join the Church, I would have thought you were ready to have your head examined."

"I know it," was my reply. "That first night you had a picture of the Catholic Church in your mind to which I was as much opposed as you were. All I did was to try to paint a different picture. Your prayers and the grace of God did the rest."

6

The Right Approach

CLARE BOOTHE LUCE
New York

EDITOR'S FOREWORD: *Few, if any, conversions in our generation have attracted more attention than that of Mrs. Henry R. Luce. She was then a leading member of Congress, where her ability as a speaker and her flair for vivid and original phrases had frequently brought her into the limelight. In addition, she had achieved a considerable reputation as a writer of plays, articles, and books in which her gift for satire frequently showed itself.*

When she disclosed in McCall's Magazine *the line of evidence and of reasoning which with God's grace led her into the Catholic Church, the nation sat up and took notice. Perhaps not since Newman's time has the publication of an apologia created a greater stir. More than a thousand letters poured in from all parts of the country after the publication of the first installment. The ever-bulging mail bag showed clearly that Clare Boothe Luce had not only a message for the general public but also a manner of putting it which gripped all who read it.*

In her presentation she combines something of Newman's calm discernment and penetrating insight with Chesterton's nimbleness in phrase making. Running through her whole story is a deeply spiritual tone and a transparent sincerity which wins the respect of both friend and foe.

When we asked for a contribution, she graciously sent us a copy of a talk on winning converts which she had given to the clerical students and priests at the Catholic University with the wonderment if it would serve. It couldn't fill our need more aptly if it had been prepared especially for our purpose. We feel both happy and privileged to put her fine paper in permanent form to carry its logic, its insights, and its beauty to many generations of readers.

Not less than twenty readers of her series on The Real Reason *have written to tell her that her articles helped to guide them on the road to the Church founded by Jesus Christ. May this beautiful and stirring article, which mirrors so authentically her lovely qualities of mind and heart and soul and her deeply spiritual nature, guide and inspire the thousands who read it to win many thousands of souls for the divine Master. In reading her little masterpiece, one comes to understand more clearly what George Eliot meant when she wrote in* Romola: *"Beauty is the finished language by which goodness speaks to us."*

∽

THE RIGHT APPROACH

THEY SAY THAT a Catholic life is a long adventure in grace. I feel this is true, though my own Catholic life is still so short. I am not even a year old yet. A mere spiritual toddler. How glad I am you can't see all the bumps and bruises I've given myself. But you must guess how awkward and shy I feel tonight, talking to young men like yourselves, sure-footed in the ways of the Lord, not to say old athletes like Monsignor Sheen. And I thank your generous hearts for asking me.

All the world, they say, loves a lover. I am no exception. And never before have I been together with so many young men who are deeply in love, for the first and last times in their lives. For you are to be the truest of all lovers, the priests of God's altars. While my own adventures in grace have been limited, to be with you tonight is surely, up to now, my life's most graceful adventure.

When your exciting invitation came, Monsignor Sheen at once suggested a subject. No doubt, he knew that if he did not I would worry and fret myself into choosing some wholly secular topic, lest my youth—you do understand I mean my spiritual youth—should handicap me in your eyes. The subject was to be "The Apologetical Approach to the Non-Catholic Mind." That sounded at first like something I could cope with—indeed, vaguely political, a little like "The Republican Approach to the Conservative Democrat." And the convert maker is like a politician, in that he is always trying to enlarge the constituency of his faith. But when one began to think about it, an amazing difference presented itself.

The politician can often gather constituents by judiciously shading the truth here or there, or perhaps by not telling all of it, or, best of all, by telling people as much of what they want to hear as is consistent, let us say, with the security of the nation or a balanced budget. But when you are seeking constituents for God! Ah, then, only the whole truth will suffice. And then one must be so very careful to state the truth with exquisite accuracy and simplicity. Now it was plain to me that what that disarming title really meant was: "What should one say to lead confused or wandering minds to God?"

Here I should like to make a little confession, as a writer. In the course of my non-Catholic years I've whipped out a good number of plays, books, articles, and speeches. Perhaps people thought them too diverse in technique or subject matter to have been written by one woman.

Or perhaps, they instinctively felt that they were not being written by the real woman. I don't know. In any case, after each new literary effort, someone always accused me of having had a ghost writer. This hurt my pride badly. And I always protested vigorously. Yet today, as a Catholic, I pray on my knees for the help of a ghost writer—the most underpaid, underworked, underestimated one of modern times, the Holy Ghost.

If anything I write or say in the future about Catholicism should ever be well or truly said, the Paraclete should be given the credit. But such is the perversity of non-Catholics, they will surely insist that it is evident by the nature of the material that the lady is no longer employing her successful ghost writer.

POTENTIAL CATHOLICS

But to return to the apologetical approach—or how does a Catholic convince a non-Catholic that he would be happier if he were not, so to speak, hell-bent on being unhappy hereafter?

The question immediately suggests another. Is every man a potential Catholic? Yes, if all men are seeking three things: truth, love, and life, even when they seem to be seeking them in the labyrinth ways of falsehood. And our blessed Lord thought all men were potential Catholics, or be would not have said, "Teach ye all nations. Go ye into the whole world and preach the gospel to every creature" (Mark 16:15). He set his apostles hard tasks, but none that were impossible.

So there must be a word that can be said to every mind, which will turn it to Catholic truth, if we can only find it. And yet, the more I thought about the apologetical approach, the less willing I became to tackle it. Why? Because, as a convert, I have increasingly come to believe that no non-Catholic was ever led into the Church by mere brainwork. Not by his own, and not by the priest's. Some of the brainiest brainworkers in the world today are conspicuously poor candidates for conversion.

On my desk at home there are ten or twenty volumes, fresh from the publishers, written by men of considerable talents and intellectual prestige. According to the blurbs on the jacket, each of them is full of closely reasoned analyses of the current aspect of the tragic human situation, which they refer to as the world crisis. They are veritable puddings of ingenious formulae, panaceas, and "blueprints." But the basic premise of each is that man can lift himself by his own bootstraps, if not into the millennium—most modern authors have lowered their sights considerably in recent years—at least out of this horrible mess called progress.

Each author seems sure that if "all mankind" would give one last final "heave-ho, my hearties!" it would save itself. I have read just enough of these bootstrap plans to know that if all mankind did do just that, all mankind would only succeed in throwing out its sacroiliac for another century. Well, I once heard of a sick man who said, "God has stretched me on my back to give me time to think." And perhaps that is the real meaning of this current world crisis.

But to lurch back to my subject, the apologetical approach with its implicit hope of a conversion. I am reminded of Mrs. Brompton's famous recipe for making hare stew. "First," she said, "you must catch your hare." Now nothing is more hare-brained than a man who is fleeing the Hound of Heaven. The only way to catch up with the mind of a modern intellectual is to wait patiently until it catches up with itself. Until that moment comes, the apologetical approach is generally futile. Even if these gifted and fertile brain-workers were not, in their spare time, all snarled up in quarrels with one another's panaceas, most of them would consider it distinctly beneath their intellectual dignity to engage in philosophical debate with you or me. I know because I've tried.

I was talking with one of these bootstrap-plan authors only the other day at a dinner party. He was a political writer with something of a reputation as an historian. He was busily tracing the causes of World War II back to a certain contretemps that Woodrow Wilson had with Clemenceau at Versailles.

GOING BACK TO THE CAUSES

"But don't you think," I asked him, "that you really have to go back farther than that little episode to get at the roots of the crisis?"

"Maybe," he said, "but if you keep going back in human history, searching for causes, where could you stop? An historian must begin his examination of the causes of this war within some familiar framework of human historical reference."

"Well," I said, "you could skip an awful lot that happened in between if you just went back to the Garden of Eden. You'd have to stop there, naturally, and then begin your cross-examination with Adam and Eve and the serpent."

He laughed heartily. And then suddenly his smile froze. He had remembered I was a Catholic. "Oh, yes, of course," he said, "you believe in Adam." He humored me with a smile. It was plain that he thought Adam was a creature of my imagination, like that white rabbit Harvey.

"Well, if you do believe in human causality in human history," I asked him, "don't you sort of have to begin with the first man?"

"You mean," he said, "you really do believe that there was a first man?"

"Well," I said, "I don't find that harder to believe than that there were a first ten thousand."

"Man," he said, with infinite pity, "evolved naturally. No doubt from the ape. An atomic mutation of genes of the simian as the result of some local discharge of, er, radioactive elements."

I said, "But look, if man evolved naturally, then he wasn't mutated, which involves outside, or atomic, agency. Did he evolve or was he mutated? And who evolved what he evolved from or mutated what mutated him?"

"My dear child," he said, "I am not interested in first causes. I leave that to the theologians. I am an historian."

"You mean," I said, "You are interested in secondary causes. You do make that clear in your book explaining how this war happened?" Rather quickly he turned to his other dinner partner—and avoided me the rest of the evening. It was precisely what I deserved.

I assure you, the apologetical approach shot cannot be played out of the sand traps of dinner or cocktail parties. And anyway, clever men are always much too clever to discuss any subject but their own specialties, which generally concern facts, figures, and statistics. Oh, they do know so much!

They seem always so on fire to know even more. Their curiosity for facts and more facts is insatiable. To be sure, they are willing to answer an infinity of questions—providing your questions concern the sensible universe. To these they are ready with an infinity of answers, which in turn raise new questions.

But the truth is they are far too busy, multiplying endlessly individual phenomena and theories to explain them, to listen to any argument you or I might have concerning the whole, the totality, of which their questions and theories can be only parts. I fear we should rather try, by taking thought, to change ourselves into angels than to hope, by mere reasoning, to turn clever men into Catholics.

I know this now: The cleverer a man is, the less one should argue with him and the more one should pray for him. For what the clever man is wanting is not brains, but grace. I am hoping that in a year or two I will be a good enough Catholic that I may add my prayers to yours in their behalf. Meanwhile I am too busy praying for myself, on account of I was once one of them.

THE HEART HAS REASONS

Now I don't mean for a second that apologetics in the mouth of a master will not put a terrific dent in any non-Catholic intellectual's armament. It is true that I accepted Catholic reasoning concerning the nature and the destiny of man in a matter of weeks. It seemed to me incontrovertible as well as sublime. But it was still a matter of months before I became a Catholic. And now we come to the crux of the matter: *the heart hath reasons that knoweth not reason!* You may win every apologetical round with a non-Catholic and still not win his soul!

Then, why, I asked myself again, after I thought this unhappy fact over, was it suggested that I write on the apologetical approach to the non-Catholic? Who knew better than he that this approach is of no avail? Or who knew it better than I?

I saw it then, very clearly; it was intended that I should figure this very fact out for myself and with you, just as we are doing. It was meant that I should review my own instructions and recollect the heart of the matter.

Now we come to it quickly: The one Catholic argument I could not controvert, the one that was not just the most important but the transcendent argument, for it encompassed the totality of Catholic thought—that was the argument he gave me, in epitome, at the end of each instruction, when he said, "God love you!"

For love is the word that begets grace, and grace alone illumines and lifts the intellect. So in the end, all conversions are effected through love. The mind is hungry for truth, but the soul is athirst for love. And it is the soul that must be touched. If the Catholic cannot successfully argue the word of love, all his other arguments fail.

All the world loves a lover. Indeed, can one love, or even long respect, anything but a lover? The priest who ceases to be a true lover, though he reasons like the Angelic Doctor himself, will make few converts.

I believe that every man and woman who has ever heard of the Church that preaches Christ crucified feels in his heart that he could be converted to it . . . if, ah, if he only met the "right priest." And every non-Catholic who encounters a priest anywhere, on a bus, a train, even on a traffic island, looks to see if he is That Man. All the prejudices and predispositions he has toward the Church of Rome are thus forever focusing and converging upon each priest he sees or meets, however casual the encounter.

This, he says, way back in his mind, this creature in black, he is an agent of that God that I do not or cannot believe in. I can now judge of my own judgment by this man, I can judge his Church by this man. I can even judge his God by this man. If it is possible, the non-Catholic begins then a conversation.

"Father," he begins, "here is something I have always wanted to ask a priest." And he asks about this or that ritual, this or that doctrine, this or that stand the Church is supposed to be taking on this or that issue. Are you wondering the whole while if he could be converted, if you said just the right thing, at the right moment? Well, he is wondering, too, if you are the man who could ever convert him.

"WHAT YOU ARE"

Emerson once said: "What you are thunders so I can't hear what you say." The non-Catholic listens. But he doesn't really hear. What you are is thundering the real answer he is seeking. For even the blackest and the most cynical of all men has a clear concept in his mind of what a man of God ought to be. He knows that he ought to be a true lover. For what is it to be a true lover? It is to be transformed, transfigured into the likeness of what one loves, to become, through the passionate efforts of one's whole being, conformed to the beloved.

The non-Catholic knows that the priest ought to be Christlike, just as he knows that the Catholic layman ought to be Christian. But how does the non-Catholic judge, in the casual encounter with the priest, whether or not he is a true lover? A man who has freedom is in love, in his love he is free, and he knows that he loves forever and is forever loved in return. The non-Catholic knows that there are always three marks upon any true lover, for did he not himself love, or dream of loving, some human, perhaps, truly? The true lover is *joyous.* He is *selfless.* He is *simple* or single-eyed. Should it be less true of the lovers of Divinity? He knows it ought to be *more* true.

All men know that the human heart must seek its joy somewhere. The glum priest, the dour priest, the sad or dispirited priest, advertises rather quickly to the non-Catholic that be has not found his joy in God. Does that priest argue to him, "Our Lord gives you his joy. His burden is light." Ah, the non-Catholic reflects, it has not given this fellow too much joy; he looks like he was carrying an insupportable burden. If this God of his can give no joy to his own anointed, how should he give it to me, a sinner? The non-Catholic turns back to the world in his own search for joy.

And all men know that the mark of the true Lover is unselfishness. "All for love, and the world well lost," was said by a man of his love for a woman. Should a divine Lover inspire less sacrifice? Only a man who has nothing and wants nothing for himself, having all in God, can convince the non-Catholic, who has laid up his treasures on earth, that he just may, after all, have chosen the worst part.

And how shall a priest who is not simple in his words and single-minded in his deeds convince a non-Catholic that he must undertake that rigorous simplification of his own life and speech, which he quickly learns a conversion entails?

Yes, all men seek truth and love and life. But three other desires seek them: the desire for power over others, the desire of the senses, and the desire to possess things. The non-Catholic learns from a so-called lover of Christ that these things are bad for the soul. With what remarkable eloquence the priest says it! The non-Catholic listens. But it is not what is said he judges or what he accepts or rejects; again, it is the priest who says it.

The non-Catholic asks, "Is he proud? Does he like to be obeyed himself? Are his own comforts as relatively important to him as mine are to me, his own possessions as dear? Is he, then, acquisitive? How is this lover of the Lord any better than I? His church has done little for him but make him eloquent. Well, eloquence is not my ambition." Only humility and chastity and poverty are utterly convincing to the non-Catholic mind. Or how shall *he* be able to do or be what you say, if *you* are not able to do or be what you say? The casual encounter ends. The non-Catholic is cordial in parting, perhaps even effusive.

"Well, thank you, Father, this has been most interesting. A great pleasure to meet you. I really must read up on Catholicism. Sometime . . . but you know, I'm very busy." In vain the priest will dream of a better apologetical approach the next time.

I expect all I am saying is that when there are better priests and better Catholic laymen, too, in the world, there will be more converts.

THE HARD WAY

All of this is familiar to you. But to me it is rather new, for I found out about these things the hard way, as a convert. When I first became a convert, I thought to convince my friends with words and argument, the apologetical approach.

I quickly learned that regardless of their apparent eagerness to argue, what they were judging was me—not my arguments. Would I stay joyful and serene and happy? How long? Would I be kinder to my friends? How much? Would I grow steadily more Christian? How fast? My actions only, I learned, had any real power to convince my friends about Catholicism. It was then that I learned the mysterious and sometimes terrifying truth about the faith I had embraced.

There is no such thing as being a neutral at the Crucifixion. A Catholic may stumble and fall, or faint from weariness, or even rest a moment to regroup his forces. But when he is not trying to shoulder the cross, he inescapably finds himself engaged in another business—the business of passing out the nails to the unbelievers.

Now that I am a Catholic, I know how terribly hard it is not to do so often. But I was harsher in my judgments of Catholics in those days. As harsh as every non-Catholic you meet all the rest of your days will be in theirs of you.

Believe me, though the non-Catholic is asking about the infallibility, catholicity, apostolicity, unicity, or organicity of the Church, what is always and ever in question in the bottom of his mind is its piety and sanctity. These he judges ever and always by the Catholics and their priests whom he meets in casual encounters.

In the end, of course, only the saints and the martyrs make converts in any number. I see now what is meant when it is said that the seed of the Church is the blood of the martyrs. If the heart hath reasons that reason knoweth not of, then it must be said that the best apologetical approach to the non-Catholic is martyrdom, for the economy of the Incarnation is the begetting of love in loving unto death, in dying that others may live. Then, too, there is another thing. There are the doubting Thomases, with their congenitally curious fingers. There must always be fresh wounds for the satisfaction of these doubting digits.

Ah, yes, asks the Catholic, but have there ever been so many doubting Thomases as there are in the world today? Perhaps not, replies the non-Catholic, but have there ever been so few martyrs? But viewed from their point of view or ours, the fact stands—the world is agonizing in spiritual starvation. Can the soul of man best be fed with Catholic apologetics? Or with the Word of Love?

"And my speech and my preaching were not in the persuasive words of human wisdom," said St. Paul, "but in showing the Spirit and the power" (1 Cor. 2:4).

And now let me tell you two little stories about two priests. I never knew or saw either of them. But their spirit and their power I can testify to.

THE WRONG WAY

The first is probably dead, God rest his soul. I learned about him from a colleague of mine in Congress. A year or so ago, when it began to be rumored I was taking instructions, this Congressman, an able and decent fellow, though often strangely irascible, took me aside one day in the cloak room. He had been born, he said, a Catholic. Did I know what I was doing? Did I know what a strain Catholicism would be on my reason? In the end, he told me his story. He was bitter with an old bitterness that you could see had festered and poisoned all the conduits of his soul.

He had been a very poor boy, an only son, who in his early teens had had to earn a living for his widowed mother, whom he adored. When he was fifteen, they moved to a strange town, where he thought he might do better. She died rather suddenly. I believe that his grief must have been very intense, for be began to cry now, forty years later.

He wanted her to have a fine funeral. He went to the priest. Then his voice shook with anger remembering that visit to the rectory. The priest was probably curt and casual. He told the boy that the money he had was insufficient to give her the kind of funeral the boy's broken heart had set itself on. The boy argued. The priest argued back. The boy shouted at the priest. The priest shouted back at the boy.

The boy ran away, frightened and sobbing with rage. But since his mother, that dearest lady of his life, had to be buried, that priest had to do it. The pitiful, scrimpy funeral, at which he was the only mourner, was a double agony for the boy. Not only his mother was being buried, but his faith. When he left the Church that day, he left forever. He married out of the Church and brought up two children in his wife's faith, though he said they really have no faith at the present.

How many other souls that priest may have lost to the Church we cannot guess. I know of four. And if that Congressman had been able to convince me out of the bitterness of his angry heart, there would have been five. All because of a few words, no doubt magnified by the anguished brain of a boy, and since that time magnified even more in years of cumulative bitterness. But in any case, they were words that could not have been Christlike. That is the first priest.

THE RIGHT WAY

And now the last story. It happened on Saturday. To me. I need not tell you that, for a convert, confession is the hardest part of the faith to accept joyfully. Of all his possessions, the secret possessions of his conscience and of his pride are the ones that the convert is most loath to part with. That habitual secrecy and pride seem to be invaded and humiliated by that stranger behind the curtain.

On the other hand, the absolution, the advice of confessors who know the convert, humiliate him in a different way. He is prone to ascribe their sweetness and gentleness in some part to the friendship they may bear him or the extra patience that might be shown the convert. And yet, his pride—oh, his wicked pride—forbids that his confessor should be more gentle with him than with others!

The stranger is, then, better. Then he takes to going into big Catholic churches, on crowded afternoons, where he couldn't be known. He wants no more from the faith than any other Catholic and wants to give in the faith just as they give. So it was with me. And all had gone well enough in these churches. According to doctrine, I was, you might say, intellectually convinced of the real necessity of this sacrament. And yes, there was always some increment of grace after. And yet, and yet . . .

I know that in speaking this way, I sound as though I did not understand that this sacrament is also a sacrament of love like all the others. Well, perhaps I didn't understand it really, until last Saturday. Last Saturday at St. Patrick's, when I had finished my confession and had made my act of contrition, there came a voice from behind that curtain, saying, "Go now . . . And God bless you!"

That is all. But how shall I ever tell you the fullness of absolution that came to my heart by those words? Because they were said with warmth and joy! Because there was in them the plenitude of charity!

All the apologetics for the confessional I have ever heard or read—and had fully accepted intellectually—never awakened in my heart the unshatterable conviction that now sings in it, because of those three, short, simple, and familiar words, said in a voice that was Christlike. I am sure that every Catholic who made his confession to that priest left St. Patrick's as I did, full of awakened zeal and resolve to be better, and to do better, and to love better.

You who are a chosen generation, a kingly priesthood, a holy nation, a purchased people! If you declare his virtues in such a voice, even though you ask only the time of day of some non-Catholic, his heart will answer, "By your voice, Father, one might say the time of day is God's high noon now!"

7

Trailer Missions

Very Rev. JAMES F. CUNNINGHAM, C.S.P., Superior General
Paulist Fathers, St. Paul's Church, New York

EDITOR'S FOREWORD: *The millions of people in the South, in many localities of which Catholics are as scarce as the proverbial needle in the haystack, constitute a challenge to the missionary zeal of the Catholic population of America. Spearheading our answer to that challenge is the work of the trailer missionary. He is at our most advanced outpost. He is our entering wedge.*

While many groups are now engaged in trailer mission work, the Paulist Fathers are the great pioneers in this field, and their accomplishments are outstanding. In this chapter Father James F. Cunningham, C.S.P., takes us on a tour of the mission field, allows us to glimpse the varied activity of the missionary without experiencing his physical discomforts, though he can't entirely spare us from his heart-aches and his difficulties.

The trailer mission is an important part of the Church's manifold efforts to extend Christ's kingdom on earth. It is arduous, costly, and difficult. It is, however, eminently worthwhile. From experience in street preaching in the Appalachian mountain regions in North Carolina, we came to realize how transient are likely to be the results if there is no follow-up to extend, deepen, and consolidate the gains. This the trailer mission accomplishes.

There are few if any pages in the annals of Catholic missionary work in America today more colorful and inspiring than those which tell of the gallant work of the forlorn soldier of Christ in the lonely mission areas of the South. We hope that Father Cunningham's vivid narrative will enlist the generous support of priests and people and bring to him and to all the other trailer missionaries the needed re-enforcements in men and in material. Once a lonely battler on the farthest front and now superior general of the Paulists, Father Cunningham will not fail to allocate to the widening of the beachheads in the South, an enterprise so close to his heart, a generous amount of the support which he so desperately needs for the far-flung convert work of his missioners and which we, please God, shall not fail to send.

INTRODUCTION

IN PRESENTING THE STORY of trailer missions I should like to emphasize at the outset what the Paulist Fathers had in mind when they undertook this special type of apostolic work. It was inaugurated by Father John Harney, C.S.P., former superior general, who was dissatisfied with the results from our parishes in the rural districts. He felt that some new approach was necessary. Trailer mission work was to carry the gospel into sections where there was no electricity, where preaching would be done in open lots and the priests would live in the trailer itself. This kind of work, it was felt, required a church and a rectory on wheels. The aim of the activity was to gain converts to the Church in the rural areas. It is important to keep this objective in mind for an understanding of the tremendous energy of individuals concerned, the consistent efforts and large sums of money expended to accomplish the task outlined.

There are two important factors in trailer mission work. One of them is the contact which is made through preaching, the other is the "follow-up." The latter must be kept before the trailer missionary at all times. There are many different diocesan and religious order groups in the trailer mission field today. The Paulist Fathers present their method in the pages that follow not because it is the best but because they pioneered the mission field with this technical equipment and have found that the program works.

THE "WORK"

Since 1939 the Paulist Fathers have been engaged in trailer mission work in various parts of the United States. During the summer of 1947 there were six trailer chapels working in Texas, Tennessee, South Carolina, Missouri, and Utah. The work is expensive. During these past eight years more than $100,000 has been expended. A large number of young priests has been engaged in the activity. The apostolic pattern is pretty much the same in each place, and, since Winchester, Tennessee, with its three hundred converts, its four chapels, and its intensive present program, has been our most successful venture, we shall use it as a means of explaining our method of working. For much of our success there we are indebted to the consistent support of Bishop William Adrian of Nashville.

Let me emphasize the word "work." Those of us who began it referred to trailer preaching as "muscular Christianity." It is difficult, physically tiring, and mentally fatiguing. Yet, there are many of us who have found it the most satisfactory type of mission work. From the day you start to distribute handbills until the day your first class has been received into the Church, you have a record of never-ceasing activities. You interest people in religion and channel that into a desire for the Catholic religion. You instruct, receive, and baptize them. You hear their first confessions, give them First Holy Communion, and present them to the bishop for confirmation. In a very large way you are a spiritual "father." You find the efforts made are rewarded a hundredfold.

LET'S GO

So let's start out on a trailer. Where are we going, and what are we going to do? You look around at the equipment and find a trailer chapel pulled by an automobile. In it are living accommodations (necessarily somewhat primitive) and an altar and vestments—a complete church and rectory on wheels. Your church is supplied with the best public address system plus a motion picture machine, films, slides, and records.

Where do we go? To any remote rural area. The chapel is to be our home unless we can find a hotel or rectory not too far away which we can use as a base of operations. You will bless that hotel with its seclusion, its soft (?) bed at the end of a long day, its shower or bath; you will regard with something akin to fondness that hostelry with its privacy. In the trailer you live like a bird in a dusty, ungilded cage, or perhaps as a goldfish in a globe of murky water. From the crack of dawn—and you will be convinced that the birds are awakened by the rural farm children—until late at night, you are seldom without visitors. What is the greatest difficulty in trailer work? My own answer would be the lack of privacy.

And now with everything ready we head for the farm districts of rural Tennessee. It may be that we will stop, as we did, at the little town of Cowan with a population of about twelve hundred. We were well received. But we find very quickly that the townsfolk are well organized religiously and that the farm people are not. In the towns there is always some form of entertainment; in the rural areas you may be the only excuse people have to get together, the only reason they have for going somewhere. Your trailer is the source of endless amazement, your motion pictures are a means of bringing not only entertainment but spiritual instruction as well.

You may be reaching people who have never seen a "movie" before. That has happened to us often. The motion pictures will be the means of quieting a hundred or more children in your audience, and you will find that, by means of the picture *The King of Kings* and your commentary on it, resentments and misunderstandings are quickly and quietly overcome. In the country your trailer is a movable church and at the same time an open invitation to "come and sit awhile" to every interested or curious man or woman of the rural areas.

Why cannot this work be done with a station wagon and a public address system? It can be. However, you may well miss a vital factor in rural convert work—that is contact. People will come into the trailer who often will not talk to you outside. You will miss the advantage of advertising which comes from the daily spectacle of the trailer on the highways. You will not have the advantage of daily Mass in the field or the assistance of a quiet place "to talk things over."

On rainy nights many will come like Nicodemus of old to talk with you when you are "rained out" and are "in" to those who wish to ask questions. In the town of Decherd on one rainy night we talked to a Sunday school class for about two hours. The result of that contact resulted in a convert eight years later who was received a few months ago after he had married another trailer convert.

GOOD WILL

Just last summer a priest told me of two friends of his who used a street-preaching public address system and gave about thirty talks in twenty-five days. They went all over a certain state. I asked, "How many converts did they get?" A logical question; if not logical, at least customary. "None" was the answer. "There were some people interested, but they did not have time to stop and instruct them." I asked what he thought was the result of the work, and he answered, "Good will."

Good will is important as means to an end, and the end is converts. We use many avenues to gain this good will. On Friday nights at Winchester during the fall we used the trailer-chapel as a broadcasting base for local high school games. We found that from then on in many of the towns we were to visit there were many who came to see us because they had seen the trailer on the football field.

The Crimson Clover Festival, which brought thousands to the town in early spring, was broadcast from our trailer. Father Frank Broome found himself on one occasion acting as public-address master of ceremonies for a rural horse show.

We found an interest in civic affairs to be invaluable if we wish to capitalize on good will. Good will helps, but we must not forget that the successful insurance salesman is the one who brings in signed policies. We are, as were the apostles, salesmen of religion, and, like all of our countrymen, we like to see concrete results.

So it is important first to know what you wish to do with a trailer. We decided it was rural mission work and in this field to seek converts. In doing this we hit hard, hit often, and, like St. Paul, kept on hitting the same place over and over again until we felt there was no more fruit to be garnered.

IN THE FIELD

Our first mission was in the little town already mentioned of about twelve hundred people. Here we learned the first lesson that must be understood by any street preacher, particularly in the rural South. You must talk the language of the people to whom you speak. The primary object of the sermon is that it be understood by those who listen. Here comes a group of boys to visit the trailer. They attended the service the night previously.

"We saw you passing out handbills yesterday afternoon," one of them said, "and heard your music at night so we came on over." The handbills he referred to were printed announcements of the "mission-revival." (Protestants call this preaching a "revival," and we call them "missions," so we compromised on a title understandable to both.) In passing out these throwaways it is a help to let the school children assist you, and often it is not difficult to put them in the mail for all box holders of the district in which you work.

The boys heard you on the first night. They liked the half hour of music with which you opened; they enjoyed and were quiet during and after the ten-minute animated cartoon, from which you selected your instruction on the importance of telling the truth. You told them that each night they would have a moving picture like that if they remained quiet during the adults' part of the program.

They cooperated perfectly, too, during the twenty-five minutes devoted to answering questions, during the talk on salvation which had an evangelical appeal understood by the rural non-Catholic.

Then the children sat quietly some more while you went back to the motion picture machine and projected the first part of *The King of Kings* with a running commentary on the sacrament of penance. This was all solid religious instruction, even if to the boys it seemed to be only entertainment.

WHO IS CHRIST?

Now they are asking you questions. You have told them more about the life of Christ, spent some fifteen minutes giving them a résumé. Yet you feel that these boys, twelve and thirteen years of age—non-Catholics all—do not understand you even though they seem interested. There is a feeling on your part of inadequacy—they just "don't get it."

All during your discourse you have used the word "Christ" in referring to our Saviour. Suddenly a light dawns on one of the boys. He turns to the others: "It is all right, fellas, he is talkin' 'bout Jesus." Then he turns to you with the query, "Is Christ his last name?" Only then do you discover that though we often use the same words they have different meanings and significance.

Your audience in the Southern rural field may have one outstanding fault—a failure to distinguish. To you sin is either mortal or venial. To them sin is something which is punished in hell. Sin is using lipstick and rouge, sin is going to the movies, sin is getting drunk or stealing or even committing murder. Sin is doing anything wrong.

"Sin is sin," said the old preacher, "and there ain't no two kinds of it." Being "saved" to you is the result of a lifetime of effort. To them "being saved" means accepting baptism or "recognizing Jesus as my personal Saviour."

COMMON GROUND

In dealing with rural people you should use understandable illustrations. You must find with your auditors a common ground. There will be no difficulty in approaching them if you both stand on the same ground—that of basic religious teaching. It is important not to antagonize your listeners. This may seem a trite remark, yet I've known of more than one case in which the preacher started out the first night by speaking on "Why I am a Catholic." In another case the lead-off sermon was on the Blessed Mother. Both talks have important places in the week of sermons—but not the introductory talk. In our first week too, we found that the larger part of our audience did not like the music we were using—classical numbers and Catholic hymns. They wanted hillbilly music and their own hymns.

The first few weeks were experimental. Decherd, our second stop, brought out well in excess of 700 on the third night, and the whole population of the town was only 850. Again we had to get used to being called "Mister" and "Brother." Yet no offense was intended; we were as surprised to be called any thing other than "Father" as they were to see us preaching in cassock and mission cross.

On our next week we had asked permission to use the ground of an abandoned "Christian" church. The old gentleman who could give the required permit was eighty-six, hardy, vigorous, and one who believed that a "revival" was a good thing for any neighborhood. That is, until he asked, "What denomination do you represent?" When I replied, "Roman Catholic," he immediately said, "Sir, under no condition will we help you or cooperate with you in any way." He was a sterling old character, a faithful Bible Christian who had "heard all about Catholic priests," but had never met one.

We had a very pleasant visit after he unburdened himself of what he had heard about Catholics. But whenever I cornered him on some piece of Biblical teaching, he would answer, without admitting we were right, "Son, I'm too old a man to argue with you about that," and change the subject.

After half an hour or so I prepared to leave. He invited me to "hurry back" but to forget all this "Catholic nonsense." By this time we were settled in our routine and decided that our next stop should be the central point around which our year's work would revolve.

ALTO

We decided on a place called Alto—the center of the "bloody ninth" district—and a very small crossroads hamlet. We parked the trailer in the school yard about fifteen miles from our home base and established there our first frontier. Night preaching, daily visiting of the people, a different place each day for dinner, and morning Mass in the trailer. Four girls were our first congregation. They had never met a Catholic priest before, but today one of them is a professed nun, a Sister of Mercy, and her three sisters as well as her mother and brother are Catholic. Today there is a chapel a stone's-throw from the original "pitch" which seats well over a hundred. It is crowded for Sunday Mass, and, of the three hundred converts received in this work, well over a hundred have come from this section.

The people here were interested. So instead of moving a considerable distance for our next week we pushed on about two miles so that those who were anxious to learn more might follow us, as they did. For a full year we conducted Bible classes, four and five a week in this district. We had a special Sunday afternoon "preaching" with a hillbilly band made up of the members of one family. The children, all non-Catholic at the outset, read prayers and questions and answers from the catechism over the public address system. All during the winter, when bad roads and the cold made trailer work impossible, we stayed with them. During the summer a vacation school was taught by lay teachers the first year and then by Dominican nuns. Only when the children were well instructed in the faith did we receive them into the Church. By that time even the smallest child knew the answer to most of the questions which they were being asked.

This same process was repeated in Tullahoma, in Shelbyville, in Brownington, in Lynchburg. During the war years we had shortages of men and material—four of our chaplains having gone into the service from Winchester. We had a camp at Tullahoma with as many as 80,000 men on maneuvers at various times. It was difficult to compete with jeeps, half-tracks, and tanks, not to mention the ubiquitous army trucks crowding the road. Since then we have moved into new and unfriendly territory. The priests work night and day, but live at a hotel in McMinnville about sixty-five miles from our original base. If the work seems blessed and the people interested enough, we will build another chapel.

Not every hamlet or town has received us with enthusiasm. In several places we worked week after week without getting a single person who showed interest, though hundreds turned out for the preaching. Possibly the largest Negro congregation of all turned out in one of these towns—averaging up to nine hundred a night. Yet there were no concrete or measurable results. If we cannot get an interest aroused, we move on, to return at a time when people might be more inclined to hear our "message."

This year, too, we have established another plan. Up to now we have been using our own priests for the follow-up. This is a work which could well be done by a community of nuns. In one sector this year, for example, we have worked ten weeks with a pastor who has several rural missions. We have done the spade work and interested a number of non-Catholics in the Church. He will do the follow-up to gather in the harvest.

EQUIPMENT AND TECHNIQUE

Our trailer chapel, as already indicated, was equipped with a public address system, a motion picture projection machine, a turntable for records, and recordings such as the "Lives of the Saints" on the *Ave Maria* program, which were used for Sunday afternoon programs. The unit had its own electric generator, which is carried in the place of the back seat of the car. The films shown were six comedy films running about ten minutes each and used at the beginning of each evening program to quiet the children, who swarm all over the field and whose cooperation is necessary if you are to have the peace necessary for preaching.

The King of Kings was originally divided into three parts, each running about forty-five minutes; this year we have divided it into four parts to give an additional evening since this film has a great "pulling power." People travel many miles to see it. In addition we use the old epic *The Ten Commandments* and a motion picture on the Mass. One of these is in Technicolor, made by Father James McVann; the other an older print originally produced by Eastman Kodak Company. The original records ran the gamut from classical to hillbilly.

At the end of a week in any number of places we have had the same statement made by our auditors that was made by "Uncle Bud" Kennedy of Alto. He was baptized by Father Abram Ryan, according to his Bible, when he was six, made his first confession and Holy Communion at seventy-two.

After hearing all of our sermons for a week he remarked, "I agree with everything you have said." Many non-Catholics say the same thing, as our sermons for the first week deal largely with basic elements in religion and try, as far as possible, except through the question box, to avoid controversy.

APPROACH

How do you reach the people from a preaching standpoint? Each night, following a short introductory motion picture, there is a brief instruction from the Scriptures, emphasizing a biblical character and stressing: "The Importance of Having the Truth," "The Need of Prayer," "What About the Bible," "Why We Ask God's Help," "The Importance of Prayer," "The Helps of the Church," "How Catholics Pray."

After the first few minutes, of course, the people know you pray, for you have distributed printed prayer sheets with the Our Father, the Hail Mary, the Apostles' Creed, and other prayers in large print. If there is enough light, you ask them to say the prayers with you; if not, you read them over the public address system or have one of the local children do it for you.

Following the brief talk, which lasts about ten minutes, you launch into the question box program. It is important that this is handled properly and that it be planned. You have placed a container for questions on the platform. You explain and answer certain stock questions the first night. You ask the people to write the questions and put them in the box or have one of the children tell the questions to the preacher. During the week, no matter what type of question is asked, it is important that the elementary field of apologetics be covered as carefully as possible.

Controversial subjects can be handled graciously here that otherwise would cause difficulty if they were the subject of the main sermon. Here, too, the technique of answering questions consists in giving the answer to what the questioner has in mind rather than to what he asks. Many questions that seem abusive and lacking in courtesy may be asked in good faith. The questioner is asking in the only manner he knows how to present the problem. In the course of a week you will be surprised to discover how much doctrine can be discussed in the question box program of twenty-five minutes each night.

The sermon is given by the second member of the team. It is typical of the old fashioned sermon of the Catholic mission. It is a moral approach. Salvation, sin, death, judgment, the mercy of God, the Blessed Mother, perseverance, the Holy Eucharist are in this class. A sermon on the sacraments or "Why I am a Catholic" is usually a part of the week's routine, with the latter sermon holding "top billing" on the last night. The Sacrifice of the Mass under the title of "What Catholics Do When They Go to Church" is discussed as a commentary on the motion picture of the Mass on the last night.

We found early in the work that with a two-man team one could well afford to devote all of his time after services to "hand-shaking," while the other took care of the equipment. It is necessary to get valuable gear under cover immediately. Dampness hurts both film and machine, while one wandering child who accidentally knocks over the screen can cause you a bit of difficulty in cleaning and repairing it, particularly if it is a beaded screen. The "contact" priest shows visitors through the trailer, takes names for a free subscription to *Our Sunday Visitor*, and explains the stations of the cross, the use of statues, the altar, and Mass vestments. He also has at hand a supply of doctrinal pamphlets to pass out to those interested.

On the last two nights of the week an announcement is made of a class to be started during the coming week at the home of one of the local farmers for those who desire a further explanation of Catholic teaching. By the end of the week the preachers have a list of names. The missionary who is to conduct the class makes a house-to-house canvass to extend a personal invitation to those who have manifested a more than casual interest. As soon as possible Sunday Mass is undertaken—a recited Mass or public recitation of Mass prayers—so that almost from the beginning they learn by means of prayers and hymns to participate in the devotional and sacramental life of the Church even before they have been received into its embrace.

At Alto, Tullahoma, Brownington, and Shelbyville, where chapels were built, and at Winchester and South Pittsburg, where churches already existed, this was the technique followed. Added to this follow-up activity there was introduced at an early stage some of the social activities, "ice-cream socials," Christmas plays, picnics, so that those who had become Catholics would find in their new group the activities they had become accustomed to in the one they had so recently left.

WORTHWHILE?

In the minds of many there is a serious question as to whether the results justify the expense both in manpower and money. There is only one answer to the question, "How valuable is a soul?" To that, of course, we can say no expense is too great to save *one* soul. Added to this is the mature judgment of the men who have engaged in this work. They say it could not be done as successfully in any other way. Trailer work looks to long-range results—rural families are large. If you can get a nucleus and hold it, one day you will people the hillsides. Despite the many who have gone north to live, or in the country at large, Winchester has developed from less than 250 people to more than 650 souls in these years.

There are many difficulties. There are bad roads, poor food often, preaching in and out of season, with the elements unkind at times. There is little or no privacy and often little appreciation from those for whom you do the most. The few Catholics in the district make mixed marriages a serious problem, and those who have been lost to the faith have fallen away for the most part because of marriage problems. Then there are the "poor whites" with whom you start not from "scratch" but from far behind that. The shallowness of their background causes you almost constantly to challenge their motives. On the other hand, some of our girls have made fine convert husbands out of the boys they married.

One of the first lessons we learned came from one of the unforgettable characters, "Uncle Bud" Kennedy. We were anxious to get Mass started in his home. After several visits and some little impatience with the old gentleman, we told him to make up his mind. Leisurely he spat out his cud of tobacco, rocked in his chair for a moment or two, and observed, "Trouble with you, young man, is that you have too much of that damyankee uneasiness."

In Rome we were told to be patient. The hills of the South and the ancient hills of Rome have that lesson in common for the trailer-missionary—be patient. Patience and kindness to those who seek pay off greater dividends than preaching, for they learn to like you. Through you they come to Christ and his Church. Not the proper approach, you say? But that is the way it works out.

Another lesson is to be learned if you are to be successful. You must take the people as you find them and accommodate yourselves to their way of living and thinking.

For years I did the work. Now as an executive I have to find means of supporting it. This we do gladly, for we feel it is a work that has much to offer and will one day be a jewel in the crown of the Catholic Church in the United States.

8

"But I Am a Protestant"

Rev. BENJAMIN F. BOWLING, C.S.P., Director
Catholic Information Center, Baltimore, Maryland

EDITOR'S FOREWORD: The big problem in convert work is the recruiting of prospects. Here the maximum of initiative and resourcefulness is required. Merchants resort to advertising on a large scale. They employ specialists to arrange in their shop windows displays of goods which they wish to feature. They will even sell a single item of merchandise at such a bargain price as to sustain a loss in order to get people into their stores. That item is called a loss leader.

Back of all their window dressing, display ads, and bargain items is the clear consciousness of the need of getting the potential customers into the store. Once the public are in the stores, the merchants rely on their clerks to sell them many articles of merchandise.

The problem of winning converts is basically one of salesmanship. Salesmen as we are of the precious treasure of Christ's truths, we must emulate the initiative and resourcefulness of the salesmen of earthly goods and adopt many of their procedures. Father Benjamin Bowling is a specialist in the art of selling the treasures of Christ. Setting up an information center in Baltimore, he proceeded to press every technique of recruiting customers into the Church.

His contribution is rich in suggestions for attracting customers, for handling them with consummate tact, and for selling them the treasures of Christ's gospel. He closes with detailed suggestions for

those beginning convert work. He speaks from a rich and wide ex-
perience in winning souls, in which art he has had outstanding suc-
cess. Priests and people will find in his chapter a wealth of practical
suggestions and detailed guidance which will multiply the fruitful-
ness of their labors in winning souls for Christ.

∽

BREAKING THE ICE

SOME YEARS AGO, as I was leaving the Paulist rectory in San
Francisco, I met a tall, handsome young man on the steps. He
was much embarrassed and stammered, "I . . . I . . . would like
to talk to a priest!"

"Well, I'm a priest; come in and have a chat."

Still the young man hesitated, fumbled at his collar, gulped his
Adam's apple, and spluttered, "But I'm a Protestant!"

Stepping back in feigned horror, I exclaimed, "Good Lord, no!
Not that!"

We both laughed, and the ice was broken. Later the young man
confided to me that he had been walking up and down before the
rectory door for nearly ten minutes trying to get up courage to
enter. I have never forgotten that incident and ever since have won-
dered how many other thousand non-Catholics are, metaphorically
speaking, walking up and down before Catholic churches trying to
get up courage to come in. The average Catholic, and perhaps the
average priest, doesn't stop to think of that—what a real effort must
be made and what a world of inherited prejudice and apprehension
must be overcome before thousands of our fellow Americans get
the courage to come to our Catholic rectories for the spiritual help
they need so badly.

CATHOLIC INFORMATION CENTERS

To help these sincere souls and others of the 80,000,000 Americans
not affiliated with any church whatever, the Catholic information

centers are filling a real need. Located in the heart of the business district of our cities, they present the Church in a friendly, informal way to those who are not ready to come to our rectories and yet who really desire to give our faith a hearing. Attractive but dignified window displays of pamphlets and books with signs assuring the passing non-Catholic of a friendly reception within, without cost or obligation, are often the means of giving him his first glimpse of the Church and his first chat with a Catholic priest.

During the first eleven months, the Catholic information center in Baltimore had between three and four thousand visitors, a large proportion of whom were non-Catholics. Some seventy-five completed their instructions and were received into the Church, and about a hundred and fifty others, after taking the classes, went away with a better understanding of the Church, which may some day ripen into faith.

HOW TO GET THEM IN

The primary problem of every priest interested in converts is how to reach them and bring them to the instruction class. Archbishop Curley, at a meeting of the clergy, spoke zealously of the non-Catholic apostolate and explained the purpose of the center to supplement the excellent work for converts already being done in the archdiocese. (Baltimore city alone had nearly 1,000 adult converts last year.) He urged the pastors to open their pulpits on successive Sundays, to allow the Paulists to speak on their work at all the Masses. This proved to be one of the most successful means of bringing prospective non-Catholics to the center.

During the last few months, it was my privilege to speak at all the Masses in some twenty of the larger churches of Baltimore, reaching between forty and sixty thousand Catholic people, and urging them to invite their non-Catholic friends to come to the center either for the classes or for private interviews and instructions. After each Mass the ushers passed out small cards upon which were printed the name, address, phone number of the center and the hours of the lectures. This we found very important, for while the average announcement in our churches is soon forgotten, the cards were kept for future reference. Many of them have come back to us in the hands of non-Catholics from all points of the city.

THE APPEAL TO CATHOLICS

The highlight of this appeal to Catholics was to urge them to bring in at least one non-Catholic friend to at least one lecture. We promised that the lectures would be of a positive and constructive nature, devoid of controversy and without any obligation of any kind on the part of those attending.

Open discussions would follow each lecture. Points like the following were stressed: You tell your friends about an interesting book you've read, a delightful movie you've seen; why not tell them about the most wonderful thing in the world, your Christian philosophy of life? (Use tact, of course; don't buttonhole them on the street and ask them if they want to be saved.) Make your invitation specific; tell them that you yourself are going to hear an interesting discussion on life after death, confession, or infallibility next Tuesday evening at eight, and ask them to come with you.

We invited specific groups to our classes. While we note the converts who are coming into the front door of the church, we sometimes forget the poorly instructed Catholics who are drifting out the back door. Many of these Catholics have been trying to answer Ph.D. challenges to their religion for years, with only grammar school answers. They have never really grown up in their faith. Urge them to come to the lectures to receive an adult appreciation of their religion and to hear a competent answer to the constant objections brought against it.

This announcement in the different churches invariably brings in a number of Catholics in need of spiritual help of one kind or other. The number of men who have come in to clear up apparent conflicts with the faith or to go to confession, after years away, has been most encouraging.

"I've wanted to talk to a priest outside of confession for years," many of them say, "but I was always afraid they were too busy or

I'd be taking up their time, and so I put it off." It is surprising how many people, men especially, are hesitant about going to confession, but who will tell you everything in an informal conversation. The portable confessional in the corner, put in as an occasional convenience, has done good service.

Current institutions and philosophies are crumbling on all sides today. Many sincere non-Catholics, seeing the constant contradictions in their own churches, are turning more and more to the old Mother Church of Christianity as the one stable religious institution in a changing world. But remind our Catholic people of the young man walking up and down before the church door, trying to get up courage to come in.

Remind them that most of their non-Catholic friends have never been in a Catholic church or spoken to a Catholic priest in their lives and, consequently, would welcome a personal invitation to attend a Catholic lecture. Time and time again in the course of instructions, priests have said to non-Catholics: "You've been a Catholic at heart for years. I wonder why you didn't come into the Church before?"

And time and time again the answer is the same: "I wanted to, Father, but I didn't know how to go about it. I was shy and timid about taking the first step. Yes, I had many Catholic friends, but not one of them ever asked me to come to Mass or to Catholic devotions or lectures. I think I would have come into the Church years ago if only I had gotten a little encouragement."

Remind the Catholic people that perhaps in their office or place of business, across the street perhaps, or even in their own homes there may be a non-Catholic who would be eternally grateful for an invitation to learn something about their Catholic faith.

Perhaps the most interested group today is the non-Catholic anticipating a mixed marriage with a Catholic. Sooner or later the question of religion is bound to arise, and the sooner the young people face the religious issue, the better it will be. I could cheerfully take out into the proverbial woodshed the type of Catholic who constantly evades the religious issue with the weak excuse of not wishing to seem to influence the non-Catholic party.

On the contrary, the non-Catholic party has a right as well as a duty thoroughly to understand in advance the obligations and responsibilities he is asked to assume in marrying a Catholic. It is definitely unfair, therefore, for the couple in such cases to become engaged and even to set their marriage date before giving the non-Catholic party a reasonable explanation of the solemn promises he is asked to sign.

Most priests would agree that mixed marriages in which the non-Catholic party has taken a thorough course of instructions in advance and has cleared up the common misconceptions about the Catholic Church are as a rule far happier than those in which the non-Catholic party has had little or no instruction. Religion in the home will be either a bond to unite or a barrier to separate the young couple. The instructions help to make religion more of a bond of union in the home and, if taken in time, often end in the gift of faith. Catholics, therefore, have a solemn obligation to their non-Catholic friends, to themselves, and to their future children to give this opportunity for the gift of faith to those whom they love.

Hearing this from the altar Sunday after Sunday in the different churches has awakened a large number of Catholics anticipating mixed marriages to the wisdom of having their non-Catholic friends take a course of instruction. And the following week always finds a few extra couples in the class.

The last appeal to attend the lectures is to those who are already members of mixed marriages. Frequently the non-Catholic party has been coming to Mass for years with husband or wife, has done his or her part in the education of the children, and is fulfilling most of the obligations of the Church. Hence we say to them: "Why not take the course of instructions, clear up your remaining difficulties, and enjoy the privileges of the Church by joining your loved ones at the altar rail?"

After making this announcement in the different churches in Baltimore, it has happened again and again the following week that individuals have shown up at the information center saying, "Father, what you said last Sunday was certainly our case. I've been coming to Mass with my Catholic family for years. I wouldn't be anything else but a Catholic, yet I always feel out of it at Communion time. So, as I'm so far in already, I might as well take those instructions and come all the way in." The results have been most encouraging.

THE DEVOTIONAL APPROACH

Many priests interested in convert work are beginning to appreciate the devotional and spiritual rather than the strictly apologetic or rational approach to converts. They find that the non-Catholics who have grown to love the devotions and prayers of the Church and who have sensed the Real Presence of our Lord in the Blessed Sacrament are, as a rule, far more interested than others in giving the Church's claims a fair hearing. The Paulist Fathers found this to be especially true in their Catholic information center in Baltimore. Their temporary center is directly across the street from St. Alphonsus Church, which is known as the novena center of the Miraculous Medal devotions for the city. Thousands of Catholics and hundreds of non-Catholics attend the novena each week.

Father Louis Mendelis, the zealous pastor, kindly allowed the Paulists to speak at the eleven novena services and to invite the non-Catholics present to attend the series of instructions on the Catholic faith given at the center across the street. There would be no cost, no obligation, no high pressure of any kind. All would be free to come, hear a kindly explanation of Catholic faith and practice, have informal interviews with the priest in charge, and thus gain a fuller understanding of the Catholic Church whose devotions they had learned to love.

The response was most encouraging. Of the seventy-five non-Catholics who were instructed and   received into the Church the first year, about one third had received their introduction and first interest in the faith through attendance at the novena devotions. Here they had learned Catholic prayers and devotion to our Blessed Mother. They had begun to feel at home in a Catholic Church. Here came the first dawn of faith in our Lord's Real Presence in the Blessed Sacrament at Benediction. Here, too, they had heard constant reference to the Mass, Holy Communion, and the other sacraments, which gave them the desire to know all the Church's teachings and to participate fully in her sacramental life.

In our classes we found that non-Catholics who had attended the novena services acted as spiritual leaven for the others, being the first to grasp the spirit of the Church's teachings and helping to clear up the misunderstanding of the others. Hence we urge non-Catholics under instructions to attend Catholic devotions from the start and especially to pray before the Blessed Sacrament as often as possible during the week, asking God for the light to see and the grace to accept all his divine teachings. As children learn to love their parents long before they can define maternity and paternity, so non-Catholics, by frequent visits to the Church, grow to love our Lord's Presence long before they have learned the theology of the Holy Eucharist.

THE APPEAL OF CHRIST

In line with the above, many of us find it most helpful to inculcate from the very beginning a deep personal love of God and of our Lord in the hearts of those who are taking instructions. The majority of people who come to us today have only a vague and indefinite idea of Christ and know practically nothing of his life.

The idea of his being the great good God come on earth in human form to be our Teacher, our Guide, and our Saviour is something absolutely new and wonderful to thousands of nominal Christians today. Make the life of Christ live for them, let them catch the spirit of his divine authority, his divine pardon, and his divine Presence, and then they will be quicker to grasp the reasonableness and the need of that same divine Christ, speaking through a living, infallible Church, forgiving through a divine priesthood, and living in the Blessed Sacrament.

To supplement our lectures, many of us give them the simple life of Christ, *Jesus of Nazareth*, by Mother Loyola, once described by Father Gillis as the most touching life of Christ he ever read. We have over twenty copies in our little lending library and intend to get twenty more, as they are in circulation all the time. I find it helps more than any other devotional book to make our Lord's life and teachings become a living reality to the average convert. It helps take away the misconception of the Church being a human dictator and makes her what she really is, the living channel through which Christ teaches and through which he gives his divine graces.

Repeatedly, converts have said something like this: "You know, Father, in the beginning I rebelled at the idea of any man-made church telling me what to do and presuming to forgive my sins. Now I realize it is Christ who speaks through the Church and hence infallibility; Christ who forgives through the Church, hence confession; and Christ who gives his divine light through the Church, hence the other sacraments and especially the Blessed Sacrament through which he is with us always on our altars."

We might remark in passing that many of our Catholic people likewise constantly need to be reminded of this truth, namely, that it is Christ who speaks with divine authority through the Church as our guide in faith and morals. Too often we hear born Catholics remarking, "I am a good Catholic, but I can't see the Church's teaching on divorce, remarriage, birth control, etc." Others, especially those marrying a second time and out of the Church, say, "Well, the *Church* may condemn me, but I know that *God* will understand." They forget—or refuse to remember—that God has spoken through Christ and that Christ is still speaking through his Church, our divine guide in faith and morals.

MOVING PICTURE OF MASS

A splendid opening attraction for the instruction class, as a "promotion" for the lectures to follow, is to show a moving picture of the Mass, with a running commentary on the ceremonies. The picture used at the Baltimore center was prepared by Father James McVann, C.S.P., St. Paul's College, Washington, D.C. It is in color. It shows the priest's preparation for the Mass with lingering shots of the chalice, paten, and host, each vestment in turn, and the altar and equipment. The picture then follows the priest through the whole action of low Mass, giving the narrator ample time to explain the ceremonies and the spirit of the Holy Sacrifice.

Advertise this picture of the Mass in the daily papers and in the Catholic press. Take a large ad if necessary (one large ad is worth a dozen smaller ones), and you can fill the Church or auditorium for the opening lecture. The Catholics, of course, will be in the majority, for they too, poor souls, are hungry to know more about the Mass. But there will be a generous gathering of non-Catholics who always find this lecture most interesting. We find that this picture creates a great interest in the Mass and makes the average non-Catholic feel more at home when he comes to Mass. Later on, in its proper place in the course of instructions, another lecture on the Mass, illustrated by slides, is found very helpful.

Some priests find a lecture on a "Tour of the Catholic Church" with explanations and question box on the altar, vestments, confessional, stations of the cross, etc., is a grand drawing card for the first lecture. Then after this lecture, as after the movie of the Mass, is the time to invite everyone present to attend the course of lectures to follow, once more insisting that there will not be the slightest obligation and urging the non-Catholics present to come to hear a kindly explanation of Catholic faith and practice, to join in the open discussions after the lectures, and thus clear up popular misconceptions about the Church. The response in attendance is generally most encouraging.

While advertisements, announcements, pictures of the Mass, etc., all help to draw converts in the first place, it is up to the priest to hold them by making the instructions alive and interesting. Religion is not simply a series of definitions to be learned. It is a life to be lived. Make it live for those present, and they in turn will pass it on to others. "A satisfied customer is your best advertisement."

HELPFUL BOOKS

Each priest will have his own favorite books that he finds personally helpful in his work. Naturally they will vary according to the age, education, and spiritual background of those being instructed. For the average convert, however, many of us like the *Catechism for Inquirers* by Malloy as a general outline for the course. Personally, I think that the little pamphlet *Words of Life* by C. C. Martindale (Catholic Truth Society) is the most helpful outline I know in preparing my own course of lectures.

After the first few talks, and after the divinity of Christ and the Church have been firmly established, many find it very helpful to give out copies of *Father Smith Instructs Jackson*. The new edition has a quiz in the back, and mimeographed copies of the answers can be made and given to prospective converts. The plan is to have them read the book during the course of the instructions, and one by one fill out the quizzes and check their answers by the key. They are asked to put a large cross before any questions that they do not understand.

Thus the priest can see at a glance their weak points and give them personal supplementary instructions. Many of us find this is a great time saver, and it also fills in many gaps or blind spots that inevitably occur in a convert's instructions. So many of them can sit through a lecture, smile sweetly, and say they have no difficulties. Filling out the quiz, however, forces them to think and to test their knowledge. The results are sometimes startling and always interesting.

The popular little booklet *I Believe* by Father Hurley, C.S.P., is generally liked by the average non-Catholic, as it is easy to read and gives a good overall picture of the Church. Chaplains tell us that during the war it went like hot cakes among the servicemen. While conducting the Catholic Answers Radio Program in Los Angeles one year, nearly 1,500 copies of *I Believe* were sent out by request to those listening in.

For the old-time Bible-loving Protestant, *The Faith of Our Fathers* is still excellent, but the average convert seems to prefer *The Faith of Millions* by Father O'Brien. *One Fold and One Shepherd* by Dr. Peatfield, the convert minister, is not well-known but is an excellent and readable summary of the faith for non-Catholics.

On the college level, *Now I See* by Lunn, *Rebuilding a Lost Faith* by Stoddard, *Truths Men Live By* by O'Brien, and *Through*

Hundred Gates by Lamping are frequently helpful. The latter is the personal story of many prominent conversions and hence is of great assistance to the earnest inquirer who often finds, among the stories, the solution of his own personal difficulties.

Many of us find that *The Question Box* by Bertram Conway is better suited as a ready reference work *after* the convert has been received, rather than as a textbook in the beginning. The average non-Catholic has enough difficulties of his own to solve without being confused with the thousand difficulties encountered by others. *The Rosary Crusade*, a delightful pamphlet giving all the mysteries of the rosary in color and having on the back an actual illustration of the rosary with a chart indicating the prayers to be said, is a godsend to everyone giving instructions. The pamphlet is published by the Holy Name Society of New York City. Finally, *From One Convert to Another*, a small booklet by John Riack, C.S.P., is a series of letters to converts which many find very practical and helpful.

SUGGESTIONS FOR BEGINNING CONVERT WORK

FIRST IMPRESSIONS. So much depends upon the impression given the prospective convert on his first visit. Remember, it may have taken him years and a hard struggle to get there, so do all you can to put him at ease and make his first visit a happy one. Friendly receptionists and kindly and tactful housekeepers can help so much here.

(Couldn't we do something about the snapping turtles in some rectories? They are terrors over the phone and holy terrors face to face! No wonder some converts never venture further than the front door!)

Assure the visitor that his coming puts him under no obligation of any kind whatever, that he is just as free during and after the course of instructions as he was before, that he is free to ask any questions or none, and that no offense will ever be taken.

Tell him with a smile that if the Catholic Church were anything like many people think it is, you, too, would have nothing to do with it. Above all, assure him that no beautiful, helpful truth in his own faith will ever be challenged, but rather strengthened and confirmed and enriched by being placed in its original setting, whence it was taken in the sixteenth century.

Point out that the spirit of your instructions will be *positive and constructive*, not argumentative and destructive—clearing up errors and half-truths which are the cause of most prejudice and misunderstandings and an earnest effort to present the spiritual inheritance of the old Mother Church of Christianity in a kindly, Christlike spirit.

APPOINTMENTS. Always make appointments definite in time and place. Asking non-Catholics to come back at "some other time" or "when Father So-and-so returns" or "when the new class begins in the fall" is often fatal. Although it isn't always satisfactory, let new converts join the class at *any* time. It's better than running the risk of making them wait.

KEEPING APPOINTMENTS. Get name, address, and telephone number on that first visit, and give them yours. Explain that sometimes it may be necessary for one or the other of you to cancel the appointment, and you would not want to disappoint them. Missing appointments has been the death of many a promising conversion. We should be as conscientious about our appointments as the doctor or lawyer is about his. Let not the "children of this world" put to shame the "children of light."

ARGUMENTS. Be prepared for some converts putting up a real argument on different points of doctrine. Don't argue. Arguments generate more heat than light! Handle arguments as you would a "line drive" in baseball. "Give" with it. Admit any and all truth in it. Go out of your way to find something worthwhile in what they say. Then build on this truth and show how its source is in the fullness of Catholic doctrine.

RECORD CARDS. Keep a personal card of each one under instruction, with name, address, religion, education, marriage status, and contact with the church. Have printed or mimeographed on the back of the card the list of the lectures to be given, and check them off as given. For public classes give a card with the list of lectures to each one, and before each class have them check off that lecture. Thus converts can make up the lectures they miss, and key lectures are not overlooked.

PRAYER—1. Urge converts to *pray* daily for light to see and grace to accept *all* God's truth! Urge them to seek God's divine compass rather than their own "cafeteria method" in religion. "Not what *I* think or feel about this doctrine, but what *God* has revealed!" Say a public prayer for light before each lecture. End with an Our Father and Hail Mary.

PRAYER—2. Exchange mementos at Mass with your fellow priests for your respective converts. Ask the sisters, especially the cloistered orders, to pray for them. Get the children in the school to promise one Hail Mary each day to bring in one new convert to our Lord. Tell them when they come in! In one city some 50,000 parochial children said a Hail Mary each day for conversions and hailed each new convert as their spiritual child!

PERSONAL INTERVIEWS. If converts are in a class, be sure to have a few personal interviews with each one before reception, giving each a chance to talk over his own personal problems. Some instructors make a point of seeing one or two personally after class each evening.

GROUP RECEPTION. Have a group reception whenever possible with solemn profession of faith at the altar rail. The profession in the back of the *Catechism for Inquirers* by Malloy can be used for this; thus give each one a copy. Explain *Extra ecclesiam nulla salus.* Let everyone make this profession including those to be baptized absolutely. (One can have the intention of not including them in the conditional absolution at the end.)

PARENTS AND FRIENDS. Urge converts to bring their parents and friends to the baptism, and make a little talk before the ceremony, largely for their benefit. Make a point of meeting relatives and friends and giving them a friendly greeting. Explain the rite and ceremony of baptism as you go along. Some rubricists may frown at this, but after all, isn't it more the mind of the Church for the catechumens and their friends to know and understand the beautiful symbolism of the sacrament?

BAPTISMAL CERTIFICATE. Have a nice baptismal certificate and a little personal gift for each convert. This means a lot coming from the priest who instructed them.

CONFESSIONAL. Before reception it is well that each convert should take a look inside the confessional (this generally comes in the tour of the church). Otherwise—strange as it may seem to a born Catholic—going into a darkened confessional and not knowing quite what to expect causes real apprehension for many converts and sometimes keeps them away from confession for a long time afterwards.

CONFESSORS. Let converts know that they are free to make their confession to anyone they like. Like Catholics born in the faith, some will prefer to come to the priest they know—in this case the instructor—or to someone else. The simplest way is to have a kindly confessor—hand-picked!—go into one of the confessional boxes after the baptism of the converts and let them go to him or you as they wish.

After twenty-five years of experience, I urge against turning converts loose after their baptism and telling them to go to confession at their convenience. I have come across converts from three to six months after their baptism who still hadn't made their first confession. Many of us think that it is a good idea even for those who have been baptized absolutely to make a general confession of devotion, letting them know, of course, that it is not an obligation but only to give them the personal satisfaction of a "general clearance" for the past along with the practical advice of the priest, which is frequently very helpful for them in the future.

SPONSORS. One sponsor is sufficient for an adult, although two are permissible. Be sure he is a practicing Catholic and will be a help to the convert. It is often helpful to get someone near his own age who lives in the neighborhood and who will thus act as a kind of big brother or sister to the convert, going with him to his First Communion and assisting in the adjustment to his new life and surroundings.

FIRST COMMUNION. Whenever possible, urge converts to have a little celebration for their First Holy Communion, inviting their

Catholic friends to receive with them and having a Communion breakfast afterwards. Some priests arrange to say a special Mass for their converts and attend their Communion breakfast. But whatever you do, don't let any convert be an orphan on his First Communion day and receive alone in some strange church.

FOLLOW-UP WORK. Keep a card index file of your converts, noting especially the date of their baptism and First Communion. A postcard or note on their anniversary or at Christmas time may mean a little extra effort on the part of the priest, but it pays good dividends (and I do mean spiritual!). Time and again it has happened that a remembrance from their spiritual father gives converts the courage to come to him in trouble and straighten out their difficulties. Advanced lectures for converts are being arranged in some of our cities, together with a letter of introduction to their respective pastors, with a request that the new convert be affiliated with his parochial activities.

Other priests, once or twice a year, have a reunion for their converts and conduct an informal question box and discussion. Frankly, most of us are remiss in our follow-up work with the newly baptized. As one convert complained, "Father, everything new gets a follow-up service these days except converts!"

WARN AGAINST "FEELINGS" IN RELIGION. Periods of dryness and apparent loss of faith will come. Like the dear old colored man, many converts expect to have always "a nice warm feeling aroun' the heart." Assure them that the Holy Father, the bishop, and *even* their instructor go through periods of spiritual aridity!

WHY I WANT TO BE A CATHOLIC. Father John Keating, C.S.P., of the information center in New York, suggests having converts, at the end of their course, write a short summary of the reasons why they wish to become a Catholic. He finds that this helps the convert to reflect deeply upon the reasons for his conversion and also gives his instructor a better spiritual insight or understanding of the convert's motives.

Even for those who do not come in, it seems a good plan to suggest that they write a short summary of what they got from the course with a statement of the truths that they still cannot accept.

Personally, I think it is a wonderful idea, and I would suggest that every convert would keep this summary of his reasons for becoming a Catholic and read them over periodically, especially in times of stress and discouragement.

FORM GOOD CATHOLIC HABITS EARLY. Remind converts that for many years they have not been in the habit of going to Mass each Sunday, receiving Holy Communion frequently, and being faithful to certain definite prayers. Make them realize that unless they form contrary habits, and form them firmly and deeply early in their Catholic life, it will be very easy for them to slip back into their old life-long habits of *not* doing these things. Impress upon their minds, therefore, that spiritual, like natural habits, are second nature. If each day their morning and evening prayers are a part of their daily schedule, if each week their Sunday Mass is *the most important thing* of that day, accompanied whenever possible by the reception of our Lord in Holy Communion, then they need have no worry about their final perseverance in the faith.

HUMAN ELEMENTS IN CHURCH. Finally, it is well to remind our converts that, while the Church is divine, those within the Church are only human, with human faults and failings. Christ did not guarantee the *conduct* but the *teachings* of his followers. There were twelve apostles and yet one-twelfth of these betrayed him, another twelfth denied him, and the other ten-twelfths deserted him in his hour of trial. The proportion of unworthy followers of Christ has never been so high in any period of the Church's history.

The wonder is that, taken as they are from every walk of life, his representatives on the whole have been so faithful to the ideals of the Master. As a dear old priest once said to his congregation, "One of the greatest proofs that the Church is divine is the priest-hood. It has stood *us* all these years and still goes on." Then he added with a chuckle, "There is only one other, greater proof of her divinity . . . It has survived you folks, also!"

9

Winning Negro Converts

The Priests Engaged in the Work in Chicago

EDITOR'S FOREWORD: *A recent nation-wide survey of convert work brought out the interesting and surprising fact that the parishes registering the largest number of converts are Negro*[1] *parishes. Almost all the cards reporting a hundred or more converts a year proved to come from pastors working among our colored brethren.*

The highest total reported from any parish in the United States came from the priests ministering at St. Charles Borromeo and its subsidiary church, St. Aloysius, both in the Harlem district of New York. They received 450 Negro converts in 1946. In June 1947, St. Aloysius was elevated to the status of an independent parish with its own pastor and curates. In Baltimore, the Josephite Fathers at St. Francis Xavier parish received 206 converts in 1946. In Philadelphia converts at St. Charles Borromeo for the same year totaled 227 and at St. Elizabeth's 104. In Detroit converts at Sacred Heart of Jesus parish totaled 180, while at St. Anthony of Padua in the Bronx, New York, they totaled 140.

In Chicago similar splendid results have been achieved for many years. Back in 1927 we featured in The White Harvest *the pioneering work of Father Joseph F. Eckert, S.V.D., who averaged more than*

---

1. See footnote on page 23.

100 converts a year at St. Elizabeth's. Today this work is being carried on with ever increasing success in the Negro parishes of Chicago, where it has been singled out for special commendation by Cardinal Stritch.

The methods which have proven so fruitful in the six parishes in the Negro districts of Chicago are here detailed by the group of priests engaged in that work. Note particularly the use made of the Catholic school as a means of winning the parents of such pupils. It makes us wonder if that can't be done elsewhere with similar results. The technique developed by these priestly fishers of men can be used not only in other colored parishes but in those of mainly white people as well.

The magnificent achievements of this group of young levites make us hope and believe that similar copious draughts can be gathered into the Master's net wherever similar zeal, resourcefulness, and determination are put forth by priests and people.

CONSIDERATIONS

SIX PARISHES in the Negro districts of Chicago have been engaged in the work of converting hundreds of people each year. The larger baptismal classes are at Christmas and Easter each year.

In each parish these classes are made up of from eight to two hundred souls. At Christmas in 1946, for example, the total of baptisms of converts was 540 for the six parishes, while at Easter in 1947 the total rose to 582.

We hope the reader does not thereby get the false impression that the Negro people are running to the Catholic Church. Such an idea brings a sad smile to the faces of the men in this work. It is a difficult work. It is difficult to get them to instructions and very difficult to have them accept the Catholic faith. It is rather a matter of the grace of God and a lot of hard work.

We should note that our methods have been used in white districts and are found successful. There is nothing peculiar to Negro work in these methods except perhaps that we have schools that are over fifty percent non-Catholic. Thus we can get to the parents of our school children and convert them in large numbers.

The first thing necessary on the part of the convert maker is a realization that we in America are not dealing so much with non-Catholics as we are with people with no practical religion. Many of those outside the fold say they have a religion of some sort, but in many cases it is a sham. Its doctrinal content is very low; its morality is hushed.

We in America must realize that we are now dealing with paganism, a refined paganism if you will, but a paganism nevertheless. The priest must realize this. He therefore must adopt a more aggressive attitude than we have had in the past. Too often we labor under something near heresy, namely, that the people around us will do all right without the Church or that we can do nothing about those outside the fold.

The first thing then is a realization that people are not coming to ring our door bells very often to seek to be Catholics. We must adopt some other means. We must adopt a more aggressive and a more vigorous approach. We are right, so we take the offensive in this matter of gaining souls to Christ's Church. I hope this approach will become clear from a reading of the following pages. We list our methods of recruiting in the order of their importance.

THROUGH OUR SCHOOLS

Our people send their children to us each September. Practically all the children are non-Catholics. These children are sent to us in such numbers that we must turn away hundreds of them each year. We simply do not have room for them. The parents come to the school. The sister superior sends them to the priest. The priest asks to see both parents before he will consider the matter. The priest knows that these parents are here because they want good Christian living and morality for their children. So he says this to them:

"We are very happy to help you in the education of your child. But you must help too. That means that we shall expect you to take a course in religion and morality from the priests of the Catholic

Church. The classes start on September 8. Please be assured that you do not have to become a Catholic; neither does your child at any time have to become a Catholic. Then we shall expect you parents to attend Catholic Church with this child each Sunday. If you do not do this, we cannot feel that you are really interested in our school and in the training the school gives."

This is not a harsh method. You have before you a modern man. He knows little or nothing about religion. Yet he will expect you to produce a good child in a religious school while he has an irreligious home, at least in the sense that there is little religion or religious teaching there. You want to know what happens in the minds of these parents when you ask them to receive religious instructions.

Practically all of them see the logic of your stand. They are more than willing to cooperate with you. This is the beginning of a real appreciation of Christianity. Our effort must be to bring families into the Church rather than individuals. Before someone uses this method, he should learn more about it. People and neighborhoods differ, but it can be used more or less in different situations.

RECRUITING THROUGH LAY APOSTLES

It can be taken almost as an axiom that all recruiting must be done by personal contact. All other methods are not very productive. Lay apostles must be used. An organization of Catholics whose *only* work is recruiting for the class must be used. We have found little success in other methods and great success from apostles who go into the highways and byways and "force" them to come to the supper. Once they come, they enjoy the meal.

It is our custom to tell new converts that one of the best ways of manifesting gratitude to God for the gift of faith is to send at least one hundred others to the instructions. I remember one good lady in her late fifties. She became a Catholic. Then she started out for her hundred converts. Her doctor and the priest later on told her to stop her work because she had a weak heart. She actually brought at least a hundred, of whom sixty-four are fine practicing Catholics today.

FOR PARENTS WHO WANT
DISCIPLINE, OBEDIENCE, GOODNESS

St. James Catholic School for Children
accepts children of all religions.
Registration opens July 15th
at 2942 S. Wabash Avenue.

The Catholic School is noted for accomplishing all this:

1. It makes the children good boys and girls.
   No fighting. Nothing rough or vulgar is
   permitted.
2. Respect and obedience to parents. Character
   training.
3. Teaching in morality and good decent living.
4. Thorough training in all branches of learning to prepare children and give them a
   chance at the best positions in the city.

NOTICE:

1. We are interested only in those families who
   will cooperate with us in forming good
   citizens of God and our Country.
2. Neither you nor your child need become
   Catholic.
3. Children for kindergarten are accepted
   at the age of five years.
4. A full day of school is given in all grades.
5. The cost is from 35 to 40 cents a week.

Registration Opens July 15th. Please Register Early.

Phone — Calumet 6315

Around her was built an organization of ten people of similar mind and similar zeal. They went around the parish and brought people to the instructions. Each one felt it her personal duty to see that her clients were at class regularly. Their cry was: "Just listen to the fathers and then make up your mind about your life. This is the only true religion."

Many times our instructions were almost humorously interrupted by an apostle, following the instruction for the fifteenth time, who would jump up suddenly and leave the hall to go for some client who was not present and who had promised to come. Such an aggressive attitude must be used if we are to convert even a part of America. Remember that we do not expect to baptize half of these people. But we will do everything possible to get them to listen to God's teachings. Be quick to bring them to instructions and slow to baptize them.

NAMES OF POSSIBLE CONVERTS

The Catholic people will furnish names of people who are interested. You will meet non-Catholics at the door of the church on Sunday. Some of the priests go from door to door during the summer time and put down the names of people who seem interested in coming to the instruction class. A book should be kept in the office of the rectory in which each priest writes down the names of prospects. Otherwise they will be forgotten. The class should be announced at Mass each and every Sunday. In this way your people will get the apostolic spirit.

If you have non-Catholics attending weddings and funerals, it is not out of place to make a short announcement about the effort of the Catholic Church to teach all in the neighborhood the truths of religion. Each and every method that comes to your mind must be used. Please don't be afraid of offending people. Always remember that you are dealing with an indifferent and pagan group. Most of them will pay no attention to you, but it is the odd one here or there that you seek. None of them is ever offended if you make your announcement tactfully.

RECRUITING THROUGH THE C.C.D.

Each priest has a select group of non-Catholic children from the public school. Because they are in the public school, their instruction period is one or two years with faithful attendance at Mass. Prudently he can ask their parents to come to the adult class. Your aim is always a Catholic family. If you are quick to get them to instructions and slow to baptize, you can get hundreds of Catholic families.

RECRUITING WITH NEWSPAPERS, "PLUGGERS," AND MAIL

Frankly we have not had much success with these methods, though we do use all of them except newspapers. We have distributed thousands of "pluggers." The results were disappointing. This brings us back to the former statement: *You must have personal contact.* We send notices through the mail to inform people of the beginning of a new class. But these are people who intended to come anyway. It is merely a notification of the start of the class; it is hardly an advertisement. The hard method, personal contact, is the one that produces results.

RECRUITING THROUGH MIXED MARRIAGES

When a non-Catholic comes to the rectory to make arrangements to marry a Catholic, he is told that it is the law of the Church that the non-Catholic party must take some instruction in the teachings of Christ. Notice that we never say teachings about the Catholic Church. Thus is avoided a resurgence of bigotry, if there is any in the person. We explain to the non-Catholic party the laws of God about marriage, not the laws of the Catholic Church. We explain to them that we and they hope for a happy marriage.

"To have a happy marriage," we point out, "some instructions are necessary. We don't want your marriage to end in divorce. Neither do you want such a tragedy. So for your own good you should take instructions in religion and marriage. Classes are on Monday and Thursday. Please be sure that you need feel no obligation of becoming a Catholic." We have converted many non-Catholics in this way. Notice that we do not mention the number of classes non-Catholic parties must attend. Usually they won't ask because they will get interested in their first real understanding of Christianity.

THE INSTRUCTIONS CLASSES

There are three courses of instructions each year. The first starts with the opening of school in September and ends at Christmas. The second class starts in January and terminates at the end of April. The last starts in May and ends in August. Instructions are held twice a week—Monday and Thursday. There are three hours at which they may come each day. They can choose any hour—10:00 A.M., 1:15 P.M., and 7:30 P.M.

Please notice that the daytime classes are made to end with the school noon period and the dismissal time. Thus wives come in the daytime with the children, while husbands come at night. Each class lasts one and one-half hours, and near the end of the course the class lasts an extra half hour for those who wish to become Catholics. It is better to have instructions twice a week, using longer periods of time; people simply cannot come three or four times a week. If the speakers are interesting, the people love the instruction. Please notice that a person can come at any of the hours, just so he comes once on Monday and once on Thursday. The same material is presented morning, afternoon, and evening.

MATERIALS USED IN THE CLASSES

It is well to start the series of classes with a moving picture. This is the first class. But be sure that the audience understands that this is not entertainment. On the first night you must explain to them the purpose of the classes, namely, to teach religion. Explain what religion is, why one must learn religion, what happens to people who neglect to learn about God and morality. (Don't mention the Catholic Church. This comes later.) The motion picture *The Song of Bernadette* can be used to prove the divinity of the Catholic Church after doctrinal matter on the Church has been presented. Cecil B. De Mille's old production *The King of Kings* can be used for the first class or the class on the life of Christ.

We use the film slides of the Society for Visual Education. Each instructor uses these as he sees fit.

We use blackboards according to the methods of the individual instructor. Each teacher teaches a little differently from another.

Two or three question boxes with pencil and paper are placed near the doors of the hall.

KEEPING RECORDS OF ATTENDANCE

We use a large sheet having two sides. On one side is the nun's report on the children of the family. It contains the following information: name, grade, teacher, attendance at Mass, studies, conduct, and whether or not the child asked to be a Catholic. On the other side of the sheet is kept a record of the father and mother and their progress in religion.

It contains these items: attendance at class, attendance at Mass on Sunday, dates of interviews with the priest, attendance at Protestant church, number of marriages, whether or not the adult asked to be a Catholic. On this sheet is given plenty of room for the priest's observations. He writes in Latin various observations he has made since dealing with the person.

Again our purpose is to Christianize a whole family. Each priest is in charge of so many families. Father L. of this parish has each non-Catholic family whose last name begins from A to H. Father C. has from I to M. Father F. has from N to Z. Everything about the family is on one sheet.

ORDER OF THE LESSONS

These are the lesson titles:
1. Introduction: Necessity of Religion.
2. The Sacrifice of the Mass.

3. The End of Man.

4. God.

5. Our First Parents Lost Grace (really a lesson on grace).

6. Sin.

7. Christ (emphasize his divinity).

8. Grace.

9, 10. The True Church.

11. The Sacraments in General.

12. Baptism.

13. Confirmation.

14. Confession.

15. The Holy Eucharist.

16. The Mass.

17. Extreme Unction and Holy Orders.

18, 19, 20. Marriage.

21. Prayer and the Sacramentals.

22. The Commandments of God.

23. First Commandment.

24. Second and Third Commandments.

25. Fourth Commandment (emphasize parents' duties).

26. Fifth Commandment.

27. Sixth and Ninth Commandments.

28. Seventh, Eighth, and Tenth Commandments.

29. The Commandments of the Church.

30. The Last Things.

FOLLOWING THE CATECHISM

You will notice that the classes follow the simple order of the *Baltimore Catechism*. You present the Mass first because you should never baptize a man unless he has been attending Mass for at least four months. At the first or second class you ask him to go to Mass. Therefore you must explain what Mass is or he will lose interest in Catholic worship.

You have two classes on the Church because this is such an important subject. You have three classes on marriage for the same reason. A person must accept Christ's Church and the Catholic morality of marriage before he can be any sort of a Catholic.

THE ACTUAL TEACHING OF THE CLASS

Motion pictures and film slides are really terribly unimportant. The success or failure of the class depends in the ultimate analysis on the teachers. The teaching must be clear, concrete, and full of animation. We are doing the most important thing in the world for our audience. They will not come back unless we can hold them. There is nothing difficult in teaching a large class of non-Catholics. They know nothing about the subject. Everything you teach is new and interesting if you are alert and animated.

The priest first of all is a teacher. He is not there to argue with people, though he welcomes their questions. Secondly, he is a missionary. He must be direct and forceful. He must use all the best methods of the missionaries we admire. The class is not just an effort at teaching the religiously illiterate. It is an effort to convert people from indifference, sin, and paganism.

Two priests teach each class. The first reviews the matter taught since the first day of instructions. *This is the most important part of the class.* Each day he must give forty-five minutes to review. The best way to review is by a simple question process in which the whole class gives the answers in unison. Repetition is the mother of learning. Our greatest mistake is to make the class a lecture course. You question the people in this simple method:

Is there a God? How do you know?

Why did God put us on earth?

How many Persons are in God?

Who were Adam and Eve?

What did they lose by their sin?

What is grace?

How many kinds of sin are there?

Name the mortal sins going on in our neighborhood? (Always be concrete. Don't teach mortal sin in general. Teach about specific mortal sins!)

Which is the first Church?

Who made it?

Each priest uses his own simple set of questions. This method gives life and interest to the class. The people are participating. No one is embarrassed. The big point is that the most unlettered people can learn the essentials of the faith in this way. We have taught illiterate and blind people by the score. Each one of them was thoroughly familiar with the essentials of the Christian life at the end of the course.

The second forty-five minutes is used to present the new matter. The priest must be well prepared, clear, and forceful. Let him be sure to come down to the level of his hearers and his neighborhood. Let him be sure not to make a double mystery out of our mysteries.

For instance, we never use the word "transubstantiation." Clarity demands that we simply say that the Holy Eucharist is the Body and Blood of Christ. We never mention the word infallibility, but we certainly have a class that understands that the Church cannot make a mistake when teaching Christ's doctrines. A mortal sin is simply a big sin that destroys all the grace in your soul. Then we have the class repeat over and over again the big mortal sins going on in our neighborhood. Thus mortal sin is not merely a word or a definition.

SPECIAL CLASSES

The class lasts one and one-half hours. Those who want to become Catholics must attend an extra half hour Monday and Thursday. The others leave at the end of an hour and a half.

During this last half hour the catechumens are taught the principal obligations of a Catholic and especially those things converts don't clearly understand. They are: Go over the profession of faith again and again; weekly Communion; confession every two weeks; obligation of marriage before a priest; terrible sin to miss Mass just one Sunday or holy day; never attend a non-Catholic church; sick calls; novenas, missions; funerals, weddings; blessings and the use of sacramentals; baptism of infants; necessity of Catholic education; fast and abstinence; necessity of belonging to parish societies; donations to the Church; get ready for confirmation next year.

PRIVATE INTERVIEWS WITH MEMBERS OF THE CLASS

It is most important to have several private interviews with each member of the class. Thus the non-Catholic families are divided alphabetically. Each priest has his share. As soon as the lesson on the Church is presented, the priests start their interviews. While one is teaching, the others interview. The purpose of the interview, in short, is to see what can be done to bring this person and his family to Christ. Does the person want to be a Catholic? What sin in his life is keeping him from our Lord? Or is he just a Hard-Shell Baptist? All these things are noted on the record sheet in Latin. (Lay secretaries keep the records for the priests.)

If the person wants to be a Catholic, you must see if he understands the Church. The paramount question that will decide the case is this: Does he understand that he must be a Catholic to save his soul? If he wants to be a Catholic for any lesser reason, you don't yet have conversion. Wait! Keep him in class. Turn him to prayer, but don't baptize him. Very often it is necessary to wait a year or two. It is better to have a good catechumen than a poor Catholic. Be quick to instruct, slow to baptize.

If the person is ready for baptism, you must be careful about his marital status, his abandonment of the heretical church, and his acceptance of the true Church. Lastly, you must examine him thoroughly to be sure he is a well-instructed Catholic. Above all, always be sure a person is leading a Catholic life before you accept him into the Church. Any other procedure means defection.

THE DAY OF BAPTISM

The day before the actual baptism the catechumens come to the church. They take the profession of faith in a solemn manner. Then they practice for the baptism with their sponsors.

A public baptism is one of the most beautiful ceremonies in the Church. It impresses one almost as much as an ordination does. The purpose of the public baptism is to impress the new converts with the importance and solemnity of the step they have taken and to gain new converts to the Church. Each convert has his own pew in the church. He is told to bring his family and friends to celebrate with him. The ceremony consists of a sermon, baptism by ten or twenty priests in the aisles of the church, and solemn Benediction. A priest in the pulpit directs the baptism. Each priest baptizes eight or ten adults.

CONFESSION AND HOLY COMMUNION

The new converts must go to confession on the six consecutive Saturdays after baptism. The purpose of this is twofold: to destroy any fear of the confessional; to impress upon them frequent confession. Frequent confession is one of the best safeguards against defection. The new converts receive their First Holy Communion in a group on the Sunday after baptism. They are given the place of honor in the church and a Communion breakfast is held in the school hall. The priest, of course, talks to the congregation about the new class which will start within a week.

PREVENTING DEFECTION OF CONVERTS

All priests who have converted people are interested in the success of their work. We actually took a census of converts only, to see if they persevered. We found over eighty-five per cent of them actually leading practicing Catholic lives. This was five years after their baptism. The first preventive of defection is a thorough course of instruction. Let the priest not baptize a doubtful convert. We confess our mistakes of ten years ago. We have had defections, but not since we were careful about baptism. Be sure the person has been attending Mass for many months. Be sure he is giving up his mortal sins. Above all be sure that he understands that he cannot save his soul outside the Catholic Church.

The new convert must be enrolled in his parish society the day before he is baptized. The officers of the parish society must know that they have an obligation to see that all the converts are at least receiving monthly Communion with the society.

By orders of the authorities of the Church, the parish priest must take a census of his parish annually. In this way he meets his converts.

Each year the parents of school children must see the priest. Then he checks on their Catholicity. In our parishes we announce each summer that registration for school will start on August 15. Both parents must see the priest. If your child attended this school last year, you must register all over again. The purpose of such a registration is to see the parents.

This last method of preventing defection has not yet been tried, but we are rather sure it will help. In the instruction class we are going to teach that new converts must come to the rectory twice a year, namely, in September and in January. Then we are going to set aside a week in each of those months to do nothing but interview our converts. Those who do not come will be contacted by letter. Then, if they do not come, the priest will go to their homes. A record of these semi-annual checkups will be kept on the parish census cards.

A WORD ABOUT PRIVATE INSTRUCTIONS

We avoid as much as possible a full course of private instructions in the rectory. Our reason is this: You cannot preach with force at one man in an office. The instructions must be missionary talks to produce conviction and conversion. Too many converts can learn the catechism without applying it to their own lives.

At the same time private work with individuals is most necessary. This is taken care of in the interviews. Thus in this method there really is a combination of group and private instruction.

10

Alertness Wins 1,300 Converts

Very Rev. JOSEPH P. DONOVAN, C.M., J.C.D., President
Kenrick Seminary, St. Louis, Missouri

EDITOR'S FOREWORD: The supreme model for all convert makers is Jesus Christ. Ranking next to the divine Master comes St. Paul, the mighty apostle of the Gentiles. The flame of his burning zeal has kindled a fire in the heart of many a priest, giving him no rest until he does his utmost to search for the sheep that have strayed from the Master's fold. Such a priest is the nameless, self-effacing pastor whose work in winning 1,300 converts in twenty-one years is described by Father Donovan.

It is only fair to point out, however, that Fr. Donovan can speak with authority in his own name and by virtue of his own accomplishments in this field. Hundreds of priests throughout the country have had their zeal kindled by the fire of his consuming passion for souls, a passion which seems to burn even more brightly as the snows of many winters pile up like a widening aureole of glory upon his priestly brow. While the snows of many winters are on his head, in his heart there is the spirit of eternal spring.

Among the several methods used by this zealous Chicago pastor in making contact with potential prospects is that of meeting all the people at the church door. In this way he gets acquainted with strangers who happen to accompany a Catholic friend or come by themselves. He makes capital use of such contacts and never fails to make the stranger feel doubly welcome and to offer to explain more of the ceremonies, practices, and beliefs of the Catholic religion to such visitors.

In Fr. Donovan's picturesque phrase, this pastor is an "in-front-of-the-church priest." It will be noticed that Father Navagh places similar stress upon the importance of utilizing for a divine purpose such contacts at the church door. Out of our own experience of thirty odd years of meeting people in this manner, especially strangers, we can add our own humble testimony to the worthwhileness of such contacts. They constitute a fruitful source of prospects for instruction. We hope the practice will continue to spread until it becomes the universal custom at every Catholic church door in America.

An enthusiastic advocate of using the Legion of Mary as an auxiliary in recruiting prospects for instruction, Fr. Donovan naturally could not resist the temptation—and we're glad he could not—to show how Legionaries can supplement the priests' labors in many fields and can immensely enhance their fruitfulness in rescuing the sheep that have strayed from the Master's fold.

∽ঌ

LIKE ST. PAUL

WHEN FATHER O'BRIEN asked me to contribute a chapter to this book, which he said was going to be a sequel to his *The White Harvest*, I felt that I should stress the Pauline method of making conversions. I mean the method practiced by the great apostle, who was always on the alert to make converts, even as an incident of some other apostolic occupation. He had no set times nor places for bringing the good news to individual souls. At Philippi he did not tell Lydia and her women companions that he would like to meet them later on and at leisure to tell them about the fulfillment of their life-long desires.

He met them accidentally, and forthwith he broke to them the glad news of the gospel. In Athens, if he were one of those apostles who has his time off as well as his time on, he might have rested up while waiting for Silas and Timothy. But he never had time off from the apostolate during his waking hours. Whether the interval that he had to wait for his companions was of days or of weeks, he made up his mind that he would spend it for souls. He visited the synagogue; he talked in the market place; and though he must have thought his chances of doing good at Areopagus were slim, still he went there and engaged the men who spent their lives in discovering new things or talking about supposedly new things.

Nor were his efforts without immediate fruits. In addition, they were the occasion of countless souls all during the life of the Church Militant learning how to turn the passing occasion toward God. The inscription on the idol "TO THE UNKNOWN GOD" furnished the mighty apostolic opportunity for instructing the faithful and unfaithful of all time on what can be said, even in passing, on the nature of the Triune God.

"IN-FRONT-OF-THE-CHURCH PRIEST"

Inquiry classes have their place in every parish, but the priest who confines his efforts to inquiry classes, no matter how successful the classes are proving, will be doing only half his work in the way of bringing outright converts into the Church, and of bringing back fallen-away Catholics, and of getting those who were merely baptized in infancy to be instructed and receive the sacraments. He will be forgetting that the Spirit breatheth where he will and that there is hardly an hour in the pastoral life of a priest that does not yield at least one opportunity for the first steps towards the conversion of a soul.

In the summer of 1945 I met a Chicago pastor who is the best illustration of this Pauline alertness, already referred to, that I can recall. He was sent, soon after the beginning of his pastoral career, to a parish that was fast running down. The neighborhood was filled with people of recent immigrant stock.

Most of these had been baptized in infancy, but relatively few of them had grown up in the faith. A considerable number of the men thought themselves militant atheists. At this prospect some pastors would have been discouraged. They would have felt inclined to mark time until the bishop moved them to a parish worthy of their supposed efforts.

This pastor felt, however, that a running-down parish could be made a running-up parish. So he started to do the things at hand and relied on the grace of God for results. Results came. Most of his 1,300 converts were made in this very parish.

When I visited him on the first of August, 1947, he already had received 36 converts in six months through individual instruction. If we call some pastors "rectory priests," we might refer to this pastor as an "in-front-of-the-church priest." From the beginning of his pastorate, winter and summer, outside of his own two Masses, he is in front of the church, Sunday morning after Sunday morning, greeting every member of his 750 families, by name for the most part, and getting acquainted with the strange faces that he meets.

UTILIZING CONTACTS

In his early days in that same parish, the pastor noticed an upstanding young man coming out of an early Mass on a hot summer morning. He approached him and told him that it was good to see him out so early on such a warm morning. The young man responded that he liked to go to Mass. "But," interrupted the pastor, "you seem to be a newcomer in the parish."

"I am not a Catholic at all," answered the young man, "but I do like to go to Mass."

"Why not come all the way?" rejoined the pastor.

"I might do that too," responded the young man.

The next night was fixed for the beginning of instructions. The young man turned out to be a medical student who was working in a near-by restaurant early in the morning and late at night. When his mother came for his graduation the following year and found that he was a Catholic, she refused to attend the exercises. The young man set up his practice in Chicago and converted the nurse, whom he afterward married. He is rearing a Catholic family and incidentally practicing medicine with success in Chicago.

BREAD CAST UPON THE WATERS

An advertisement brought a couple to the mission from a near-by suburb. The first night of the women's meeting, the pastor saw a cultured and gracious woman coming out of the church. He felt sure that she was a stranger, so he spoke to her in a friendly way. She reciprocated his greetings. She told him that she was not a Catholic but an Episcopalian and that she had been drawn to attend the mission by the advertisement in the *Chicago Tribune*. She said also that her husband had driven her in and was riding around the streets until she came out. That husband, she informed the pastor, was baptized a Catholic, but was never instructed and never attended the Catholic Church.

The pastor expressed eagerness to meet the husband when he drove up and thought that he might be talked into coming to the men's mission the next week, a plan in which the Episcopalian wife heartily concurred. The pastor went so far as to suggest that, after the men's mission, the husband might be gotten into an instruction class and his wife also. And that is just what happened.

After some weeks, the Episcopalian wife became a Catholic, and the uninstructed Catholic, baptized in infancy, was made into an intelligent and practicing Catholic. They insisted on coming to the church of their conversion since they had not taken up permanent quarters in the suburb. The pastor remarked that they had already given, in their separate envelopes each Sunday, more than enough to pay for the advertisement in the *Chicago Tribune*. His initial outlay was as bread, cast upon the waters, that came back a hundredfold.

The pastor, being a man of faith, relies on the prayers of the congregation, asked for at different seasons of the year, especially Lent, the Pentecostal season, the Epiphany season, and Advent. Last Epiphany, no one had been brought to the Church on the feast of the Epiphany or before the Feast of the Epiphany in response to the prayers asked for and the prayers offered. So, after supper on the feast, the pastor bethought himself of a young woman who lived in the same block with the rectory and who was unbaptized, though other members of the family were Catholic. He had always made it a point to be sociable, even cordial, in meeting her. He had noticed during the Christmas season the very fine Christmas tree displayed through the window in the house where this girl lived. After supper then he went to inspect this Christmas tree at close range.

The family was naturally gratified to have the pastor come to see the Christmas tree, and the prospective catechumen showed him the fine points of the display. When she was asked before the priest left whether she had seen this year's Crib at the church, she admitted that she had not, for she had not been at Mass either on Christmas Day, Circumcision, Epiphany, or the intervening Sunday. The pastor suggested, therefore, that he turn on the lights in the church and that she come over and view the Crib. This sacramental had its effect. Before she left the church, she was signed up for instruction and has long since been a Catholic.

SOWING THE SEED

Then, during the war, the pastor made remote preparation for converts in the years to come. Each morning, he read the deaths of servicemen in the paper, servicemen whether Catholic, non-Catholic, or Jewish, living within the limits of the parish. That very day he made it a point to visit the bereaved family and extend his condolences. Whether the seeds thus sown have already sprung into catechumens or neophytes I do not know, but I am sure that he brought the first grace toward conversion in every one of those homes and in the homes of the neighbors and friends who heard about his welcome visit.

Two years ago, when I first met this zealous priest, he expressed one regret of his priestly life. He was sorry that during the years of his active pastoral work, he was not able, nor did he make it a point, to spend two hours each day in personal contacts. I am sure that the people of his neighborhood do not feel, as many non-Catholics do, that they are not welcome in the nearby Catholic church.

This priest, in his humility, feels that be is but reaping the harvest that others have planted and even watered. He attributes much to the constant circulation of Catholic pamphlets, to Catholic radio talks, national and local, and to the lending out of Catholic books. He feels that we of this generation are enjoying the fruits of the labors of our predecessors. This is largely true, as was indicated in a Springfield, Illinois, inquiry class where thirty-eight of the ninety-four who attended the first week registered as desirous of becoming Catholics.

APOSTOLATE OF PRAYER

There is another phase of prayer for converts that might be developed. As the Legion of Mary is starting auxiliary units in grade schools and high schools, nothing prevents, in devotional seasons of the year, the active auxiliaries from prevailing upon their classmates to go to Communion every day, or as often as an individual can be prevailed upon to go, for the conversion of relatives, friends, or of acquaintances of each pupil.

Last year at the Mercy High School in Chicago, the first group of the auxiliary units heard this gratifying report: Two girls were advised to walk around the block where a person lived whose conversion they were desirous of bringing about and say the beads quietly to themselves for that intention, and they did not do this more than a week or so before the conversion was made. The apostolate of prayer will help universalize the apostolate in the next generation of American Catholics.

Our own pastor, I surmise, as well as most pastors, has overlooked the fact that he must in justice save a relatively large number of adolescents to the faith. In big cities, we are finding that boys and girls in Catholic high schools are in all too many instances missing Mass on Sunday.

We are finding that the best of the Catholic high school pupils are going to Communion for the most part only once a month in an age when the Church is urging the generality of her people to go daily or at least frequently (five times a week). In other words, the flowers of the flock are not even potential apostles, to say nothing of being active apostles.

JUNIOR LEGION OF MARY

But what about the vast majority (some say as high as seventy percent) of our Catholic youth in public high schools, who are so lacking in spiritual formation as to be unable to hand down the faith to another generation except by accident? How are these, at least sixty percent of all our Catholic youth, going to be saved to the Church? I answer by using an organization that has done even harder things in every part of the world, even in foreign missionary lands. I refer to the junior Legion of Mary, made up of youth from twelve to eighteen years of age and presided over by a senior Legionary, if possible recently out of the Junior Legion ranks.

That this is feasible can be seen from what Father Francis J. Ripley did in a Liverpool parish with twenty boy junior Legionaries from fourteen to eighteen years old. His problem was to make sure that about 180 boy adolescents would attend Sunday Mass and go to Communion in a body monthly. Immediately, every adolescent in the parish was contacted weekly by two junior Legionaries. After three months, only a handful of boys were not going to Sunday Mass and monthly Communion in a body—and this in a parish where vast numbers of the parents were not going to Sunday Mass at all.

Father Ripley went further and used two Legionaries for every group of adolescents engaged in temporal activity under parish auspices, such as the Boys' Club, the Girls' Club, the Cycling Club, the Hiking Club, etc. In other words, Father Ripley promoted first the kingdom of God and his justice and incidentally the temporal activity of the girls and boys of the parish. In American parishes, on the contrary, too often it looks as if the temporal activities are promoted first and the spiritual activities hoped for as an incident. Willing pastors and assistants all over the country have been trying every effort to tempt newly fledged souls of their parish to the skies of the devout life, but most of these same fledglings are still on the ground. And they need not be. Ruby Dennison, the Legion of Mary envoy to South Africa, writes me from Johannesburg, South Africa, the very day I finish this chapter to this effect:

"Mary Duffy was my first president, and she beat me by three months being first Legion Envoy. Edel Quinn came to help me but gained her laurels in a very short time and died a saint. I enclose one of our recent reports and a little composition to let you see how well our dear black ones understand the Legion."

"SOLDIERS OF MARY"

The girl's composition reads:

The Legion of Mary is the army of Mary. This means the Legionaries are the Soldiers of Mary. The Legionaries have to fight for our Blessed Lady. This does not mean that the Legionaries fight against each other. We have to fight, together with our Blessed Lady, against her enemies. Her enemies are the devil and his servants.

There are many people who are tempted by the devil. They follow him. They hate God and serve the devil by doing bad deeds. We have to try our best to get them away from the devil, back to God.

Here on the mission we cannot do as much as we are bound to do, because we have not enough time to visit the villages, to seek people who lost their faith, but we can do other things. There are many rules to be observed in a boarding-school. Some pupils do not want to obey. We have to tell them and show them by example as much as we can that they are not allowed to disobey authority.

In the villages are old people who are not able to work for themselves. They need somebody to help them. After my school I like to help them by giving them clothes and food. They will be very glad when they see such actions. They will talk among themselves that I am different from others. They will like their children to act likewise. The children will be jealous and want to do what I do. They will imitate me. So progress is made in the world. The world will become better.

To help make the world better is the work I do for God in union with our Blessed Lady. If we had many more Legionaries, God would be served much better.

THE LEGION HELPS WIN CONVERTS

The following is the report of *Praesidium "Mary Our Hope,"
Elizabethville, Belgian Congo:*

> The six-month report of our Praesidium, which is held in Kiswahili.
> The meetings of these native women are held in the Sacred Heart
> School each Sunday after High Mass.

Spiritual Director .... Dom Albert, O.S.B.
Active Members 12

LEGIONARY ACTIVITIES

People brought to Sunday Mass 2,501
Those returned to Sunday Mass 102
New family visitations 359
New members for Confraternity of the Holy Rosary 91
New members for First Fridays......................... 29
New members for First Saturdays....................... 27
Baptisms performed 19
Family prayers started............................... 12
Ave Maria in the mornings............................ 11
Catechumens brought in............................... 9
Marriages rectified 3

The above Belgian missionary added this note to the report:
"We read that the Legion is progressing rapidly in Belgium and with
great encouragement from our Cardinal. God be praised. Without
doubt if the Legion spreads, our Country will be saved."

What the Legion of Mary is accomplishing, in the districts of
the Belgian Congo in which it is established, it likewise can do in
the parishes of our country where pastors will establish it. It provides every pastor eager to win converts with a zealous group of
lay workers who are constantly bringing prospective converts for
instruction.

11

Charts for Convert Instruction

Rev. JOHN A. O'BRIEN, Ph.D.

SAYING IT WITH PICTURES

IN THE INSTRUCTION of converts, carefully devised charts are a powerful help. They give concreteness to truths which to the neophyte may seem abstract. They enable him to visualize a series of facts along with their relationships and thus to assimilate them more readily. What stories and illustrations are to homilies for the faithful, charts are to instructions for non-Catholic inquirers. They add clearness, enhance the interest, and put the point across more effectively. *Iter longum per praecepta, breve est per exempla.* The journey is shortened likewise by the skillful use of graphs which tell the story in pictures and enable even those who run to see and understand.

The enormous appeal of the cinema lies in the fact that it tells a story pictorially, thus supplying a richness of imagery which mere words do not possess. Words are but slender and feeble bridges to concepts and ideas. Many cross those bridges haltingly, while others stumble and fall and never get across at all. This is true in almost direct proportion to the abstract character of the words employed.

Teachers of college and university students are often distressed in finding that three-fourths of their students are left behind when the lecturer persists for any appreciable length of time upon the purely abstract plane. The dullness that creeps into the eyes, the waning attention, the growing restlessness are the tell-tale signals that it is high time to come out of the stratosphere and down to earth. As nature abhors a vacuum, so the minds of all but a few highly trained logicians abhor imageless or near-imageless thought. "Get out of the clouds," "Come down to earth," are what most students are saying when their professor tarries long in the empyrean blue.

If this be the case with students with a university background, how much more does it hold for the masses without their training in abstract reasoning? It is well known that children must be taught with pictures, stories, chalk sketches, and all the elaborate technique of presenting knowledge in a concrete manner. Most adults are but children of a larger mold. They still clamor for the picture, the story, the concrete illustration. Because it is part of the technique of making the abstract concrete, the chart is welcomed by classes of prospective converts as an aid to clearness and ease of understanding.

A GRAPHIC PRESENTATION

In the instruction of converts over more than thirty years, we have found ourselves constantly seeking means of presenting the credentials of the Catholic Church in a graphically arresting form. As this phase of the instruction is of crucial importance, we have concentrated most of our efforts upon the graphic presentation of those facts of history which make the divine origin of the Church stand out in bold relief. Once this fact is clearly established, the remaining truths find ready acceptance. If the Catholic Church be proven to be the one true Church founded directly and immediately by Jesus Christ, it follows with the force of a self-evident truth that she alone is worthy of the belief and loyalty of all mankind.

Accordingly, we shall present some charts with the hope that they will prove helpful to our brothers in the presentation of the claims of Christ and his Church to our non-Catholic countrymen. The first is the precipitate obtained by the distillation of the nineteen centuries of the Christian era. It is basic and all-important.

CHART NO. I—THE VOICE OF HISTORY

The Divine Origin and Continuous Growth of the Catholic Church as Contrasted with the Human Origin and Short Durations of Other Faiths.

Explanation of chart: The vertical lines indicate the centuries of the Christian era. The horizontal lines represent some of the larger and more important of the many hundreds of religious denominations that have arisen during the past nineteen centuries. These lines indicate the duration of the various sects by beginning at the respective dates of origin and ceasing when they disappeared. The width of the line shows the approximate size of the denomination.

The chart shows that the Catholic Church was founded by Jesus Christ in A.D. 33 and has continued its amazing growth through the centuries to its present membership of 431,428,000. It depicts some of the leading heretical sects, such as the Montanists, Novatians, Arians. These have disappeared from the earth, leaving only their names and the memory of their errors to posterity.

In presenting to a Protestant the claim of the Catholic Church to be the true Church, we have found it well to point out that the question boils down to this: Whom are you to believe—Christ or Luther? That is the question which confronts every Protestant. If he reflects carefully upon it, he will not fail to see the wisdom of choosing to believe God instead of any mere man. The following chart is designed to help him in his thinking.

CHART NO. II—CHRIST OR LUTHER?

The Divine Origin of the Catholic Church and the Human Origin of Protestantism.

Explanation of chart: This chart shows the foundation of the Catholic Church by Jesus Christ at Jerusalem in 33 and the starting of Protestantism by Martin Luther in Germany in 1524. Compare the divine origin of the Catholic Church, its continuous growth, and its marvelous unity, with the human origin of Protestantism

Chart I

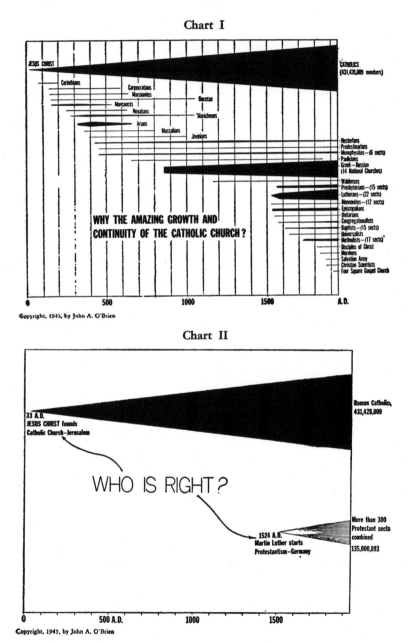

JESUS CHRIST

CATHOLICS (431,428,009 members)

Corinthians
Corpocrates
Marcionites
Montanists
Docetae
Novatians
Manicheans
Arians
Massalians
Jovinians

Nestorians
Predestinarians
Monophysites—(6 sects)
Paulicians
Greek—Russian (14 National Churches)
Waldenses
Presbyterians—(15 sects)
Lutherans—(22 sects)
Mennonites—(12 sects)
Episcopalians
Unitarians
Congregationalists
Baptists—(15 sects)
Universalists
Methodists—(17 sects)
Disciples of Christ
Mormons
Salvation Army
Christian Scientists
Four Square Gospel Church

WHY THE AMAZING GROWTH AND CONTINUITY OF THE CATHOLIC CHURCH?

0   500   1000   1500   A.D.

Copyright, 1945, by John A. O'Brien

Chart II

33 A.D.
JESUS CHRIST founds
Catholic Church—Jerusalem

Roman Catholic,
431,428,009

WHO IS RIGHT?

1524 A.D.
Martin Luther starts
Protestantism—Germany

More than 300
Protestant sects
combined
135,000,893

0   500 A.D.   1000   1500

Copyright, 1945, by John A. O'Brien

and its ceaseless splitting into hundreds of different sects which have continued to change, so that even their own human founders would not recognize them today.

This chart focuses attention upon respective founders of Catholicism and of Protestantism. As one reflects upon the divine character of Jesus Christ and the human character of Martin Luther, he can scarcely fail to realize that one is God-made, the other is man-made. If God is to be obeyed rather than man, then it is clear that one is under an imperative obligation of embracing the religion of Jesus and of rejecting the creed of any human founder.

So important and far-reaching in its consequences is this truth that we have presented this substantial truth in another chart which emphasizes the tell-tale lapse of fifteen centuries between the origin of the Catholic Church and the appearance of Protestantism. In the preceding chart the contrast was between God and man. In the following chart the contrast is between the first-century origin of Catholicism and the sixteenth-century origin of Protestantism.

CHART NO. III—A SIGNIFICANT GAP?

Chart Showing the Gap of Fifteen Centuries from Christ's Foundation of the Catholic Church at Jerusalem in 33 to Luther's Establishment of Protestantism in Germany in 1524.

Explanation of chart: This chart focuses attention upon the telltale gap that stretches from the divine origin of the Catholic Church at Jerusalem in 33 to the establishment of Lutheranism, the first form of Protestantism, by Martin Luther in 1524.

Christ not only founded the Catholic Church, but he promised to be with her "all days, even to the consummation of the world." The chart which shows the continuous expansion of the Church to her present size of 431,428,009 members according to the Catholic World Atlas, quoted in *The Sign*, February, 1936, proves that Christ has kept his promise. In discussing the matter with our countrymen, it is well to point out the amazing vitality of the Church in the United States in contrast with the decline in Protestantism. This we do in the following chart.

Chart III

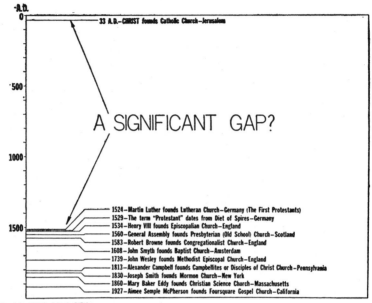

Chart IV

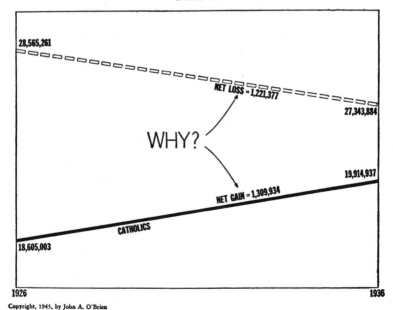

CHART NO. IV—THE VITALITY OF THE CATHOLIC CHURCH

The Growth of the Catholic Church in the United States Compared with the Net Loss of the 13 Principal Protestant Denominations from 1926 to 1936 as Shown by the U.S. Federal Census.

Explanation of Chart: The United States census reported a total membership for 13 of the principal Protestant denominations of 28,565,261 in 1926 and of 27,343,884 in 1936—a net loss of 1,221,377. Compare this with the net gain of 1,309,934 for the Catholic Church in the same period. The denominations are the Baptists (includes 3 groups), Methodist Episcopal (5 groups), Presbyterians (2 groups), Episcopalians, Lutherans (6 groups), Churches of Christ, Christian Scientists, Church of the United Brethren, Congregationalists, Disciples of Christ, Evangelical Reformed, Evangelical Church, Church of the Latter-Day Saints.

Another indication of the vitality of the Church in the United States is the number of converts whom she has drawn to her fold. While the preceding chart reflects the growth from births, the following chart shows the growth from conversions. It is impressive and well calculated to jolt any non-Catholic from his apathy into serious thought concerning the character of an institution which could draw so many people into her fold.

CHART NO. V—THE PULL OF TRUTH ON THE OPEN MIND

The Annual Increase in the Number of Converts to the Catholic Church from 1926 to 1945—a Total of 1,126,658 in 19 Years.

Explanation of chart: In 1926 the converts totaled 35,751; in 1934, they totaled 63,845; in 1943, they reached a peak of 90,822 —making a grand total for the 19-year period of 1,126,658.

The marvelous growth which characterized the Church in other ages and in other lands is continuing in America today. The most gifted minds among the scientists, philosophers, artists, and litterateurs are flocking to her. "The cold clear light of reason," observes Arnold Lunn, "is all the guidance a man needs to find his way to the Church."

The truth of his words is evidenced by the roll call of the brilliant Americans who thought themselves into the Church. That line we trace from Orestes A. Brownson, one of the most profound thinkers America has produced, to Bishop Frederick J. Kinsman, one of the most scholarly of all Anglican divines, down to Professor Carlton J. Hayes, the leading historian of our day. The reasons which brought this galaxy of brilliant scholars, as well as the other 1,126,658 converts into the Church, can all be reduced, as G. K. Chesterton pointed out, to one reason: "Catholicism is true."

"The other day," wrote William Lyon Phelps, "I read as a piece of news that in fifty years science will have destroyed religion, so that there will be nothing left of it except a memory. Meanwhile conversions to the Roman Catholic Church continue in such quantity and quality as to excite the attention of all who are interested in what is called the trend of modern thought. I recommended to those who wonder how any intelligent man can become a Roman Catholic a little book called *Restoration*, written by Ross J. S. Hoffman, a professor of history in New York University, who tells us how he went from nothing to everything."

The noted author John L. Stoddard thus summarizes what his conversion has brought to him: "The Catholic Church has given me order for confusion, certainty for doubt, sunlight for darkness, substance for shadow." Therein is reflected the experience of all converts.

CHART NO. VI—MARVELOUS GROWTH OF THE CHURCH

Membership in the Catholic Church in the United States as Compared with That of Other Organizations, as Shown by the U.S. Federal Census of 1936.

Explanation of chart: There is food for reflection in the fact that the Catholic Church has grown so rapidly to the position of overwhelming numerical superiority in our country. The continuous misrepresentation of Catholic teaching by her enemies and the waves of anti-Catholic bigotry, which periodically sweep our land as a result of propaganda by such notorious organizations as the

Chart V

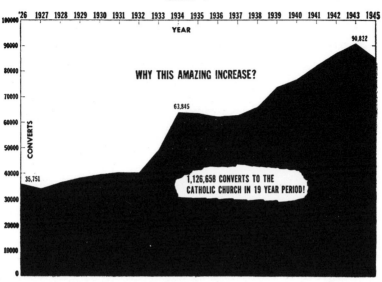

WHY THIS AMAZING INCREASE?

1,126,658 CONVERTS TO THE
CATHOLIC CHURCH IN 19 YEAR PERIOD!

Chart VI

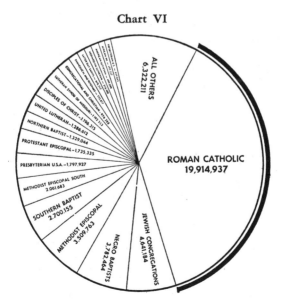

American Protective Association and the Ku Klux Klan, have not been able to counteract the pull of truth nor the unfailing aid from on high. No searchers for truth can fail to be impressed by the chart prepared by the United States Census Bureau showing how the Catholic Church stands above every other religious group in America. The statistics are for the year 1936. While they certainly do not represent the full membership in the Church at that time, they suffice to show how far she outstrips all other organizations. Christ is keeping his promise to be with the Church unto the consummation of the world.

CHART NO. VII—THE MAKING OF THE NEW TESTAMENT

The Catholic Church—Mother of the Bible.

Explanation of chart: This chart presents in outline form the essential historical facts about the origin and formation of the New Testament. In showing how it came into being, the chart shows how it owes its existence to the Catholic Church, the mother of the Bible. The chart brings out into clear relief the following facts:

1. The New Testament was written in its entirety by Catholics.

2. St. Peter, the first pope of the Catholic Church, is the author of two of its epistles.

3. The Catholic Church determined the canon or list of books to constitute the New Testament.

4. The declaration of the Catholic Church that the books of the New Testament are all inspired by God constitutes the sole authority for the universal belief of both Catholics and Protestants in their inspired character.

5. The Catholic Church existed before the New Testament.

6. The Catholic Church is the mother of the New Testament.

DETERMINING THE CANON OF NEW TESTAMENT

If she had not scrutinized carefully the writings of her children, rejecting some and approving others as worthy of inclusion in the canon of the New Testament, there would be no New Testament

Chart VII

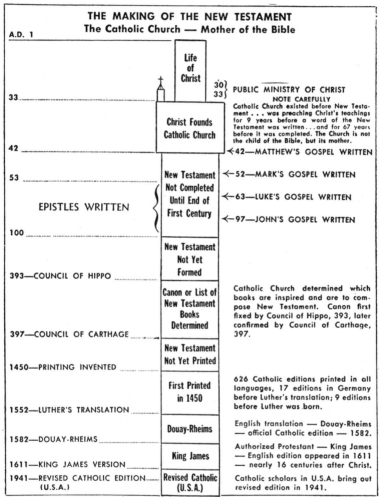

THE MAKING OF THE NEW TESTAMENT
The Catholic Church — Mother of the Bible

A.D. 1

	Life of Christ		
	✝	30 } 33 }	PUBLIC MINISTRY OF CHRIST
33			NOTE CAREFULLY
	Christ Founds Catholic Church		Catholic Church existed before New Testament . . . was preaching Christ's teachings for 9 years before a word of the New Testament was written . . . and for 67 years before it was completed. The Church is not the child of the Bible, but its mother.
42			←42—MATTHEW'S GOSPEL WRITTEN
53	**New Testament Not Completed Until End of First Century**		←52—MARK'S GOSPEL WRITTEN
			←63—LUKE'S GOSPEL WRITTEN
EPISTLES WRITTEN			←97—JOHN'S GOSPEL WRITTEN
100			
	New Testament Not Yet Formed		
393—COUNCIL OF HIPPO	**Canon or List of New Testament Books Determined**		Catholic Church determined which books are inspired and are to compose New Testament. Canon first fixed by Council of Hippo, 393, later confirmed by Council of Carthage, 397.
397—COUNCIL OF CARTHAGE			
1450—PRINTING INVENTED	**New Testament Not Yet Printed**		
	First Printed in 1450		626 Catholic editions printed in all languages, 17 editions in Germany before Luther's translation; 9 editions before Luther was born.
1552—LUTHER'S TRANSLATION			
1582—DOUAY-RHEIMS	**Douay-Rheims**		English translation — Douay-Rheims — official Catholic edition — 1582.
1611—KING JAMES VERSION	**King James**		Authorized Protestant — King James — English edition appeared in 1611 — nearly 16 centuries after Christ.
1941—REVISED CATHOLIC EDITION (U.S.A.)	**Revised Catholic (U.S.A.)**		Catholic scholars in U.S.A. bring out revised edition in 1941.

The Catholic Church—Mother of the Bible.

today. If she had not declared the books composing the New Testament to be the inspired word of God, we would not know it. The only authority which non-Catholics have for the inspiration of the Scriptures is the authority of the Catholic Church. If the latter be rejected, there remain no logical grounds for retention of the cardinal tenet of all Protestants—the inspired character of Scripture.

With the possible exception of St. John, none of the apostles ever saw all the writings which now make up the New Testament. If the Church did not preserve the Bible, shielding it from the attacks of barbarians, copying it in her monasteries throughout the long centuries before the art of printing was invented, the modern world would be without the Bible.

THE CHURCH EXISTED BEFORE THE BIBLE

The chart shows that the Catholic Church, founded by Jesus Christ, was teaching and preaching the word of God for nine years before a word of the New Testament was written and for sixty-seven years before it was completed. The truths enunciated by her divine Founder were deep in her heart and fresh in her memory. She was busily engaged in imparting these orally to mankind.

Christ wrote nothing. Neither did he command the apostles to write. He commissioned them to teach his doctrines to all mankind. "Go ye into the whole world," he said, "and preach the gospel to every creature" (Mark 16:15). The apostles fulfilled the command of Christ by their oral preaching.

Three of the twelve, Peter, Matthew, and John, supplemented their preaching by writing. It is well to remember, however, that the Church was a going concern, a functioning institution—teaching, preaching, administering the sacraments, saving souls—before the New Testament saw the light of day.

THE MOTHER OF THE BIBLE

The chart shows vividly that the Church is not the child of the Bible, as many non-Catholics imagine, but its mother. She derives neither

her existence nor her teaching authority from the New Testament. She had both before the New Testament was born. She secured her being, her teachings, her authority directly from Jesus Christ.

If all the books of the Bible and all its copies were blotted out, she would still be in possession of all the truths of Christ and could still continue to preach them as she did before a single word of the New Testament was written. Those truths are deep in her mind, heart, and memory, in her liturgical and sacramental life, in the traditions, written and unwritten, which go directly back to Christ.

The Church has brought the Bible into being. She reveres it. She loves it as a mother loves her child. She declares it to be the inspired word of God. She urges its reading upon all mankind with the power and authority bestowed upon her by her divine Founder when he said: "All power is given to me in heaven and in earth . . . Going, therefore, teach ye all nations . . . Teaching them to observe all things whatsoever I have commanded you: and behold I am with you all days, even to the consummation of the world" (Matt. 28:18–20). As the Founding Fathers of our country established the Supreme Court to interpret with authority the Constitution for all our citizens, so Jesus Christ established the Catholic Church to interpret with infallible authority all his teachings, both oral and written, for all mankind.

CHART NO. VIII—TITLE DEED OF THE CATHOLIC CHURCH

Unbroken List of Pontiffs from Peter to Today.

Explanation of chart: The chart lists the names of the pontiffs, beginning with St. Peter and continuing in an unbroken line through nineteen centuries to the pontiff happily ruling today. It shows when each pontiff ascended to the chair of Peter and when he died. This unbroken list of pontiffs constitutes the title deed of the Catholic Church's exclusive jurisdiction over the divine deposit of truth. It drives home to the spectator at a single glance the connection between the Catholic Church of today and the Catholic Church as founded by Christ and governed by Peter, the chief of the apostles and the first pope.

Chart VIII

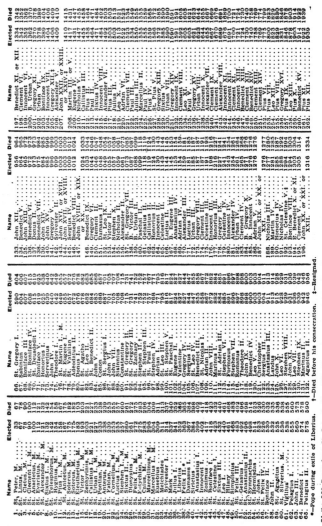

Unbroken List of Pontiffs from Peter to Today.

We have found a number of prospective converts who entertained some doubts and difficulties until they beheld this impressive chart, which allowed no further room for doubt. The title deed of a family to the property upon which they live, to be valid, must go back to the original owner, namely, the United States government. If the title stops short of the original owner, it is invalid and worthless.

No Protestant church goes back beyond the religious revolt of the sixteenth century. Hence, no one of them possesses a valid title deed to the jurisdiction and administration of the truths, authority and laws established by Jesus Christ to guide all mankind safely to their eternal home in heaven.

It is hoped that the use of these charts will be of help to our brother priests in the instruction of converts and in the winning of the "other sheep" to the fold of the divine Master. All the charts presented in this chapter are reproduced in the writer's pamphlet, *How To Find Christ's Church*, published by the Catholic Information Society, New York City, at ten cents each and with generous discounts on quantity orders. It will be well to provide each individual with a copy for detailed study and reflection so that, after he has absorbed these outstanding truths, he can explain them to others and thus recruit prospects for the next class. For use by the instructor in the class, these charts are reproduced in large and impressive form by the Catechetical Guild, St. Paul, Minnesota. They are also suitable for use in Catholic schools.

12

The Inquiry Forum and the Legion

Very Rev. Msgr. CHARLES H. HELMSING, Diocesan Director
Society for the Propagation of the Faith, St. Louis, Missouri

EDITOR'S FOREWORD: One of the most encouraging aspects of the convert movement in America is the zeal and enthusiasm with which young priests and young laymen and -women are throwing themselves into this work. In virtually every seminary, methods of winning converts are now being presented either in a formal class on the subject or in informal talks and discussions. The Brownson Club at Kenrick Seminary has fired the enthusiasm of hundreds of young priests for convert work, and the fruits are becoming increasingly apparent.

Think of a priest, ordained only a dozen years, who has been privileged by God to lead five hundred people into the Church of Jesus Christ. Yet this is the achievement of Monsignor Helmsing. Other former members of that Brownson Club are accomplishing similar results.

Young priests and older ones too, as well as seminarians and lay people, will find in Monsignor Helmsing's story inspiration to cast their nets out into the mighty deep in search of a copious draught that will fill their nets to the overflowing.

Note, too, the important role played by the Legion of Mary in this inspiring achievement. The use of these Legionaries on an ever-increasing scale is the promise and the guarantee of vastly increased results. To every priest searching for the sheep that have strayed from the Master's fold, we say respectfully and earnestly: Use the Legion of Mary to help you recruit prospects, and yours, too, will be a harvest similar to that gleaned by this young and zealous disciple of Christ—Monsignor Helmsing.

SOURCES OF INSPIRATION

I T IS A JOY to tell the story of a dozen years reaping in the white harvest of souls. That reaping under God's grace flows from lofty inspiration and opportunity—the inspiration coming primarily from the intellectual and spiritual training of Kenrick Seminary, further enhanced by an extracurricular activity of the Kenrick Missionary Society. A study group under that Society, dedicated to the great American convert, Orestes Brownson, undertook a thorough perusal of *The White Harvest.*

That study and discussion threw open to us young theologians a vista of apostolic work that was made concrete by the splendid example of experts in convert-making. During our vacations we had the further inspiration of seeing an inquiry forum in operation. It was under the pioneering direction of the late Father Burke, S.J., pastor of St. Francis Xavier College Church, St. Louis, who was aided by the Jesuit theologians then attending the university.

REALIZATION OF AN AIM

The opportunity came after ordination. On temporary assignment during the absence of an older priest, I found myself entrusted with a small class of converts, recently baptized but still in need of some instruction. I learned that it was just as simple and easy to instruct four persons as one.

Before long I was suggesting to my superiors the possibility of larger classes, but more experienced confreres counseled against the plan on the plea that the instruction would not be thorough enough and that the converts would slip away. Accordingly, for two years I was content to give individual instructions. In retrospect, these instructions proved to have been invaluable both in learning the difficulties and problems of prospective converts and also in outlining a personal course of instructions.

Class instructions were inaugurated through force of necessity. Transferred to an almost full-time teaching assignment in a high school, while living and working in a large parish, I soon became acquainted with an increasing number of prospective converts. About this time I had the opportunity of listening to a conference of Monsignor Fulton Sheen on priestly zeal. In it the zealous priest-orator recounted how a single advertisement telling people to come to an inquiry forum on the Catholic faith had resulted in a hundred converts. That talk gave the immediate incentive. The problem of how to cope with the increasing number of inquirers and at the same time not to infringe on classroom duties was discussed with the local pastor, Right Rev. Msgr. Nicholas W. Brinkman. His advice and assistance proved invaluable. It was decided to hold an inquiry forum to begin in late September and to conclude early in Advent.

PUBLICITY AND PROCEDURE

An announcement was made in the secular press. Advertisements in the parish bulletin and the diocesan paper were followed by pulpit announcements. The result far surpassed all expectations. There were twenty-two converts as a result of that first class. Since then three inquiry forums have been conducted annually in the St. Louis cathedral parish. I have had the happy privilege of conducting some thirty of them. The first forum is conducted immediately after January first, concluding during the Lenten season; the second begins immediately after Easter and ends at the time of the annual priests' retreat; the third runs from the end of September to the early part of December.

The lectures are held on Wednesday and Friday evenings from 7:45 to 8:45 P.M. There are twenty lectures plus a Sunday afternoon detailed tour of the church. One of the regular lectures, running from an hour and one-half to two hours, is an illustrated explanation of the Holy Sacrifice of the Mass. Opportunities for conferences with the instructor are given before and after the regular lectures and by appointment at other times. Classes that are missed by anyone who has expressed a desire to become a Catholic are made up privately.

A record of the attendance is kept simply by asking those in attendance to sign their name to a blank card and drop it in a box at the door as they leave the class. In this way those who come merely to listen do not have to identify themselves, their anonymity can be respected. It goes without saying that the private interviews are absolutely essential, and even after the twenty lectures some souls require many hours of private instruction. Others are practically ready for baptism at the conclusion of the public lectures.

LECTURE CONTENT

The forum is conducted as an informal lecture. The advice of Cardinal James Gibbons given in *The White Harvest,* enjoining expository rather than the argumentative style, is scrupulously adhered to. The opening lectures are concerned with a statement of the problem of happiness, the *why* and *wherefore* of human life, and an attempt is made to clarify the ideas of God, man, religion, Christ, the God-man, the Church with its attributes as we find it depicted in the gospel story. Then, after an explanation of the sources of revelation, Scripture and Tradition, the dogmas or teachings of the Church, as they are given in outline form in the *Baltimore Catechism Number Two*, are taken up individually.

Personally I am convinced that a thorough appreciation of the Church as the divinely authorized teacher of revelation is absolutely essential for the convert's future. However, I am not certain whether it is better to give the complete apologetics of the Church early in the course—that is, the identification of the Catholic Church with the Church of the Scriptures by means of the marks of unity, holiness, catholicity, and apostolicity—or whether that phase of the teaching should be reserved until the article on the Church in the

Apostles' Creed is reached in the catechism study. It seems that too great an emphasis on the one true Church before presenting the other dogmas may repel some inquirers. I am also undecided as to whether it is better to teach Christian morality before the sacraments and prayer. Since the perfect fulfillment of even the natural law is impossible without revelation and grace, perhaps it is better to give priority to the sacraments and prayer.

TEXTS

The guide book given to the prospective converts is the *Baltimore Catechism Number Two*, merely as an outline for orderly procedure, not a book to be memorized. I try to emphasize to the class that they are expected to understand, not to memorize, and that they are free to ask questions on any matter that the lecture does not clarify.

For supplementary reading they are given Bishop Noll's book *Father Smith Instructs Jackson* and the little book of Father Martindale's, *Words of Life*. As soon as the positive teachings of faith are reached, great stress is placed on prayer and each class member is given a Sunday missal, for an attempt is made to link up doctrine and devotion and to make the lectures resemble as closely as possible the conferences of a retreat.

ROSARY AND THE LIFE OF CHRIST

Experience has proved that the ordinary inquirer knows very little about the life of Christ. The facts of his life given in connection with his Incarnation and Redemption are further taught by means of the rosary. The rosary is exhibited as a practical method by which the Catholic knows and applies to himself the life of Christ through meditation on the mysteries.

Instruction in the use of the missal, Father Stedman's simplified form, is given in connection with the instruction on the Mass. In private interviews great stress is laid on vocal and mental prayer. Experience proves that where a prospective convert either refuses to pray or takes the obligation lightly, that his dispositions can be seriously doubted. It goes without saying the priest merely plants and waters through his instructions. God alone can give the increase, and the grace for this increase comes through prayer.

TANGIBLE RESULTS

The question suggests itself: How has the stream of inquirers kept coming during the years? Baptisms during the dozen years number well over five hundred. Occasionally there trickles in a report about a harvest reaped elsewhere as the result of our sowing. The original method of advertising is still continued.

Parishioners, as a result of the frequent announcements, are conscious of the opportunities that their parish presents to them for bringing non-Catholic friends and acquaintances. Practically every non-Catholic is brought by a Catholic. The best recruiters have been and continue to be persons who became Catholics through the inquiry forum. This is especially true of converts who have been inducted into the Legion of Mary.

ROLE OF THE LEGION OF MARY

Membership in the Legion of Mary has been a great boon to new converts, giving them the sterling example and charitable companionship that they need in the early days after their baptism and confirmation and at the same time giving them an outlet for their zeal and gratitude by affording them opportunities to bring to others the benefit that is theirs.

The Legion of Mary has worked consistently with the inquiry forum at the St. Louis cathedral. Its members are constantly making a census of the parish. These census calls bring them into contact with very many persons who with a modicum of encouragement welcome the opportunity of learning something about the Catholic faith.

The Legionaries on their part are always alert to the opportunities of bringing prospective members to the class. Moreover, they compile a list of persons who have expressed an interest in the faith, and prior to each new series of classes they address an invitation to these persons and try to follow it up by a personal call before the opening class.

It has been found that members of the Legion who have been Catholics from infancy have, through their charity in accompanying others to the classes, received for themselves an adult's appreciation of their faith, becoming thereby more intelligent in their zeal. They have also found the inquiry forum a wonderful opportunity for bringing back fallen-away Catholics.

Many of those who have lapsed in the practice of the faith have done so through a kindergarten knowledge of their faith. They are amazed to hear their faith taught from an adult's point of view, and many have been the returns to the sacraments, marriages validated, and children brought to adequate instruction through the Legionaries, who bring the spiritually poor to the inquiry forum.

AN APOSTOLIC LAITY ESSENTIAL

The years have convinced me that if the Legion of Mary continues to grow not merely in numbers but especially in quality of membership, converts will of necessity be multiplied. For this reason I consider the actual work of instruction less important than the training of lay apostles. My own experience and that of many of my confreres would recommend the Legion of Mary for this training. Like the work of convert instruction, the task of working the Legion system to the best advantage means "tying one's self down" to a regular routine of methods. The Legion system itself is foolproof, provided it is scrupulously followed in every detail. Every instance of failure has been failure on the part of the priest to adhere to the system.

Results, not excuses! The Legion carries this modern business slogan into the more important business of salvation and sanctification. A holy apostolic laity will effect countless conversions and by converse action will help the priest foster his own apostolic spirit. A priest who is persevering in Legion direction will be constantly edified by the zeal of his lay co-workers. A holy emulation will inspire him to give in priestly service without the slightest avarice of leisure time.

Everywhere that the Legion has been truly operative direct results are outstanding. The hidden, indirect leaven of Legionary action and interaction can and will increase the spirituality of every parish. Thus will be eliminated the fear that has too often stifled the apostolate for the "other sheep"—namely, that time and effort spent on convert instruction would interfere with the spiritual care of those already in the Church. The Legion operating in a parish keeps alive the true apostolic character of the Church, of being on the alert for every opportunity to bring souls to the knowledge and love of Christ.

APPROXIMATING THE MISSION CATECHUMENATE

It has been a consolation to me to know that in the year that new duties have taken me from this work the classes continue flourishing more than ever under priests more enterprising in organizing their methods. Systematic efforts are now being made to circularize the non-Catholic spouses of mixed-marriages. In addition, persons who come to the rectory expressing a determination to study and embrace the faith are not made to wait until the beginning of a new forum.

Special convert classes are begun each month by an assistant priest of the parish, and these classes have greatly increased the number of converts, while the inquiry forum continues as usual in its task of sowing the seed in the hearts of those who perhaps have not as yet made up their minds to embrace the faith. Private instructions continue and will always continue in every parish, but it is my opinion that the priests of America must more and more imitate the methods and zeal of the foreign missionaries who use the catechumenate for the class instructions of their converts.

13

Instructing Converts

Rt. Rev. Msgr. FULTON J. SHEEN, D.D.
Catholic University, Washington, D.C.

EDITOR'S FOREWORD: No priest in America stands less in need of introduction than Monsignor Fulton J. Sheen. His success in leading converts to the feet of Christ is almost legendary. He has pressed the radio, the lecture platform, the pulpit, and the pen into the tireless quest for souls. In this brief but pregnant article, he lays bare the crotchets of the modern mind and shows how the truths of Christ can be most effectively presented.

∾

INSTRUCTING CONVERTS

THE DIFFERENCE between the convert of a few generations ago and the modern convert is that the latter has nothing to be converted *from*, i.e., he is without fixed allegiance, definite principles, and a clear-cut creed. This is one of the reasons why there is a decline of bigotry in the world and an increase of hate. Bigotry is dogmatic; hate is emotional.

When you bump into a bigot, you bump into a creed; when you meet hate, you are face to face with a spleen. The old bigot at least could give you fifty bad reasons for the faith which was in him; the modern soul could not give you one bad reason for his absence of faith. This means that the strictly rational approach to religion which was so popular years ago has less appeal today. It is no longer Protestantism from which we convert souls; it is confusionism.

CONFUSIONISM

The modern soul is not going to God from nature. He is no longer impressed with our traditional arguments for the existence of God based on motion, order, contingency, efficient causes, and graded perfections. This in part is due to the fact that nature seems less friendly to man today than it did to our forefathers, who were prepared to accept the sacramental character of the universe.

The atomic bomb is a symbol to the modern soul of how nature can operate against man. This, of course, does not mean the invalidity of the approach from nature, but it does mean that today it has little appeal. In its place the modern man is going to God through himself, not his subjective self, but rather his disordered, frustrated, complicated, confused, bewildered self. Under the pressure of wars, insecurity, revolution, and chaos, people are coming back to a consciousness of guilt and sin. They may not see it as such, but they do see it as fear.

It is from this intolerable tension within their souls, such as was described by Ovid, who saw and approved the better things and followed those which are worse, that the soul seeks release. Modern theology confirms this as the principal burden of the contemporary spirit. Kierkegaard first pointed to it in the last century; then came Brunner and Barth in Germany, Joad in England, Niebuhr in America—each of whom pointed out the civil war that goes on inside the soul.

As Joad put it, none of the explanations given of evil at the present time, such as the economic or the psychological, explain the fact. "Evil is endemic in the heart of man." What is Marxism but the admission of conflict and tensions in the language of economics?

Contemporary psychology is wrestling with this problem too, describing the tension inside man as the conflict of self and environment, the conscious and subconscious, or the erotic urges and conventions, none of which are very profound. But they are, however, closer to the true nature of man than were the liberal philosophers who denied guilt and believed in inevitable progress. In literature too there is an attempt to return man to Paradise after an obvious Fall. Lawrence would reintegrate man through sex, Hemingway through soil and blood and subscription to a totalitarian ideology, Huxley through an eclectic mysticism, Joyce through imposed literary forms. In general they are describing man in terms of the Old Testament without the New.

Stating all this in strong language, it is true to say the modern soul is coming to God through the devil. This should not surprise us, for there are two ways of knowing how good God is, one by remaining with him in innocence, the other by losing him. Mary Magdalene, the woman in sin, the young man of the Gerasenes, and countless others came to God the second way. That is the way many are coming back to divine love today. As a matter of fact, the very vacuity which some sins engender in themselves is a negative preparation for coming to the divine embrace. As Muir expresses the mood of the tension of good and evil in one of his poems:

> Hell shoots his avalanche at our feet,
> In heaven the souls go up and down
> And we can see from this our seat
> The heavenly and the hellish town,
> The green cross growing in a wood
> Close by old Eden's crumbling wall,
> And God Himself in full manhood
> Riding against the Fall.

ORIGINAL SIN

This means that the most important tract in theology today, so far as the modern soul is concerned, is titled "Original Sin." There is a suggestion of this approach in St. Augustine, St. Thomas Aquinas, and Newman, but a more evident use of it needs to be made today. Modern theology, literature, psychology, and economics are all playing on the fringes of original sin. It is with the fact of tension or guilt that we best approach the soul in search of God. In the older generation where society was good and evil the exception, we had to explain the problem of evil. Today the argument is the other way around. Evil is no longer an objection against religion, but a proof in favor of it. As St. Thomas argues in *Contra Gentiles*, because there is evil in the world there is a God. This disorder in man has all the evidence of being due to abuse of free will; man cannot get out of it any more than he can lift himself by his own bootstraps. Only the intrusion into the historical order of the eternal and the divine can release man from this servitude.

The new apologetics with this starting point has not yet been written. A dim beginning was hinted in Rosalind Murray's *The Good Pagan's Failure* and Newman's *Grammar of Assent*, but the real treatise awaits an author. Practically all our textbooks on apologetics and our pamphlets are still battling Protestantism, as our philosophical textbooks are beating the dead dogs of Kant and Hume. Not until our schools and universities rise above a philosophical insight which thinks that a student is learning something when he writes on "The Criteriology of John Locke" or the "Theory of Knowledge of Hume" or the "Apologetic Method of Nicholas de Cusa" will they be ready to meet the contemporary world.

The modern man, like the boy in the mountains, is isolated from himself (his name is "Legion"), from his fellow man (he lives in the tombs), and from God ("Art thou come to destroy us?"). This triple divorce of the soul from itself is the *fact* with which we must start. In other words, our times are no longer concerned with the "Problem of Man," but with "Man as a Problem." That is why the I-II of the *Summa* of St. Thomas is the key to the apologetics of the future. Therein St. Thomas begins a study of the tensions within man, then the mechanics of the tension, then its causes, and finally the remedy. But we will have to put that thirteenth-century truth in twentieth-century clothes.

SUGGESTIONS CONCERNING METHOD

Never mention any sect in the course of instructions nor make any reference to Protestantism unless an inquiry is made. If one presents the Church as the prolongation of the Incarnation, as the Mystical Christ living through the centuries, as Christ speaking his truth through his Body, as he once spoke it through his human nature, forgiving sins through his new Body as he forgave them through his human nature, then there is no need of refuting a sect that came into existence 1,500 years after the death of Christ.

Prepare instructions so as to be able to talk in an intensely interesting and inspired manner for thirty minutes without interruption. Then give the inquirer all the time he wants to ask questions on the particular subject and present his difficulties. Instructions from the catechism by going over each question are not apt to give him as coherent and integrated a picture of the faith as the one outlined. The priest should make a notebook of instructions and from time to time add new developments to each subject and those best calculated to convince the inquirer.

Instructions are dull when there is a communication of a fire without heat or a truth without love. As Horace said, "If you would make me weep, you must weep first." Unless we cast a few sparks, how shall the convert catch fire?

The convert should be given considerable reading matter according to his intelligence, both books and pamphlets, and they should all be given *free*. The pamphlet rack in the back of a church should have the money box taken out of it, and all the pamphlets should be gratis. If you wanted to know something about communism, the communist headquarters would send you a subscription to the *Daily Worker* free and flood you with literature, but when a non-Catholic wants to find out about the Eucharist, he has to pay a dime.

No gratuity should ever be accepted from a convert, not even a stole fee at baptism. They will hear plenty of money sermons later on, and it would be a good idea to start them off with a memory of never having heard money from the priest who instructed them.

14

Into the Highways and Byways

Rev. WILLIAM J. QUINLAN
St. Sabina Church, Chicago, Illinois

EDITOR'S FOREWORD: At St. Sabina's Church in Chicago, the pastor and his four assistants were busy with the customary duties of a large city parish. Since they were located in a Catholic section of the city, conversions were not too numerous. Then, in 1944, at the suggestion of the pastor, Father William A. Corey, there was organized a Legion of Mary unit. Things began to happen—and happen fast.

The Legionaries called on mixed-marriage families to interest the non-Catholic party in a course of instruction. Forty responded favorably. Other non-Catholics were interested. As a result, the first inquiry class was established, netting twenty-four converts. It was a convincing demonstration of what can be accomplished when the Legionaries of Mary are enlisted in the work of winning souls for Christ.

Now the public inquiry class is a feature at St. Sabina's. Instead of waiting for prospects to ring the rectory doorbell, priests and people go out into the highways and byways in search of them. Placed in the neighborhood stores are hundreds of attractive placards announcing the series of public lectures on the Catholic religion. Notification cards and programs of the lectures are passed out to the parishioners. Hundreds of personal letters are sent to prospects. Advertisements reach 90,000 people.

The results, while not perhaps spectacular, are gratifying and encouraging. In the four inquiry classes held thus far, 190 people were instructed and 93 have entered the fold. Similar methods, zeal, and hard work will bring like results in virtually every parish. Winning converts is not a spectacular, grandstand performance. It is a long, hard pull.

With God's grace, however, results are sure to come. In this chapter Father William J. Quinlan tells of the joint efforts of priests and people to reclaim the sheep strayed from the Master's fold. Priests and people in every parish will find therein many hints and suggestions for the enhancement of the success of their labors in this apostolate, so close to the heart of Christ.

❧

INTRODUCTION

WHAT PRIEST or even what devout Catholic layman is there today who is not appalled at the mass of the American people outside the Catholic Church? In the large cities, having concentrated Catholic populations, we are impressed and encouraged by the throngs which fill our churches; but let a priest walk the downtown streets through the crowds of shoppers and business people, and the unknowing stares of the vast majority will soon diminish this just pride.

In rural areas and smaller cities where Catholics are but a handful, this appalling sight saddens even more the heart of a lover of Christ. Five-sixths of the American people do not really know God as he would be known! For them much of Christ's work has been in vain. Their religion, of whatever sort it be, is a poor and deficient substitute for the fullness of Christianity which can be found alone, we all know, in active membership in the Catholic Church.

Needless to say, we are all eager and willing to change this picture. We are heartened by the 100,000 American conversions, as reported in *The Official Catholic Directory* for 1947. We sense an awakening of interest in religion, as men see their hopes for a better world of their own making grow dimmer. Perhaps a change is at hand. What can we do to hasten the day? In the hope that there may be some effective methods in the procedure followed in convert work at St. Sabina Parish in Chicago, we submit the following report.

A NEW APPROACH

In 1943 in this large city parish we had very few conversions. I don't believe I instructed a single person. The other four priests may have had two or three each. In a way we might explain this by noting that we are in a very Catholic neighborhood. In 1944, however, at the suggestion of our pastor, the Reverend William A. Gorey, we started a Legion of Mary unit, a group of six men and eight women, who, under the guidance of the chaplain, assist the priests in contacting lax Catholics of every sort. Through a weekly meeting featuring prayer, assignments, and reports, these good people, traveling in pairs, take care of whatever work the priest judges worthy of their attention.

After having them check back for many months on a previous census, we proposed that they call on the mixed marriages of the parish and in a friendly, tactful way sound out the non-Catholic party on his interest in the Catholic religion. One hundred were thus contacted. Forty showed some interest. The question arose as to what we could offer those interested, and the St. Sabina inquiry class, a series of twenty-six lectures on the Catholic faith for non-Catholics, came as the answer. Of the forty, twenty actually came the first year. Twelve of these entered the Church at the conclusion of the course, and a few more have followed since. Twelve other non-Catholics came through publicity. Thus the first inquiry class brought twenty-four converts.

In succeeding years the Legion workers have called back on those who showed promise but did not attend. They, of course, are always careful not to offend and drop the cases of definite disinterest. After covering the mixed marriages pretty well, they have gone on to contact non-Catholic families. Ringing door bells, they take a little religious census of the neighborhood, inquiring into the family's religion, its possible contacts with the Catholic Church, and so on—anything to establish a friendly relationship. The response has not been too great, but a few conversions have already resulted, and God alone knows the ultimate effect of such visits.

On all these visits, literature is distributed wherever people are inclined to receive it. Programs of the inquiry class, pamphlets, and leaflet copies of a few of the instructions—confession, the Mass, and other subjects likely to interest them—are distributed as widely as prudence permits.

PERSONAL CONTACT

Personal contact seems mainly responsible for conversions, and so we use every possible means to promote it. Legion people, for example, accompany prospects to the class. Through a lively campaign of announcement and preaching, the people are urged to interest their non-Catholic friends and relatives and bring them to the classes. The response at first is apathetic. People hesitate to try, but after hearing of a successful class many acquire new interest and confidence.

Large, eye-catching signs are displayed in the vestibule of the church. Programs are made available in great numbers—2,500 for a class—and all seem to disappear. Notification cards are placed in the pews. People are asked to jot down the names of those they think might be interested. Then a personal letter of invitation with a program and sample lectures are sent to these and to all other possible prospects. As many as 400 have been mailed out for a class. In four years there has been only one violent reaction and that in the case of a family with Catholicity in its background. We have found that each of these various methods accounts for the presence of a few at the instructions.

The sisters in the school are enlisted in the campaign. In a prudent way, children of mixed marriages are encouraged to interest the non-Catholic parent. Their prayers for the success of the class are solicited. The whole parish in fact is urged on to a crusade of

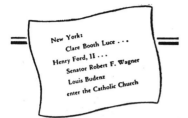

New York:
Clare Booth Luce . . .
Henry Ford, II . . .
Senator Robert F. Wagner
Louis Budenz
enter the Catholic Church

—But they are just a few of the

100,000 Americans per Year

who discov

Truth, Satisfaction, and Happiness in the CATHOLIC FAITH

You Owe It to Yourself to Investigate at the

ST. SABINA INQUIRY CLASS

A Series of Twenty-six Lectures on the Catholic Faith
TUESDAY AND FRIDAY EVENINGS
8 P.M.

Sept. 17th to Dec. 13th

ST. SABINA AUDITORIUM .

78th and Throop Streets

Admission Free

HAPPINESS

a will of the wisp?

A REALITY

Happiness seems to come accidentally to many people. It seems to be a condition that is here today and gone tomorrow. To the Catholic it comes as the direct result of his religion.

If you are searching for a plan that will give you daily happiness, you will find it in such lectures as these . . .

● A Soldier Meets His God
● Religion: Pure and Simple
● Grace Divine Help for Human Weakness
● Men at Work at Worship
● Confession: The Relieving of a Human Heart
● The Biography of a Priest or Nun
● Matrimony in the Eyes of God
● Man's Duties to Himself and Neighbor
● Virtues: The Finer Things in Life
● Saints: The World's Great Heroes
● The Mass, Divine Worship by Human Beings
● You Need the Church: the Church Doesn't Need You.

AT THE

St. Sabina Inquiry Class

A series of twenty-six lectures on the Catholic Faith

TUESDAY AND FRIDAY EVENINGS

8 P.M.

Sept. 18th to Dec. 14th

ST. SABINA SCHOOL HALL

78th and Throop Sts.

Inquiry Class Advertisements in Chicago Newspapers.

prayer. The sick are asked to join in. Masses are offered for this intention.

IT PAYS TO ADVERTISE

Publicity among non-Catholics is attempted in every possible way. A hundred attractive, informative posters are placed in neighborhood store windows, the library, and hospitals. These are especially effective. Many converts report their interest aroused by them. News items in the neighborhood papers are very valuable. We try to have a number of them prior to the class and then additional ones for subjects of particular interest, like confession.

For a few weeks before the class a series of four or five large advertisements appears in two papers. Professional help is enlisted for effective advertisements. We try to stay away from the religious page to appeal to the non-church going people, which is the big field today. The dividends on this form of advertising are difficult to determine. A few attribute their interest to it. The long term effects would seem to make it worthwhile. Non-Catholics get to know that there is such a thing as an inquiry class and that conversions are a common thing. Legion members find, in making calls, a general knowledge of it among non-Catholics even though there be no interest at present. This in itself would seem to be worthwhile.

All this costs money, as everybody knows. Surely here, however, it would seem that the Church, where it is possible, should be ready to spend. This work would seem to deserve a generous place in "running expenses." Without doubt the Master would have us use to the utmost the great modern methods of communication. The results, furthermore, seem to sanction the expenditure.

WELCOME STRANGERS

With all this fanfare behind him, the instructor eagerly awaits the first trickle of people into the auditorium on the opening night. The classes are held twice a week for thirteen weeks, on Tuesday and Friday nights at eight o'clock, from the middle of September to the middle of December. This is our large class. This past year we added a second class after the first of the year. Intended mainly as a carryover for late comers, it picked up an additional dozen through the mere announcement. In some places, no doubt, three or four classes a year are feasible. The arrivals come in rather sheepishly, of course, feeling their way in strange surroundings. We try to be friendly with them but not over friendly too soon. We are careful to avoid giving the impression we are after them.

Our appeal has been to come in and investigate. "Come in and look into the matter. There are no commitments, no questions asked. Stay as long as you wish." We omit prayers for the first few times, and then only the priest says them. We thereby avoid an embarrassing division of the crowd. You will have sincere people who will not even stand up for the opening prayer of the priest. The people will of their own accord gradually join in the prayers as the class progresses. Incidentally, we stress that the class is for non-Catholics especially. Reluctantly, we almost discourage Catholics from coming because we have found that the non-Catholics feel lost in a large group of Catholics and are much more at home by themselves. We purposely call the class "inquiry" and not "convert," for while many have made up their minds when they come, many too have not.

THE PURPOSE OF THE INQUIRY CLASS

This brings up the whole question of the purpose of the class. It is not intended primarily as a substitute for private instruction, although in a large, busy parish that might be a necessary purpose. Single converts are not saved up for the class. Here each priest keeps his own instructees. The class is intended especially for those who are undecided, just interested, maybe only curious—like the Protestant lady who came to find out what her Catholic grandchildren were being taught and finished the class with, "Well I have learned a great deal, but, when you are brought up one way, it is hard to change." Nine months later she entered the Church and is now a member of a third order.

Another woman at the announcement of the class was remind-ed by her husband, "Well, here is your chance. You have often said you would like to find out about the Church," and she came. Half way through, upon inquiry, she didn't know; three-fourths of the way she was lying awake nights trying to decide; now she is a daily communicant.

In another instance, a gentleman, whom the Legion of Mary men called on because the baptismal slip showed him a non-Catholic father, invited them in and proceeded to floor them with every non-Catholic objection in the books. After answering as best they could, they invited him to the inquiry class. He came to most of it, questioned often, and still has fifteen pages of objections. He is, however, sincere, and so we have hope.

The class, therefore, is for people who will not at the moment enter the rectory and ask for instruction. There are many such in-quirers, and we cannot reach them by offering private instruction. Then too the class, set for a definite time and place, with plenty of forewarning, brings out many who have been thinking about the Church for years.

We try to make the class feel at home. We remind them of their complete freedom of movement. Only after a few classes do we approach them for simply their names and addresses and religious affiliations. Thereafter we make up an attendance roster and have them check in each night as they enter the class. This is very nec-essary to keep track of classes missed so that they can make them up. It also obviates the delay of a roll call. A more detailed ques-tionnaire as to their marriage status and so on can await the latter part of the class. Too early, it might scare some away. Last year we had two who wouldn't even leave their names.

CONVERTS' READING MATTER

We give them a catechism the first night—Father Deck's *Number Three Baltimore*, Father Connell's, or *The Catholic Faith*, Cardinal Gasparri's catechism in English. We ask them to study this carefully, keeping up with the subjects of each lecture. It is very important to get them to do the work and not have them merely come and listen. The memorizing of the key questions seems necessary. As the class proceeds, copies of *I Believe*, by Father Hurley, C.S.P., are distributed.

All are urged to read *The Faith of Millions* and *The Faith of Our Fathers*, which are made available to them along with numerous other apologetic books and pamphlets. Sodality girls check them in and out. A number of instructions have been synopsized in leaflet form, and these are distributed at the various classes. Two of these, *Bill Jones Meets God* and *Religion Pure and Simple*, are now printed by the Catholic Information Society of New York City. Many of this society's pamphlets and charts are distributed as the class progresses.

HELPFUL ADDITIONS

Variety is most important in the classes. Straight lecturing could be monotonous. One or two instructors would seem to be necessary for the continuity of the class, but a change once in a while, a guest speaker every fourth talk, for instance, seems to help. Illustrated lectures add a great deal. The Bible, grace, the sacraments, the Mass, Church history all lend themselves easily to diagram and illustration, and one need not be an artist.

Where the size of the room and the lighting make blackboard work difficult, mimeographed sheets of diagrams are second best. Movies and catechetical films provide an interesting change and an effective mode of teaching. There doesn't seem to be too much available, however, at the present time.

The King of Kings, an old Cecil B. De Mille silent film, modernized with a musical sound track, is a wonderful life of Christ. A picture of the Mass, to which a running commentary can be added, is fine. There are lives of the saints, but these all seem to be foreign films. Some of the catechetical film strips are good, but really nothing comparable to the secular movies. Nothing with Hollywood technique seems to have been done as yet in the religious field. A priest friend remarked once, "Oh, what Walt Disney could do with that *Baltimore Catechism.*" Some of us have talked of making our own film strips, but we have not gotten around to it as yet. The inquiry class eagerly awaits some effective work in this field.

QUESTIONS

The instruction consists of a forty-five minute lecture. An informal perusal of the questions and answers may be an occasional alternative, but the general lecture seems more effective. Fifteen minutes are left for questions, and interesting questions may prolong the period.

A question box is placed at the entrance of the hall. Not too many ask questions from the floor; people are a little self-conscious. This is, of course, a serious drawback, but it can be remedied to a certain extent by placing on the chairs cards on which they may jot down their questions as they come to mind. They deposit them in the question box as they leave.

Occasionally a heckler or a sincere fanatic may cause a little commotion, but they are generally not too difficult to handle. They may have to be stifled if the argument is too prolonged. Limiting questions to the subject at hand or to matters previously covered is wise. Repeating the question asked so that all may understand is also necessary. The good that all derive from the answering of the various questions is one of the great benefits of the class. Private questions are always welcomed, of course, after the class.

KNOWING YOUR PUPIL

Regular attendance is urged for a proper understanding of the matter. Those who miss occasionally for various reasons are invited to make up the classes in private conferences. This gives the instructor a splendid opportunity to get to know the prospect and to ascertain how he is progressing.

After a few weeks the instructor begins to meet the individuals as they arrive for the class. Their apprehension in talking to a priest slowly disappears, and a friendly relationship is then set up. It is

Mr. and Mrs. Non-Catholic!

Are You Interested in
Religion?

No! · · Well, that is not unusual these days; but have you ever stopped to think that it might be because you have never known real religion?

Yes! · · That's fine; but are you sure you have the right one? You must realize that out of the thousands of present day religions only one can be God's own, for one God and one human race add up to one religion.

Whether you answer YES or NO, you owe it to yourselves to investigate the Catholic Church's claim to being God's own.

Now in making your investigation don't rely on hearsay evidence, superficial criticism of uninformed outsiders.

Get the facts first-hand at the

ST. SABINA INQUIRY CLASS

a series of twenty-six lectures on the Catholic Faith

TUESDAY AND FRIDAY EVENINGS
8 P.M.

Sept. 18th to Dec. 14th

ST. SABINA SCHOOL HALL

78th and Throop Streets

FACTS ABOUT THE CLASS

1. These classes are especially for non-Catholics. Kindly dismiss, therefore, any thought of uneasiness or embarrassment at being all alone among a crowd of Catholics. Almost all of last year's regular attendants were non-Catholics. We assure you that after the first class any feeling of hesitancy will disappear.

2. Mere curiosity, inquisitiveness, mild interest or avid interest—even antagonism if you will, any reason at all for coming is acceptable.

3. By attending this class you are not making any commitments on joining the Church. This is an "inquiry" class, not a "convert" class. Whether you will enter the Church at the conclusion of the course God alone knows. We are anxious only to have you hear of the Church; the rest we leave to God, for faith is from God alone.
    The decision of joining or not joining the Church should normally come not at the beginning but at the end of the class.

4. You may come and go as you like. Sixty-one non-Catholics attended some of the lectures last year. Thirty attended regularly. Twenty-two of these entered the Church last Christmas. Some remained apparently unconvinced; others wished to think it over a little longer; but all, we feel sure, left at least friendly to the Church.

5. Tolerance, charity, respect for other religious opinions will be the predominant note of the lectures.
    We realize every one must follow his own conscience; we wish only to inform what we know are uninformed consciences.

6. Lectures will appeal to reason not emotions. Religion must have intellectual foundations. We desire to foster convictions not prejudices.

7. No questions will be asked of those attending. At the completion of the lecture you are free to ask questions and open discussion with the speaker.
    A question box will be available for those who might not wish to ask a question publicly.

8. The course will feature religious movies and demonstrations.

9. All kinds of religious literature may be borrowed for further study.

10. Lectures will begin promptly at 8 P.M. If, however, you happen to be late, don't hesitate to come in.

11. Classes unavoidably missed can be made up privately.

12. There is no fee for any lecture, literature, or service.

13. You may bring any one you wish with you. Have a Catholic friend accompany you the first time. After that you will find it unnecessary.

P.S. If you should prefer private instruction rather than the public class, simply call at the Rectory at any time.

Sponsor, REV. W. A. COREY, *Pastor*
Director, REV. W. J. QUINLAN

interesting to note the growing friendliness of the crowd as the weeks pass.

After getting in deeply, let us say about the beginning of the last third of the class, private interviewing is begun. The invitation for a private conference is extended to all. We try to see each one sev eral times. This is difficult, of course, on the priest as well as on the people; they are already coming two nights a week. The perfect system is probably something like Monsignor Helmsing's at the cathedral in St. Louis, whereby people attend a class for two months and then their instructions are completed privately. The difficulty is that we are generally finishing up at Christmas or at Easter, and we hesitate to pass up the psychological benefits of entering the Church at these times.

There will be some, of course, who will avail themselves of the privilege of leaving or of dropping in on just a few of the lectures. Last year we had about sixty-five non-Catholics registered. Forty came regularly. Thirty-five entered the Church. Marriage cases, of course, always prevent a few, and bigoted home conditions delay and at times prevent conversion. Some simply remain unconvinced, for the present at least.

ELABORATING ON THE CATECHISM

The subject matter of the lectures is simply the catechism. However, an elaboration of the simple answers does seem necessary. The more instructing you do, the more and better ways you devise to demonstrate the divine truths. Grace, for instance, would seem to call for ingenuity in presentation.

This development of technique is one of the great benefits of the inquiry class to the instructor. It seems a fact that the instructor will quite naturally give better instructions to a class than to the individual. You simply work harder at speaking to a crowd. The instructor picks up ideas, examples, stories, and so forth from various sources, but one in particular is worth mentioning. *Outlines of Religion for Catholic Youth*, by Father Rosenberger, is excellent. Unfortunately only the first volume, *Catholic Belief and Catholic*

Morality, is published as yet. Here in a few pages you have available in order all the essentials on any given topic. It is very helpful.

As the class approaches its conclusion, the instructor tries to sound out the prospects on their intentions. He begins to estimate the possible conversions. He counts the sure votes and then at times is pleasantly surprised at the intentions of some of whom he was doubtful. He does a lot of praying to the Holy Ghost these days to sway their decisions. At the end of the last class comes the announcement of additional sessions for those entering the Church, during which the catechumens are drilled on confession, Communion, the missal, the rosary, and so on. In a final session they are shown through the church and trained for the baptismal ceremony. A private oral examination is also given each one these last days.

A ROYAL RECEPTION

The reception of the converts on a Friday evening is a very impressive thing. A sermon of welcome and felicitation by the pastor opens the ceremony. There follows a solemn profession of faith by the converts.

Then the group baptism is conducted at the altar railing. With thirty-four persons to be baptized last Christmas, five priests in unison across the sanctuary baptize six or seven neophytes apiece. A sixth priest, in the pulpit, directs the ceremony, guiding the priests and the people through the various parts of the ritual and explaining everything for the benefit of relatives and friends assembled. Benediction closes the ceremony. This wonderful spectacle leaves a lasting impression on the converts and all who witness it. Those who have been baptized conditionally make their first confession immediately afterwards.

First Holy Communion is received on the following Sunday morning. The new Catholics with their happy friends and relatives are given the place of honor in the church. After Mass a Communion breakfast is served. A few words of congratulation are offered, and then each is called upon to say a few words. "It has taken me thirty years to come to this, the happiest day of my life." "I don't know why I waited so long." Expressions like these vouched for by tears of joy bring to a happy ending the long road of the inquiry class.

Contact thereafter is often difficult. Many move away. We try to get them together two or three times a year through an alumni association. Various types of meetings—movies, lectures, and tours through Catholic institutions—have been tried. A day of recollection once a year would seem to be a fine thing. Some sort of contact is necessary because defection or lukewarmness shows up in some cases. Converts are urged to recruit prospects for future classes. Prior to each class they are sent literature in time for such work. A few like to come back for further enlightenment, and some have brought new prospects each year.

A HUNDRED CONVERTS MULTIPLIED

This, then, is the story of convert work here at St. Sabina Parish in the last three years. The total of converts for three large fall classes and one small spring class this year is ninety-three. The total of non-Catholics who registered at these classes is one hundred and ninety.

As to the chances of those who didn't enter the Church, it is difficult to say. God's grace works slowly at times. In the small class of twenty we have hopes of six more joining the eight who entered at Easter. We have had reports of one or two finishing elsewhere after a class. Only God knows the ultimate results.

In closing we would again emphasize that this crowd of non-Catholics has been reached in a thoroughly Catholic neighborhood. It is in a parish where individual requests for instruction are not very numerous. If in these circumstances the inquiry class has reached the mass of non-Catholics in some small way (it is indeed small, with the circulation of our advertisements being 90,000), surely in less Catholic areas, with so many more souls to work on, the results should be much greater. They are, in fact, as is shown in the cathedral parish in Springfield, Illinois, where classes on a similar plan are dwarfing our figures.

ALL OUT FOR THE HUNDRED MILLION

It may well be that the apparent opportunity for Christianizing, which ultimately means Catholicizing, our beloved America calls for a mighty offensive, a great crusade. We may have to go out after these people. We must, of course, avoid the crude propagandizing of the fanatic sects but also the mere passive reception of only those who ring the rectory doorbell. Our times seem to cry for the dedication of our talents, clerical and lay, to the launching of a mighty stream of the best possible literature, films, advertisements, radio work, and all the rest which will envelop the mass of non-Catholics in America. Father Keller's Christophers, with their ambition to "bring Christ into the market place," are working toward this goal.

Lastly we would emphasize the part of the laity in the movement. They alone can make most of the contacts with non-Catholics. They will, if reminded, if spurred on and, if organized for the work, do much to change the sad picture of five-sixths of our people outside the fold of Christ and 100,000,000 Americans with little or no religion at all.

15

The Brooklyn Approach

Rev. JOHN J. O'CONNOR, Secretary
Brooklyn Diocesan Apostolate

EDITOR'S FOREWORD: In Brooklyn convert work is organized on a diocesan scale and is called the Diocesan Apostolate for the Instruction of Non-Catholics. Founded by Bishop Molloy in 1937, it has fifty centers located throughout the diocese, where priests conduct a five months' series of weekly instructions for non-Catholics. Each year there is staged an impressive Converts' Confirmation Ceremony at which a vast army of converts appear and manifest the rich fruition of the zealous work of the priest instructors. In the first ten years of its operation, the Apostolate has brought 5,850 converts into the Church. The organization so clearly set forth by its secretary, Father O'Connor, may offer valuable suggestions for incorporation in organized convert work in other dioceses and cities.

ॐ

THE BROOKLYN APPROACH

THE CATHOLIC CHURCH'S apostolate to non-Catholics is admittedly an integral part of its general apostolate. The Church's approach to the non-Catholics of the United States, however, presents a practical problem.

The practical problem is this: How can this apostolate reach rather directly the greatest possible number of non-Catholics? This problem is most pressing in the large dioceses and big-city parishes, where so many varied demands are made upon the time and effort of the clergy. It is likewise a problem in the smaller dioceses and parishes, as may be concluded from correspondence received from all sections of the United States and even Canada and Australia.

While acknowledging that there is no one approach to non-Catholics and fully appreciating that the only invariable influence in conversions is the grace of God, the Diocese of Brooklyn has faced the practical problem of how to reach the greatest possible number of non-Catholics. Its answer to the problem has been a diocesan-wide organization, the Brooklyn Diocesan Apostolate for the Instruction of Non-Catholics.

ORGANIZATION IS THE KEY

Organization is characteristic of all achievement. The success of big business is dependent upon systematized organization. Organization is found necessary for the successful production of stage drama, symphony concert, or radio broadcast. Labor organizes. Industry organizes. There are medical societies and associations of lawyers. In political circles they talk of the "organization man."

Strong organization propagates the untenable errors and diabolical falsehoods of communism. The advance of dictators is on the wheels of powerful organization. There is organization in legitimate government. Organization is evident in the army, in the navy, in the police force. We are familiar with organization in the sport world and to a lesser degree in much of social life. Why even the individual, and the specialist too if he would be successful as an individual, must organize at the very least his own life, his own talents, his own skill. And since human ingenuity cannot outsmart divine Wisdom, Jesus Christ himself made adequate provision for the organization of his Catholic Church.

Without judging the objective worth of the purposes to which organization has been put in the instances cited or in any others of which we can think, we must admit that organization contributes directly to the achievement of purposes and to the attainment of goals, no matter the absolute or relative merit of these purposes or goals. The fact is, success is proportionate to proper organization.

Whatever success the Brooklyn Diocesan Apostolate already has had, or in the future will have, may be attributed in large part to its carefully planned organization. The Brooklyn Apostolate is organized in its physical make-up, its administration. It is organized on its more spiritual side, the actual presentation in objective fashion of Catholic teaching and practice to interested non-Catholics.

The external organization of this Brooklyn approach to non-Catholics is most apparent.

CLOSE EPISCOPAL GUIDANCE

The Brooklyn Apostolate for the Instruction of Non-Catholics is immediately under the inspiring leadership of the Most Rev. Thomas E. Molloy, bishop of Brooklyn and founder-moderator of the Apostolate. Bishop Molloy's public statements indicate his direct supervision and personal guidance of the work of the Apostolate. Among the countless matters that require his official attention, the bishop repeatedly has advised, there is none in which personally or officially he has greater interest than the Apostolate.

Founded in 1937, the Brooklyn Apostolate has had as its diocesan director since the beginning Rev. James J. McGowan. It has fifty centers conveniently located throughout the diocese, where priests, appointed as associate directors of the Apostolate, conduct a five months' series of weekly instructions for interested non-Catholics. At the conclusion of each annual course of instructions there is a diocesan Converts' Confirmation Ceremony, at which the bishop confirms those who have become Catholics at the various centers. This Confirmation Ceremony is held at a different church each year.

The external organization of the Brooklyn Apostolate is reflected in the Apostolate's attempt at systematic presentation of the truths of the Church. In this attempt "to systematize the work of instruction as well as to offer some standard guide of instruction-matter for the convenience of the associate directors," Father McGowan has published a printed syllabus, copies of which have been sent to the directors. This syllabus lists as the textbook to be used at all the instruction centers *A Catechism for Inquirers*, by Rev. Joseph I. Malloy, C.S.P., published by the Paulist Press.

Allowing for the widest possible variation of development of subject by the individual director, the instructions to be given at the centers are divided in the syllabus into two major classes, apologetical and catechetical. For each instruction topic there is included a suggested outline of treatment, together with a listing of the pamphlets to be used as supplementary reading and of certain references which may be helpful. The latter part of the syllabus is devoted to suggestions for the directors in the conduct of their courses, bibliography of pamphlets and books, and summary information concerning the workings of the Apostolate. This present syllabus or outline is intended by Father McGowan as a temporary working plan. A more comprehensive and informative outline is planned for the near future.

The pamphlets, to which reference is made in the syllabus, are given free of charge to those attending the instructions. In this manner each one receives a copy of every pamphlet listed as supplementary reading. Thus it is that the Apostolate gets organization and system not only into its administration but also into its presentation to non-Catholics of Catholic truth.

As you read the details of the organization of the Brooklyn Apostolate, you may wonder why all the fuss. Hasn't the Church by the grace of God and force of the gospel always had converts? Haven't priests in every parish by their own zeal and labor and without any central direction brought converts into the Church? Then to what purpose so much organization and so much systemization?

The only answer to the first two questions can be a quiet "yes."

The point is there are today, perhaps more than ever before, hundreds and thousands and millions of people still outside the true Church—but waiting only to be asked in. Most of these people will never come to a rectory for instruction. They are not Catholics, and they do not know how to go about the matter. If they have Catholic friends, they may hesitate to ask these friends for fear of assuming a kind of obligation to become Catholics. With regard to them, we must remember that, were we in their position it is just likely we ourselves would shy from ringing a rectory bell and asking for a priest. There really are such interested and rightly disposed people, but not every one of them is a Clare Boothe Luce, so you never hear of them. If, however, you prefer cases, consider for a moment the following.

THREE RANDOM CASES

Here is what one young man told a priest of the Apostolate after registering at one of the centers. "This may sound funny to you, Father," he said, "but I've been going to Mass for ten years, and yet I never thought of taking any instructions until I heard of the work of the Apostolate. In fact, I wasn't sure I could."

Some years ago *The New York Herald Tribune* carried a news item on the opening of the annual course of instructions for non-Catholics under the auspices of the Brooklyn Apostolate. Within twenty-four hours, three letters asking for further information were received. One of these came special delivery and another was from outside the diocese. Other inquiries followed.

"And they never told us!" A non-Catholic said that of Catholic neighbors. The non-Catholic was a woman who just happened to meet a priest. She chanced to mention her "desire to know more about the Catholic Church." When the priest told her of the instructions for non-Catholics conducted by the Diocesan Apostolate, she expressed her surprise at the Catholics next door. "Strange, we're such good friends," was the way she put it, "and they never told us!"

These are three random cases. Yet the implication is the same in each. If the Church is to bring "many more souls to the knowledge, love, and service of Almighty God," as Bishop Molloy put it, if she is to make easily available to all who are interested the true picture of herself and of her teaching, then she cannot wait in her rectory parlors. She must go out to the non-Catholics.

True, there is no sense in supplanting the work of the individual parish or the effort of the individual priest. But there is reason in supplementing this work and this effort with an organized and systematized campaign, whereby those whom the individual parish and priest may never contact will have, without any obligation on their part, access to the evidence for the Church and its truths either to their enlightenment only or by the grace of God to their conversion as well. Such a campaign is the purpose of the Brooklyn Diocesan Apostolate.

Setting up the machinery of the Apostolate was no serious problem. The real problem was to reach the very people for whom the Apostolate exists. Here again organized effort has proved the best method of dealing with the problem. Accordingly, the Brooklyn Apostolate has enlisted the assistance of the Catholic laity, has attempted to contact directly the non-Catholic parties to mixed marriages, and has made use of the press and the radio.

Affiliated with the Brooklyn Apostolate are a Ladies Auxiliary, which raises necessary funds, and the Diocesan League of Converts, which is the follow-up organization of the Apostolate. Both these organizations have their own directors.

We know that converts must be made. That is the divinely appointed mission of the Church. Encouraged by a direct invitation, non-Catholics will be inclined to seek instruction, particularly since they will know that they incur no obligation by attending instructions, that other non-Catholics will be present, and that the instructions will be given the same evening every week for a stated period of time. The existence of a diocesan apostolate for the instruction of non-Catholics will make an entire diocese convert-conscious as well as aware of the importance of the apostolate to non-Catholics.

16

The Rural Apostolate

Rev. JAMES J. NAVAGH, Director
The Missionary Apostolate, Diocese of Buffalo

EDITOR'S FOREWORD: *For many years far-seeing bishops and priests have been greatly concerned with the exodus of dwellers from the rural areas into the cities. In that exodus Catholics have shared to such an extent that now Catholicism is rooted chiefly in the cities. But the population in urban centers is notoriously unstable, mobile, and tends to burn itself out—unless constantly fed by emigrants from the country.*

Father Navagh gives us a new approach to the solution of the problem of enlarging our rural Catholic population, namely, by the conversion of rural dwellers. From his headquarters in Mayville, New York, Father Navagh directs the missionary labors of a group of priests ministering in scattered country parishes and outmissions. Since the Catholic population in these areas is very small, increases must be achieved largely by conversions.

Father Navagh outlines a plan well calculated to enhance the fruitfulness of the labors of every priest ministering in rural areas. It is a plan tried and tested by years of experience and by many priests. Carefully worked out in all its details, it offers specific suggestions and guidance to priests in the winning of converts.

That it is not limited in its practical application to the rural areas in New York State but is equally valid in the mountainous

182

mission areas of North Carolina was evidenced to the writer who saw it in partial operation in the missions among the Tarheels of the Appalachian regions. We think that every reader, priest, and layman, city dweller or living in rural areas, will find in Father Navagh's article helpful suggestions for the winning of converts.

THE SITUATION

P REOCCUPIED as the Catholic Church has been in the United States with our large urban Catholic populations, the conversion of rural America has never been seriously tried. There have been spot attempts, of course, but, generally speaking, vast sections of our country districts have been abandoned to Protestantism. The reasons for this are varied.

There is and has been a lack of appreciation of the importance of rural communities as sources of population. There have been physical difficulties, long distances to travel and poor roads made further impassable by weather conditions. Beyond that there is the poverty of many small country groups, with the resultant need of subsidization for the bare necessities of religious service.

SPECIAL RURAL PROBLEMS

There is no essential difference between conversion problems in country and city. The gospel effectively preached has the power to change the hearts of all men. However, in the rural communities there are certain special differences which require solution.

The first is that in most small towns there are fixed thought patterns, and in these public opinion is definitely anti-Catholic, a feeling which persists even where the practice of Protestantism has been dropped. Secondly, the natural conservatism of our rural districts opposes conversion to Catholicism. Even those who will admire the Church adhere to the opinion that a person ought to stay in the religion of his fathers.

Finally, actions which would pass unnoticed in the city are noticed by the entire community in the country. If a person begins instructions, all his neighbors know it, and reception into the Catholic Church is a public event which calls down upon the head of the person received the disapproval of the entire community. We have, for example, the remark of a mother to her daughter who was about to become a Catholic: "If you must have some religion, why does it have to be the Catholic?"

CONTACT IS THE ANSWER

The extensive and successful convert effort in country districts, then, must take into account not only the few possible interested persons but the community as a whole.

The effort must be systematic. It must be an effort which will carry the priest from the quiet of the rectory to the people and the homes of his parish. Constant home visitation is the key which will open the individual minds of the community to the attractiveness of the Catholic Church.

These visits should not be long—fifteen minutes are sufficient. They should be planned to accomplish a specific purpose. They should be made in a friendly but efficient, business-like fashion that assures the person of the regard in which he is held without giving the impression of aimless wandering about. Moreover, as he deals with people the priest must act on the firm conviction that God's grace, channeled through his priestly efforts, will change the face of the community.

"THE OPPOSITION"

Sometimes we hear talk about "the opposition" to the Catholic Church, talk of a force menacing but vague and abstract. We should realize that opposition does not exist in the abstract but very much in the concrete. It exists in individual men and women. So the first effort of the priest in the country who desires converts is to analyze the district.

He ought to have down before him, in black and white, the leaders of the religious, educational, economic, social, political, and recreational groups in the town. He ought to know the people of consequence—all who can influence public opinion. He ought to sort them out into opponents, friends, or neutrals. He ought to consider how to make the friends of the neutral individuals and how to win the good will or at least neutralize the opinions of his opponents. He ought to keep in mind what I have said above, that there are few individuals in this world whom persistent efforts will not change.

THE HEART OF THE PROBLEM

A survey of public opinion in the average American rural town will show three and sometimes four principal reasons which keep people from considering the claims of the Catholic Church. They are:

1. Deep-seated prejudice against Catholicism.
2. Attachment to some heretical sect.
3. Indifference to all religions.
4. Sometimes public or private immorality.

Where the second, third, and fourth reasons exist, they are usually accompanied by the first. The problem arises, then, how are we to combat prejudice? The usual answer is to broadcast information about the Church, usually in the form of literature. A little thought will show how comparatively useless this is. This envisions an appeal to reason, but the prejudiced mind is closed to reason. So the effort is usually lost. The only solvent of prejudice is Christian charity—and so the love of God above all things for his own sake and the love of neighbor for the love of God, shining forth in the life of Catholic priests and Catholic people, is the appointed remedy to combat prejudice.

THE PART OF CATHOLICS

In this article there is not space to outline all that Catholic people can do in order to spread the faith. It will have to suffice to point out that few non-Catholics consider the Catholic religion in the abstract. It stands or falls in their opinion as they see it in the lives of their Catholic neighbors.

The best advertisement of the Catholic religion is a good Catholic. The worst argument against the Catholic religion, in their opinion, is one faithless to his religious duties. The rural priest who wishes large numbers of conversions must put the Catholic members of his parish in such spiritual shape that it will make the non-Catholic long to be one with them. He must labor vigorously to bring back the waifs and strays.

His Sunday Masses must be filled with all his parishioners, and attendance on weekday mornings must convince outsiders of the drawing power of the Catholic faith. His number of Communions must soar to great heights. The children in his parish must be extremely well instructed, and the adults who are deficient must be given that knowledge of their faith which will enable them confidently to set it forth to the stranger.

The families in his parish must be Catholic in fact as well as in name. Catholic reading material in the home, very especially the Scriptures, and family devotions, especially the rosary, must make an outsider understand that the Catholic family is different and better. They must be trained in real charity toward their fellow Catholics and toward strangers too.

Such a program is the work of years. It does not have to be completed before work on outsiders has begun, but the two ought to go hand in hand, one program aiding and assisting the other. Essentially the priest's part in it is a constant contact with his people, encouraging them, reproving them, suggesting further efforts, in brief, as the father of old and young, rich and poor, prominent and obscure, trying to do some spiritual good to each as he meets them.

As we consider the problem of influencing the community in favor of the Church, we ought to say a word about the children of the town. Pope Pius XI has said, "Kindness to children is the shortest way to the affections of all men." Remembering what was said above, that the non-Catholic judges Catholicism as it exists in the individual Catholic, we can be sure that nothing will popularize the Church more than the good opinion which children have of the local priest. In dealing with children the priest should remember that the children's opinion of the Church will make it or break it in the next generation. The children, Catholic and non-Catholic, are the most important part of the priest's charge. The practical procedure is this:

1. The priest should make fast friends of his own Catholic children.

2. He should speak in a friendly fashion to all the children he may meet, being very attentive even to the smallest.

3. It is an excellent thing to visit the public school yard during noon hour to converse with the children, showing an interest in the things in which they take interest, their sports, clubs, report cards, and everything else.

4. He should make the acquaintance of the non-Catholic children and be seen about town frequently with numbers of children. He should treat them occasionally in the town store and be present at school affairs.

THE AGED AND SICK

The next vulnerable spot in the shell of anti-Catholic prejudice is the sick and the bereaved. He should visit the sick and the aged; if possible, when well acquainted, he should leave little gifts of magazines or fruit. He should visit the homes where there is a death, expressing his sorrow to the relatives. During these visits, which should be made as far as possible to all irrespective of their religion, he should mention religion only casually and naturally, as he would if he were dealing only with Catholics. He should try to make these people his friends.

THE POOR

It is most important to be both cordial and helpful to the poor. By personal kindness and by a charity that transcends the limits of the

Church, not only will the poor be attracted to the Church, but such aid will attract the attention of the rest of the community. Many people are cynical nowadays. "What is the angle?" "What is in it for him?" Such are questions asked about many things we priests do in this world.

All can see that by this form of charity there is no personal advantage, and quite easily the continuous charity of a priest will open hearts otherwise impenetrable. One result of such zeal, observed on a number of occasions in small rural towns, was that the non-Catholic social workers have called on a priest to care spiritually for the non-Catholic old and friendless, so that a number were instructed and baptized on their deathbed.

THE INFLUENTIAL

The next logical effort would be, having consulted the survey, to make the acquaintance of the important people around town, introducing himself as the Catholic priest in charge of the local parish. The result of a friendly visit will be to leave a good impression of the Church, and, if the priest is able to make friends of these people, the least result will be the suppression of hostile remarks from them about the Catholic religion.

VISITATION

Following this effort it is expedient that a house to house visitation be made through the town and the surrounding countryside. The purpose is:

1. To meet the non-Catholics and give them the opportunity to meet a priest.

2. To find any fallen-away Catholics.

3. To discover any non-Catholics who may be interested in the Church. If there exist any apprehensions about the reception of the priest on such a visitation, they may be laid aside. The experiment has been tried in the north and in the south. The overwhelming majority of people welcomed the priest to their homes.

A FRIEND TO ALL

A few more hints are set down here which experience has taught to be useful in combating prejudice. Walk, do not ride, about town. You will meet many more people. Speak to all whom you meet, even if they do not respond—eventually they will. *Learn to smile as you greet people.* In conversation speak well about the town. People have deep attachments to their hometown and sometimes deeply resent the criticism of outsiders.

Constantly speak well of the people, the families, the homes you have visited. Nobody can keep a permanent grudge against those who speak well of them and praise their good qualities. Attend community meetings, introduce yourself to the people there, and try to learn their names. As the campaign progresses, keep an accurate record of the well-disposed with as complete information about them as you can gather.

It might be asked, does all this work? I answer that it does— where it is really tried.

One priest who had tried it out for only two years, in a formerly bigoted town without a Catholic church, was accompanied on his round by another one a summer afternoon. At the end of several hours spent in the town the visitor remarked: "I didn't know there were such friendly Catholic people living here." The pastor truthfully replied, "This afternoon we haven't spoken to one single Catholic."

WHAT INTERESTS PEOPLE IN THE CHURCH?

When prejudice begins to dissolve, the next step is to proceed systematically to scatter about some accurate knowledge of the Catholic faith. It might be asked now: What interests people in the Catholic Church? In a survey of a number of converts, their answers fell into three groups. The largest group was first interested in the Church by contact with a good Catholic priest or layman.

The second group was first interested in the Church by attending a Catholic service.

The third and smallest group became interested in the Church by reading some piece of Catholic literature. It would seem then that in this phase of our efforts we have to concentrate pretty much on these three things.

CONTACT

With regard to contact with non-Catholics, it is the work of the priest as well as the people. His efforts are better in some cases, theirs in others. The practical steps to be taken are these:

1. The priest is to continue his contacts with friendly non-Catholics, but he is to begin to introduce religion into the conversation. A good way is to lead them into giving their ideas and then, in a kindly fashion, correct them. These visits should be uniformly short. They should be planned. A priest ought to have in mind, before he enters, at least one point he intends to drive home, and he ought to leave each time some pamphlet which will arouse further interest in religious discussion.

2. The priest ought to greet people at the door of the church at the end of Mass and at every other church service and speak for a moment with strangers and invite them to return again.

3. With regard to the great body of his parishioners, he ought to drive home the idea that they are never to let any remark on the Church pass, but rather to answer it at once or, if the answer is beyond them, to come to him immediately and get the answer so that they may pass it along to the other. He ought to urge them continually to bring to the rectory those who wish to discuss religion or show some interest in the Catholic Church.

4. A few exceptional Catholics should be trained to search out non-Catholics and impart to them some knowledge of the Catholic Church.

THE WELCOME SIGN

Many non-Catholics are of the opinion that the Catholic Church is closed to all except her own members. It is necessary to do away with this opinion in order to attract outsiders to the Church which God has prepared for them. For this purpose a priest should make the non-Catholics he knows acquainted with the fact that they are welcome to Mass on Sunday, and he must remind his people of their duty of bringing their non-Catholic friends to Mass with them.

He ought to emphasize in his newspaper notices that all are welcome, and he ought to give the schedule of services. Especially ought he invite, personally and through their Catholic partners, the non-Catholic party to a mixed marriage. Finally, he ought to make it plain by his own efforts, and through those of his people, that non-Catholic children are welcome to Catholic religious instruction classes or to the Catholic school, if there is one.

LITERATURE

The idea of spending parish funds for the purchase of literature for distribution may seem strange to some priests, but the apostolic parish will find this a necessary expenditure. The literature used must be very pro-Catholic, but it should not be anti-Protestant in tone. People are principally interested in what we have to offer and very little in the reasons why we dislike Protestantism. Pro-Catholic literature will plainly state the Catholic position and answer Protestant difficulties without hurting the feelings of other people. A sound literature program for an apostolic parish is as follows:

1. A monthly Catholic paper sent to every home, non-Catholic as well as Catholic, through the mails.

2. A special pamphlet at least monthly to those who have shown good will to, or interest in, the Church.

3. Periodically an informative article on matters of current religious information to the leaders of public opinion.

4. Paid advertisements in the local papers on points of Catholic doctrine at least weekly.

5. Comprehensive newspaper reports, incorporating pertinent doctrine, on happenings such as baptisms, marriages, and funerals.

6. Through groups of Catholic laymen, Catholic books and periodicals supplied to the public library.

LEARNING RELIGIOUS A-B-C'S

These efforts will gradually result in arousing a tremendous interest in things Catholic. The next phase of our activity will consist in getting people who have become interested to take instructions in the Catholic religion. The practical steps towards this end are:

1. At least twice a year, from the pulpit in church, the priest ought to explain just what a person has to do to become a Catholic.

2. He ought to keep it always before the minds of his people that he is always willing to give private instructions if they are desired, and he ought to set aside a night each week on which people will always find him at home to discuss religious difficulties and to give instructions if desired.

3. In country districts, in the beginning instructions must be given in the instructee's home, for non-Catholics consider that they are marked men once they enter a Catholic rectory for this purpose. The priest must suggest this in cases where experience teaches him the only probable reason for not taking instructions is the inconvenience or their unwillingness to take them at the rectory.

4. He should resort to the home study course in religion, if necessary, in order to start people on their instructions.

5. He should aim from the beginning to conduct regular instruction classes. Experience has taught that it takes some years of effort in places where the Church has not been well established to get these classes going, but experience also teaches that persistent effort will make the classes possible and will result in increasing numbers of converts.

6. A person who once starts should never be abandoned. Many difficulties, which the born Catholic cannot understand, cross the path of the inquirer into the Catholic religion. Experience proves that continued, tactful contact eventually will bring the majority of people who start instructions into the Church.

17

The Information Center

Rev. VINCENT F. HOLDEN, C.S.P., Ph.D., Director
Paulist Information Center, New York

EDITOR'S FOREWORD: *Persons who have been passing the corner of 59th Street and Columbus Avenue in New York for years have noticed of late a surprising transformation of the corner store. The old drug store has passed out of the picture. So, too, has the empty, down-at-the-heels look the building had for a considerable time after the drug store proprietor had folded his tent like the Arab and silently moved away.*

In its place the passer-by sees an up-to-date office with attractive displays of religious truths in the windows. If he enters he sees an inviting reading room, well-stocked with magazines, pamphlets, and books, and a friendly receptionist to help make him feel at home. It is the Catholic information center, sponsored by the Paulist Fathers and directed by Father Vincent P. Holden, C.S.P.

Centers of this type are now operating in many cities and bid fair to blanket the country in the next decade. Even a city as modest in size as Grand Rapids now boasts a thriving center with two zealous young Paulists in charge.

When we visited there this fall, they had donned workmen's clothing to complete the rehabilitation of the building. With characteristic Paulist resourcefulness they allowed themselves to be photographed by the local newspaper while thus laboring in workmen's attire. Now, without a penny of expense to the Paulists, the whole city and the surrounding countryside are aware of their presence and of their willingness to supply information about the Catholic religion and to help all who have the slightest curiosity to find out the truth about Christ's Church.

Young, resourceful, zealous Father Holden has given a convincing demonstration of the usefulness of such a center. In the first year of its operation 42 converts were received; groups of 62, then 110, then 120 followed the last three years, with 139 fallen-aways being reclaimed. An army of 31,865 visitors in the four-year period has received helpful information. The Catholic Information Center fills a long-felt need and shows all of us priests and people new ways of winning converts for Christ.

∾

THE INFORMATION CENTER

I T USED TO BE A DRUG STORE, and then an empty building, but since the fall of 1943, the corner location on 59th Street and Columbus Avenue, in the shadow of the great Paulist church in New York City, has become increasingly well known as the Paulist Information Center. It is one more apostolic step toward the fulfillment of the high ideals set forth by convert Isaac Hecker when he founded the Paulist Fathers.

"Our vocation," he said, "is apostolic—conversion of souls to the faith, of sinners to repentance, giving missions, defense of the Christian religion by conferences, lectures, the pen, the press, and like works . . . to supply the special element the age and each country demand." Faithful to those words, the Paulists recognized that here was a chance to meet the man on the street who would like to know what the Church has to say on the many questions puzzling him. As a means to meet that need, the Information Center was opened November 21, 1943.

The following day I was sitting in the reading room when a gentleman came in and inquired, "Father, what is this place?"

With enthusiasm I explained that it was an information center where the average American, Catholic or non-Catholic, might obtain authoritative information about the Catholic faith. He looked at me with a rather puzzled, almost incredulous expression and exclaimed, "Why, what's wrong with the rectory? Let people go there and ask their questions. Why go to all this trouble and expense?"

This observation came from an interested, well meaning layman, but he is not the only one who has voiced that opinion. Perhaps because so many have witnessed duplication of effort and multiplication of organizations, they are skeptical of the venture and ask, "What good does it do? Is it worthwhile?" Experience and facts are the best answers to these questions.

PROBLEM OF CONTACT

To begin with, it is one answer to the problem of contact. Whenever anyone attempts to interest non-Catholics in the tenets and practices of Catholicism, he invariably comes face to face with the question: "How can I reach them? How can I bring the fullness of the revelations of Christ to their attention?" That has been the question from the very beginning of apostolic times. The answers of two thousand years have been in fundamental agreement.

They have agreed upon an active, at times even an aggressive approach. St. Paul answered it by going into the synagogues of the Jews and by holding forth in the acropolis of the pagans. He carried his message to the people and flaunted it before their eyes. He created his own opportunities to make others aware of Christ and his teachings.

It is this same line of action that the information center imitates today. It attempts to bring to the attention of non-Catholic Americans the truths of the Catholic Church by providing a readily available source for accurate information about Catholic faith and practice. It is a new and basically sound approach to the persistent problem of contact. It would be foolish to claim that it is the only sound approach. It is an easy error to allow personal association to magnify the proportions of a project to the belittlement of other worthwhile endeavors. Frequently when a specialist is working in his chosen field, whether it be economics or education, preaching or pamphlet distribution, he becomes so absorbed in his own efforts and successes that he regards his specialty as the "only" thing of the moment. When discussing its possibilities, he can marshal superlatives with alarming ease. Not infrequently he creates the definite impression that this activity is the only hope for the success of the Church, and oftentimes he does not hesitate to exclaim: "This is everything."

I would not make such an exaggerated assertion about the information center. I do not believe that it is everything, or that it is the only hope for the Church in this country. No one familiar with the field would be unaware of the many admirable methods now in operation for reaching non-Catholics. But, I am firmly convinced that alone, or in cooperation with existing methods, the center can assist the spread of the Church in a very tangible manner.

OF EASY ACCESS

Even before this conviction was supported by facts, it seemed certain that such an establishment would answer the common need of many non-Catholics by providing a place of easy accessibility. How many earnest seekers of truth, in their restless, questioning days, have been able to reach a source where they can bring their problems and their difficulties for solution? The well-known financier John Moody, in his volume *Fast By the Road*, readily acknowledges that even when he was vitally interested in the Church, the only ones he could find to discuss Catholicism with him were "numerous Protestant friends."

What about the rectory? Certainly, the non-Catholic knows he can find a priest there who will be more than willing to assist him. Quite true, he can find the priest if he will call. But for so many that is a very formidable task. The rectory is a private home and the average person hesitates to just "drop in," particularly when he doesn't know any of the priests. He feels a natural reluctance, unless he has an invitation to come in for a chat. The center, however, is more or less public. By its very nature and setup, it invites any individual to stop by, whether he has an explicit reason for doing so or not. He has no more hesitancy in coming into the center than he would in entering a library or a book shop. It is for him a "natural."

When I first began this work, I was rather surprised to meet so many people who had gone as far as the rectory, but who could never muster sufficient courage to ring the bell and ask for a priest. One woman, now a devout and ardent Catholic, tried four times to conquer this foolish fear. She was determined not to succumb the fifth time she set forth.

Bravely she mounted the steps and rang the bell, but then her heart started pounding, her hand began to tremble, and her mouth was so dry she couldn't speak. She turned and fled before anyone could answer her ring. Yet this very same woman walked into the information center without any misgivings and had no hesitation in asking about instructions. Why did she find it so easy? Because she was coming into a comfortable reading room, clearly visible from the street, and one that appeared very inviting.

To this woman, as to many others, the Paulist Information Center is "easy to come into." It has a friendly, cheerful, and familiar environment that attracts rather than repels. In the New York center—the one with which I am most familiar—a visitor who enters it comes directly from the street into a reading room which is designed to make him feel at ease. It is restful in color, and its comfortable appointments are arranged with studied carelessness.

A series of bookshelves along one wall contains a fine selection of over 500 volumes dealing with apologetics, dogma, morals, devotion, liturgy, history, hagiography, and biography, as well as standard works of references. On the other side of the room is a large pamphlet rack filled with the better of those invaluable and succinct treatments of specific questions and religious problems. A long table in the center contains current Catholic newspapers and magazines. And always on hand is a gracious and trained receptionist, ready to aid anyone who approaches her for information.

From the reading room one passes into a second section of the center which contains a lecture room and two offices. The lecture room, which comfortably holds forty people, is used for continuous series of instruction courses. Interviews and private instructions are given in the well appointed offices. Naturally, there is more formality about the lecture room and offices, but these are not the things the visitor first sees. He comes into this outer, informal reading room, of which he has already obtained a clear view through the large display windows facing on the street.

WINDOW DISPLAYS

These windows are unquestionably an important feature of the center, because it is one of the means at our disposal to bring Catholic teaching to the attention of the man on the street. We all recognize the tremendous part advertising plays in the business world.

Commercial firms spend thousands of dollars year after year to bring their products to the attention of the public. They use placards, posters, newspaper ads, and the familiar, though oftentimes annoying, radio "plugs." Experience has taught them "it pays to advertise." Here we are trying to bring to the attention of the casual passerby the greatest good known to man—divine truth. Why shouldn't we employ the same business technique?

Across the street from the Paulist Information Center is one of Schulte's chain stores. He is selling shirts and cigarettes, and we are in a modified way selling religion. He advertises his product, we must feature ours. He attractively arranges his stock in the window, we do the same.

During the past three years we have featured displays on such vitally important subjects as marriage, Catholic education, confession, purgatory, the Bible, the sacraments, and the papacy. Our technique is to give solid information on these and other phases of Catholic doctrine, but not completely to satisfy the passerby. We want him to come in and inquire further about these doctrines or to ask for literature. On an average, the displays are changed once a month to give them a freshness in appearance and a vitality in idea.

An interesting incident occurred two years ago which brought home to us how much attention the windows attract and how far the knowledge of them can travel. When *The Song of Bernadette* was playing on Broadway, we had a window display on Lourdes and miracles. Within a week after the window had been arranged, I received a call from the manager of the theater in which the picture was showing, complimenting me on the theme we had used and offering me tickets for the production. Broadway had become conscious of us through our windows.

NEWS STORIES

However, we do not depend solely upon this medium to remind people of our existence. We reach out to others through the press. Surprisingly enough, we have little difficulty getting stories into the New York papers. They are looking for items of interest and are always fascinated by the human interest angle. The center is certainly a "natural" for that. We are dealing daily with human beings and their ever perplexing conflicts with life and its problems. Catholic, Protestant, and Jew, old and young, find their way easily into our office and seek help in their difficulties. Some of these are amusing, some tragic; some are trivial, others are tremendous; but they make interesting copy, and that is what the newspapers want.

Not a year has passed since we opened that we haven't been written up at length in at least one metropolitan daily. The first year *The New York Sun* sent up a reporter who did a two-column spread with a prominent, bold type head. The second year *The World-Telegram* carried a very interesting account written by one of their staff, a Presbyterian minister's daughter. This year *The Journal-American* followed suit with a full page story accompanied with pictures. This entirely free publicity in daily papers having a huge circulation helps us tremendously, and we always experience an increase in callers after the story appears.

Whatever the means which attracts them—window displays, newspaper stories, paid ads, circulars, or word of mouth—increasingly large numbers of Catholics and non-Catholics have found their way to the information center. In the four years of operation an accurate count made by the receptionists shows a total of 31,865 visitors. They come from every walk of life, profess a variety of beliefs and disbeliefs, and explain a bewildering range of problems.

It would be difficult to say whether there is any specific type of question that troubles the majority of interested inquirers. For some, it is a question of confession, for others the papacy, for still others the historical credibility of the Gospels. Our inquirers ask questions from the simple catechism variety to the most intricate type that have absorbed theologians for centuries.

One gentleman, a lawyer and a confirmed skeptic, who has since, thanks to the grace of God, come into the Church, brought in a typed list of questions summarizing his religious difficulties. They were questions that not even a professor of dogmatic theology would ask of a student preparing for a theological degree. I happened to show them to such a professor during a visit to a seminary, and he remarked: "This fellow touches the core of all religion. He needs a Thomas Aquinas to answer them."

VARIETY OF VISITORS

Of the number of visitors who have come into the center, there is a surprisingly small percentage who have had no contact with any religion whatsoever. From my observation, I would say that only about six per cent of the entire number using our facilities at the center have not been associated with any organized religion.

About 84 per cent have had some training in religion or association with various religious groups, but not in any intensive way. The remaining ten per cent not only have a knowledge of their respective religion's beliefs but have also faithfully adhered to its practices.

As a general reaction, I have noticed with all of these inquirers that they are finding Protestantism inadequate. They are puzzled and confused with its changing attitudes on various questions. They want certainty, they seek divine comfort, and they have not found it in their own groups. They turn questioningly to the Catholic

Church to see if she can supply it. At the same time, while they investigate and while they search, they like to feel that they are incurring no obligation. We set their mind perfectly at ease on this point. We make very clear to them that we are not under the impression that they "intend" to become Catholics, but that they are here to investigate and to learn what the Church says of herself. If, when they have completed the instructions, they sincerely want to become Catholics, we assure them we will baptize them.

We explain that if, at the conclusion of their study, they find that they have a better understanding of the faith and a better appreciation of what Catholics believe but cannot accept it, then no attempt will be made to force their assent. Even with this result, we point out that no time will have been lost. At least they will know considerably more of the beliefs and practices of the Catholic Church than a number of their fellow men.

With this basic understanding we begin the instructions which are given only by the priests associated with the center. There is an idea current among certain Catholic groups that lay people should take over this work and bring the prospective convert to the priest when he is ready for baptism. This method has never been adopted at the Paulist Information Center in New York.

Our experience has shown that many questions that arise about confession, marriage, birth control, and sin demand more of a background than even the instructed and trained layman can give. Furthermore, we have noticed a decided reluctance on the part of the inquirers coming to the center to discuss their questions with the receptionist, who is not a cleric, or to accept an authoritative answer from one who is not a priest.

CONVENIENT HOURS

The Paulist Fathers who are assigned to the center do all the interviewing and instructing. The New York Center is open every day from 12:00 o'clock midday until 9:00 o'clock in the evening. There are classes four evenings a week, on Monday and Wednesday at 8:00 o'clock, and on Tuesday and Thursday at 6:00 o'clock. The earlier hour is more acceptable to those who come for instructions immediately after office hours and have the rest of the evening free. The later hour attracts those whose duties at home occupy them until the family chores are completed. There are also many individuals who are unable to make the scheduled classes, or who begin their investigation after the classes are well under way. These receive individual instruction when they are free to come.

Whether the instruction is given in class or individually, there are a minimum of twenty-two instructions. At times it is amusing to hear people say: "A friend of mine was received after ten instructions. Why must I take twenty-two?" It reminds one of the comparison between sales in rival bargain basements. Nevertheless, at the New York center we insist upon the specified minimum for a well grounded knowledge of the Catholic faith and practice, especially since we realize that this is probably the only instruction the person will ever receive. Neither in class nor in private do we use the catechism method of taking each question, explaining it, expanding it, and then moving on to another.

We employ the practice of a connected, integrated lecture, and then we answer questions or difficulties at the conclusion of each instruction. To supplement what we have discussed, we give a pamphlet covering the subject matter of the evening, and we ask the individual to read it carefully. This we find far more desirable and effective than handing out an overall treatise of Catholic faith in the beginning. That is advisable at the conclusion, after each fact has been separately and individually studied.

What has been the effect of this method? The first year the center opened its doors to the public, 42 were received and baptized; the second year, 62; the third year, 110; the fourth year, 120. In a sort of local distribution, we have noticed that by far the greater majority do not come from the area adjacent to the center. They are residents of localities where a Catholic church is within convenient distance, but who do not go to their own communities, where they are known.

They prefer to preserve their anonymity until they make up their mind about becoming a Catholic. Hence, they come where they are not known, and where their interest can remain unknown to their neighbors and friends until their decision is made.

AFFILIATE THE CONVERT WITH A PARISH

Once they become Catholics, they are sincere, ardent, and enthusiastic. We attempt to solidify this enthusiasm by identifying them with Catholic groups, particularly in their own parishes. We never have had any convert group associated with the New York center. Of course, there are others in convert work who have had remarkable success with such organizations and who have found them extremely helpful.

Up to the present we have followed the plan of parish assimilation because we fear that such groups may take the individual away from his proper cell of Catholic activity—the parish group. It seems to us advisable and desirable to have the recently received Catholic absorbed by his own parish organization, whether it be the Holy Name Society, Rosary Society, Sodality, Legion of Mary, or whatever opportunity his own locale offers. To facilitate this absorption, we usually give the newly received Catholic a personal letter of introduction to his own pastor.

The formation of a convert group—in fact, even the use of the term "convert"—leaves me with no enthusiasm. It seems unwise both for the recent and the cradle Catholic. It gives the newly received Catholic the impression that he is not really quite a full-fledged member of the Church, but a sort of special species, a *rara avis*. It often affects the cradle Catholic with the reaction that this person is not yet proven, but a sort of "half-baked" Catholic. This is why I advise and suggest that one who embraces the faith should refer to himself always as a Catholic, not a convert.

The center has proven its effectiveness by the number of fallen-away Catholics who have returned to the sacraments. We know definitely from our records of 139 who have gone back to confession after an absence of from two to thirty-one years. The reaction of this group is interesting. It seems almost as though they are the most hesitant and fearful. They come in to look around, to "catch a glimpse of the priest to see what he is like." They quietly and nervously inquire of the receptionist if he is "strict or understanding, grumpy or regular." Many of these have been involved in invalid marriages and have hesitated to do anything about it. They labor under the misapprehension that they will have to go up the aisle to the unwelcome strains of "Here Comes the Bride." Once they realize that convalidation is a quiet and private affair they are very much relieved.

This, then, is the work of the Paulist Information Center. The distinctive type described in this account was established by the Paulist Fathers first in New York, then in Boston, Baltimore, and Grand Rapids. With certain modifications, as a result of space, personnel, and location, it functions also in San Francisco, Chicago, Minneapolis, and Toronto, Canada.

The center reaches out to the non-Catholic in a way which appeals to him. It aids the lapsed Catholic in a manner that draws him back to the bosom of the Church from which he has strayed. In the four years of its operation, the New York center has more than fulfilled its promise. Yes, it is "another" agency to spread the truth of Christ, one that has tremendous possibilities, one that has definitely proven itself.

One of our most discerning and constructive critics has said of it: "I have watched it grow from its very modest beginning, I have known the doubt with which some viewed it from the very day its doors were opened. I remember the half-hearted enthusiasm it received from well intentioned visitors, but I have also seen all that changed. Now there is no lack of congratulations, no absence of encomium, no paucity of praise. It comes from all quarters." How goes the adage? "Nothing succeeds like success." The Paulist Information Center is succeeding because it is a success.

18

Conducting an Inquiry Class

Rev. WILLIAM J. GRACE, S.J.
Gesu Church, Milwaukee, Wisconsin

EDITOR'S FOREWORD: *As a result of our nation-wide survey of convert work, our attention was drawn to the splendid results being achieved at the Gesu Church in Milwaukee. The pastor, Father Richard A. Cahill, S.J., had recently instituted the group instruction plan and found what every pastor who has tried the plan has discovered, namely, that the number of converts was greatly increased.*

In 1946 Fathers Finnegan, Grace, and Morgan, who alternate in giving the instructions, received 169 converts. It was a striking demonstration of what can be accomplished when a recruiting campaign for prospects is launched with vigor and determination and the class of instruction is conducted in a systematic and well-organized manner. At the Gesu Church every detail of procedure is worked out in advance with great care.

At the end of each of the three courses conducted during the year, Father Cahill arranges for the public reception of the converts with impressive ceremonies. They are similar to those conducted at St. Sabina's Church in Chicago and are fast becoming universal. A priest in the pulpit directs the proceedings. Candidates recite the profession of faith in unison at the altar rail. Then they stand and are baptized. The ceremony closes with solemn Benediction. Each convert is presented with a certificate of baptism. A group photograph

*is taken; each convert receives a copy as a memento. Similar cere-
monies are held for the group reception of First Holy Communion.*

*In some parishes the reception of converts, while carried through
in its entirety on the preceding day, is reenacted in a summary but
impressive manner at the Sunday Mass for the edification and inspiration of the congregation. It never fails to move the parishioners
profoundly, and it enlists their efforts in recruiting prospects for the
next class. Whether held in connection with the Mass or on Sunday
afternoon, it is eminently worthwhile to have as many of the faithful
in attendance as possible.*

*At the Gesu Church, Father Eugene P. Mullaney, S.J., organized
the convert guild to provide the indispensable follow-up. Father William J. Grace, S.J., has made us all his debtors by favoring us with
a clear and detailed exposition of the manner in which the inquiry
class is organized and conducted. We think it safe to say that in parishes where no group plan is employed the adoption of the essentials
of the plan here outlined will double or triple the annual total of
converts.*

❦

CONDUCTING AN INQUIRY CLASS

C ONDUCTING AN INQUIRY CLASS seems to be within the compe-
tency of almost any parish priest in ordinary circumstances
and of some who are not directly in the ministry. One has to
lay aside an hour on each of two evenings a week for the instructional work, during a period which need not exceed twelve weeks.
Suitable textbooks, pamphlets, and charts are available. Every
priest has a ready knowledge of the subject matter, and most have
often enough covered it in guiding individuals into the Church. It
is as easy to say it to a hundred as to one, and as a matter of fact,
a busy pastor finds that he actually saves time by taking many together rather than separately.

By holding classes regularly and by persistently publicizing the
fact, he will almost certainly receive more converts into the Church.

Although he will no doubt still have mixed marriages, he will not have so many of them. By means of the class he will more frequently succeed in inducing the non-Catholic party to study the entire catechism instead of limiting his interest to the few instructions which are required by Church law. If the mixed marriage takes place before the entire course is completed, the non-Catholic party may more easily be led to resume instructions later on. Having a ready opportunity each Sunday to announce the subjects of the talks for the coming week, the pastor can soon make his congregation convert-conscious.

Only one who has tried the group instruction plan can know how fascinating the work becomes. It is the way of leading couples to the altar steps instead of to the rectory parlor, of bringing the nuptial blessing to spouses who have been united perhaps for years after entering into a mixed marriage, and of preparing for First Holy Communion adults who were baptized in the Church as infants and who for some reason got no further. Experience shows that the ordinary attendance case is that of the Catholic young person who brings the non-Catholic sweetheart and the Catholic husband or wife who accompanies the non-Catholic partner.

INDIVIDUAL VERSUS GROUP INSTRUCTION

Individual instruction provides the advantage of easy opportunity for checking, quizzing, and answering personal questions. But even if equal numbers of catechumens could be drawn to such instruction—and they cannot—a priest who is attempting to teach, say fifteen individuals, just cannot find thirty hours a week for their accommodation.

The group plan, besides being a time-saver, has several other advantages. The visitor feels more at ease when he seems to be lost in the crowd. He gets inspiration, too, from the discovery that he is not singular in evincing interest in the teachings of the Catholic Church. He senses that if he wishes to drop out of the scene he can do so without embarrassment. The teacher himself, when addressing a group, is likely to prepare more thoroughly and consequently to provide more interesting and profitable instruction.

A study of records from the inquiry forum classes of the Church of the Gesu in Milwaukee shows that, during a given period of time in which 48 adult inquirers were received into the Church, four others completed the course but for various reasons were not received at its conclusion, and 50 who attended more than one meeting dropped out before the end of the series. Of the 50 who dropped out, it is estimated that close to one-third were preparing for a mixed marriage at an early date, and it is hoped, and rather expected, that a goodly proportion of them will be received later on.

How do you get an audience? This question is admirably answered by Father John T. McGinn, C.S.P., in this symposium. Certainly any pastor can use the ordinary means of circulating a printed invitation and making announcements from the pulpit.

Instead of attempting to indicate how a class should be started and operated, the writer will simply tell of the methods used in the only type of convert class with which he has had personal experience. This is the inquiry forum of the Church of the Gesu. While the reverend pastor of this large parish is able to assign three assistants to look after the inquiry forum, there seems to be no serious reason why the average parish priest, who is alone or has one assistant, could not follow the general lines of the system, accommodating details to the exigencies of his particular set-up.

THE FIRST MEETING

Before the inquirer enters the classroom for the opening session, his eye is caught by the pamphlet rack, on which he may notice copies of Father Hull's *What the Catholic Church Is and What She Teaches* and Father Harney's *Why I Am a Catholic*. On subsequent visits he will often observe these same five-cent pamphlets on display, since they are regarded as of fundamental importance and interest and are well written.

On the arm of the chair at which he is seated in the lecture room he finds the four basic texts which he is urged to acquire and familiarize himself with. They are (1) *A Catechism for Inquirers*, by Father Malloy (Paulist Press); (2) *Father Smith Instructs Jackson*, by Bishop Noll (Our Sunday Visitor Press); (3) *The Greatest Prayer, the Mass* (Bruce Publishing Company); (4) *The New Testament* (St. Anthony's Guild Press). The four texts may be purchased for a total outlay of two dollars.

Father Malloy's *Catechism for Inquirers* has been adopted because it is a modern book, attractively printed, and made up specifically for adults. Special features are the chapter on the Bible, the insertion of appropriate Scriptural quotations following many of the answers, and the inclusion of the formula for the profession of faith.

Father Smith Instructs Jackson is written in simple language, in the manner of dialogue between an inquirer and a priest, making it much easier reading than head-on instruction, page after page. This text is widely used today, having proved attractive to service men during the war. It has the very important advantage that a series of six printed tests on the subject matter is made available through the Home Study Service, St. Louis, Missouri.

The Greatest Prayer, the Mass, containing as it does numerous and excellent photographs of the priest at the altar, together with brief explanations and prayers, enables the neophyte to begin finding his way through what is to him the puzzling action of the Holy Sacrifice.

The New Testament is assigned through the syllabus for reading at the rate of eight chapters per week during the twelve weeks.

On his armchair the registrant finds also three papers which he is invited to retain gratis. The first is an announcement folder. This provides some essential information concerning the inquiry forum and specifies the date and topic of each meeting in the fall, winter, spring, and summer series of lectures.

It calls attention to the fact that, in case an inquirer is permanently prevented from attending one of the fixed weekly meeting days, he may nevertheless complete the course by continuing through two successive series, since the odd-numbered lectures are offered on Mondays in one series and the even-numbered lectures on Mondays in the succeeding series. The second piece of printed material offered gratis is the syllabus, which indicates the textbook assignments for each lesson. The third free paper is a prayerbook-size picture of Christ knocking at the door, with a prayer for light on the reverse side. The inquirer is asked to recite this prayer each day.

REGISTRATION

The inquirer and companion now proceed to register by filling out a mimeographed four-by-six card, white for the non-Catholic and blue for the Catholic. This card has been handed to them as they entered.

It calls for the name in full, with designation of "Mr.," "Mrs.," or "Miss," street address and zone number, telephone number, and occupation. It asks whether the registrant has been baptized and, if so, in what religion. Catholics are asked whether or not they have received First Communion and confirmation. There is a line for insertion of the date of first attendance at the forum.

Should one have been in attendance in a previous series, he merely writes his name on an attendance slip. His registration card will later be pulled out of the "dead" file.

STARTING THE MEETING

Whether it is well to open with prayer is a question for each director to decide in view of circumstances which may vary in different localities. The writer believes that generally it is advisable to omit prayer and to restrict the program to an objective exposition of the claims, credentials, and doctrines of the Catholic Church.

After welcoming the guests, the speaker proceeds to develop the nine topics which the syllabus suggests for the introductory talk. These topics are:

1. The *purpose* of the inquiry forum.
2. Reasons why the course should be *interesting* and *profitable*.
3. What *faith* is and how it is acquired.

4. The necessity of *prayer*.

5. An introduction to the four basic *textbooks*.

6. The advantage of becoming familiar with the *Bible*.

7. How the *syllabus* is to be used.

8. The manner of treating *audience questions*.

9. The *registration cards*—their purpose and filling them out.

The talks are intended to be informative, not controversial. No one's religion is to be attacked. The Catholic position and doctrine, correctly and clearly stated, speak for themselves. Care is taken at all times to avoid wounding the feelings of non-Catholics or causing embarrassment to their Catholic companions.

Any sincere inquirer is welcome to sit in, if he so chooses, as an auditor, without any money expenditure whatever. It is pointed out, however, that one would not expect to master a school subject by such procedure, and it is made plain that any person who proposes to become a member of the Catholic Church is expected to use the textbooks as essential tools for acquiring the needed fundamental knowledge.

Some inquirers presumably come to their first class on the alert lest they be softly cajoled or gently pushed or pulled into the Catholic Church. For their benefit the speaker stresses the fact that no one can be received unless and until he spontaneously asks for admission, that to please another would not be sufficient warrant for joining the Church, that a priest is not allowed to admit a candidate without being satisfied that he is reasonably well instructed, that a further prerequisite is that the aspirant be prepared to make a sincere profession of faith, and that, finally, he must be ready to pledge himself to live and die as a good Catholic.

With a view to forestalling misunderstandings and disappointment, particular attention is called to the status of a divorced person or one married to a divorcee, should such a one become a Catholic while the validly wedded spouse is living, and to the gravity of the promise required of such a candidate regarding attempted marriage or company keeping in the future.

At the first meeting the manner of handling audience questions is explained. Anyone may, of course, put a question to the director at any time outside the lecture hour. If for any reason one prefers not to do this, he is asked to withhold his question until the proper subject matter is reached in due course. He is encouraged meanwhile to study the catechism and "Father Smith" on the subject, to delve into Father Conway's *Question Box*, and even to consult *The Catholic Encyclopedia* in the public library. Finally, he may find the answer in one of the pamphlets or in the lecturer's discourse when the topic is treated.

Should the question remain unanswered after this search, it is to be written out and dropped into the question box which is kept available for the purpose. The speaker will either give the answer privately or, if he judges the matter to be of sufficient general interest and importance, will report back at the next meeting.

This system works! It keeps at a minimum the number of questions which demand a public answer, brings the queries in at the appropriate point, saves time for more essential purposes, and satisfies everyone. Moreover, it effectively forestalls the likelihood of disagreeable heckling and controversy.

CLOSING THE FIRST MEETING

As the audience files out after the lecture, the registration cards of newcomers and the attendance slips of the others are collected at the door. Those who wish to purchase textbooks carry them to the corridor, where lay volunteers, previously supplied with change, are ready to take care of the business.

The conduct of the opening session has been described in some detail for the obvious reason that it is of the utmost importance to provide so interesting and profitable a meeting that the maximum number of those in attendance will be eager to return and be inclined to invite others and to see to it that the mode of procedure and certain facts and principles are made clear from the start. The first meeting, if well advertised, is likely to bring out a large crowd, and hence the special importance of preparing a definite line of thought for presentation and of making a favorable initial impression.

When the registrant returns for his second and subsequent sessions, he is given an attendance slip on which to write his name. Should one resume attendance in a later series, he does not register second time, since his original card has been kept on file.

As soon as convenient after each meeting, the priest who is responsible for keeping the records encircles the proper numeral on the registration cards of those who were present. The numerals from 1 to 25 are printed on the cards. A second set, of six numerals, is for recording tests taken and passed. The cards are kept in an alphabetical file.

Underneath the numerals and on the reverse side of the card there is ample space for noting points of information which may be gathered from time to time regarding the registrant. Memoranda are made there, for instance, of the name of the companion who comes with him, the date on which candidacy for reception is announced, and in due time the dates of baptism, First Communion, marriage (if later contracted), and confirmation. There is freedom in making entries, since after the evening of his first attendance the card will not again be in the hands of the registrant. These cards may therefore become valuable miniature case records.

SUBSEQUENT MEETINGS

On his return each time the registrant finds that the pamphlets in the rack have been changed to correspond to the topic of the evening. And since new inquirers may begin to attend at any point in the series, sets made up of the four basic texts, the announcement folder, the syllabus, and the prayer for light are stacked on a table before each meeting so that they may be conveniently carried, for the sake of examination, to the seats taken by new registrants. Thus the essential materials come to the attention of all without delay.

It is found to be practically necessary to allow new inquirers to join the class at any time when they may apply, and as a matter of fact there is seldom a meeting without the appearance of new faces. Newcomers are held after nine o'clock on the evening of their registration to allow the director an opportunity to synopsize for their benefit the "nine points" which he stressed at the first meeting. This is a procedure of great importance.

From time to time in the course of the lectures, additional reading materials are distributed gratis. Such, for instance, is the illustrated mimeograph sheet indicating how to recite the rosary, given out after the assignment of the Apostles' Creed as a memory lesson. *Face the Facts*, graphically picturing the fourth mark of the Church, is a leaflet which is passed to all when the lesson on "The Church of Christ" is reached. Purchasers of the prayer book *The Greatest Prayer, the Mass* receive a little card telling "When to Stand, Sit, and Kneel at Low Mass."

SELLING THE PAMPHLETS

Discovering soon that the meetings actually begin at eight o'clock, patrons learn to time their arrival with accuracy. Few put in an early appearance, and the majority leave without delay at the end of the session. They come and go, therefore, pretty much in a crowd, and not many take time to examine the contents of the pamphlet rack.

For this reason, beginning with the second meeting a pamphlet relating to the topic of the evening is placed on the arm of each chair. Since practically all the auditors attend in pairs, two pamphlets of different titles are so placed that no two contiguous chairs hold the same title. This arrangement affords each couple an opportunity to examine both pamphlets and encourage alike reading and purchase. So likewise does a judicious word of recommendation from the speaker. Inquirers, like the general public, are not immune against the arts of advertising and salesmanship!

"MAKE-UP LESSONS"

Because in a large class there are likely to be some absentees each time, a "make-up" lesson is offered as part of the routine, nine days after the regular class session on each subject. These "make-ups" are scheduled for every Wednesday evening and Sunday afternoon. They make it possible for occasional absentees to catch up without delay, and enable some persons to complete the course with the class in spite of the fact that other engagements regularly prevent their attendance on one or other of the fixed evenings.

Another advantage of the "make-up" device is that as a result there remains toward the end of the series but little "mopping-up" to be done for the sake of candidates who still have a lesson or two to account for. At each regular meeting a blackboard announcement advertises the "make-up" opportunities of the following week.

LEARNING THE MASS

Now and again after the first meeting, reference is made to the Mass, and the advice is repeated that inquirers, and especially prospective converts, should attend each Sunday, seek a favorable place not far from the altar, and use the little book *The Greatest Prayer, the Mass* for identifying the parts and reviewing the explanations. After the lesson on "The Sacrifice of the Mass," copies of Father Stedman's *My Sunday Missal* are distributed to those present, and demonstration is given of the ease and satisfaction with which the missal can be used. Invariably thereafter a notable number of Catholics as well as non-Catholics begin using the missal at Mass.

SPEAKER'S PREPARATION

Although he may at times judge it to be useful to make a brief hook-up with the preceding lesson or section, for the rest the speaker aims definitely to restrict himself to the evening's subject and to cover it as comprehensively as time may permit. This purpose is not likely to be carried out effectively unless he prepares at least an outline of related and cohesive points.

As in other forms of public speaking, the speaking out of apt illustrations and searching of the memory for personal experiences and incidents having a bearing on the subject is of the greatest help for keeping the audience alert. A humorous anecdote, or one with a note of human interest, narrated briefly and to the point, is invaluable for holding and renewing attention.

Memory being as treacherous as an experienced public speaker knows it to be, the jotting down of memoranda in proper form and sequence is a practical necessity. Some speakers choose to write out their lectures in full and to work them over carefully before each new presentation. This is the most laborious system, but no doubt it brings the best results, and these good results are cumulative and preserved.

Needless to say, there should be no mere reading from the manuscript, than which nothing could be more boresome. Here, as in all things, there is a golden mean. A brief jotting to jog the memory will at times recall an illustration or incident that can be recounted most effectively without further reference to the prepared paper. Audience contact must be preserved continuously. For effecting this an easy conversational manner is a great help.

CALL FOR CANDIDATES

Since with the completion of lessons nine ("The Church of Christ") and ten ("The Divine and Human Elements in the Church") the credentials have been shown and the preamble to the presentation of Catholic doctrines completed, it is openly suggested at this point that those who think seriously of joining the Church indicate the fact by writing the word "candidate" on the attendance card. It is made clear that in so doing they do not commit themselves with any finality. They are encouraged to express their choice either of the director or of any other priest who may be available to act as personal guide and counselor during the remainder of the course.

The priest who is so named proceeds without delay to establish personal contact. He is made completely responsible for the ultimate acceptance or rejection of the candidate. He arranges for personal conferences in sufficient number to meet the need of each individual. He checks on such matters as matrimonial status, study and mastery of the texts, attendance at Mass, progress in understanding the Holy Sacrifice, and memorizing the common prayers. He inquires about personal problems of a religious nature and answers questions.

TOUR OF THE CHURCH

A tour of the church building is offered periodically and is made in groups of a convenient size. This affords one of the most enjoyable features of the instruction. The disciple, learning simultaneously through eye and ear, is likely to absorb more knowledge and to be more stirred religiously during this hour than in any equal amount of time devoted to reading or to academic instruction. The tour, made on Sunday afternoon, is an integral and required part of the course. On the record card it is numbered 25.

The tourists listen eagerly to information not only on the various objects of devotion, but concerning the history of the parish and of the church building, the architecture and art, and various related facts and statistics. They are shown the confessional, inside and out, as well as the baptistery. They are taken into the sanctuary, where they get a close-up view of the detail of the altar and appurtenances. They enter the sacristy, where they see the altar breads, vestments, and sacred vessels.

The possibilities of effective instruction in this leisurely and informal visit to the church are many and inviting; in fact, they grow on the guide until his problem is to point out and explain without unduly prolonging the time. And meanwhile the visitor, who perhaps was never before inside a Catholic church, is beginning to feel at home.

OTHER VISUAL AIDS

The wise catechist, of course, makes use of visual aids at other times, as opportunity occurs. While explaining extreme unction he shows the oil-stock and the sick-call burse, with pyx and host. If he is clever at "chalk-talk" he has a definite advantage. An audience is interested in seeing the priest clothe himself in the Mass vestments, accompanied with explanations by himself or a confrere.

Charts, providing as they do an orderly and comprehensive outline of essentials, may be used to good purpose, especially by a teacher who is new at the work of giving catechetical instruction.

They are most serviceable when employed with a class of a size which permits all to read the lettering with ease. Good charts are available and at no prohibitive prices.

PERIODIC TESTS

Students in inquiry classes have this in common with college students and with the rest of us, that they need the stimulus of an impending examination as an incentive to master the subject. And therefore, since the oral quiz is impracticable except with very small groups, the administration of periodic written tests is regarded as essential.

Right here is a strong selling point for *Father Smith Instructs Jackson*. The publishers of this book provide six tests based on the text. Following lesson ten, on "The Divine and Human Elements in the Church," the first of the printed tests is presented to each candidate. There is nothing terrifying about the experience of being tested, since the examinations are taken at home and at leisure, and the textbook may be consulted freely. In fact, strange to say, here is an examination which even the average student thoroughly enjoys.

It is a challenge which he is capable of accepting with confidence. He can gain a grade of 100, probably for the first time in his life, if he is very careful. The object is, of course, to compel him to study the text, and this objective is really accomplished. For the teacher the task of marking the tests is a brief one, simplified by the use of a "key" which is provided. In due time all candidates and others who are interested take the remaining five tests.

APPROACHING THE CLOSE

On the evening of the twenty-second meeting the candidates remain after the regular session. They first fill out record slips with information which is later to be transcribed into the baptismal register. Next they look through the baptismal rite, under direction, being supplied for the purpose with copies of *The Gift of Life*, a fifteen-cent booklet published by the Liturgical Press, St. John's Abbey, Collegeville, Minnesota. They are encouraged to purchase a copy of this booklet so that they may study the beautiful ceremonial at leisure. Finally, they scan the formula of the profession of faith, while the director reads it aloud and explains unusual words and technical expressions. This formula is printed in Father Malloy's *Catechism*.

In a nine o'clock special meeting of candidates following the next to last session the foregoing matters are brought in again. On this occasion the profession of faith is read aloud and in unison, for practice. Then, following the final meeting of the series, the candidates go to the church for a rehearsal of the program for reception. This rehearsal is followed by practice in receiving Holy Communion.

RECEPTION INTO THE CHURCH

With a view to attracting wider interest in the inquiry forum and eliciting the zeal of the faithful, an endeavor is made to secure some prominent convert-priest or convert-maker to address the congregations at the principal Masses on the Sunday when the catechumens are to be received. The reception itself takes place at three o'clock in the afternoon. A printed program is provided. The priest in charge of the inquiry forum directs proceedings from the pulpit. The priests who are to administer baptism, one for each candidate or pair of candidates, take their places at the Communion rail, facing the congregation. Between each two priests all the necessary materials have been placed on a table.

The candidates, who with their sponsors have been seated on chairs in front of the first pews, are invited to kneel at the Communion rail and recite the profession of faith in unison, while the priest in the pulpit reads the same formula aloud in the interest of the congregation. The baptisms follow, the ritual prayers being read from the pulpit and the ceremonies explained, so that the people in the pews may follow the proceedings and the ministers of the sacrament may be kept at an even pace.

At the conclusion of the baptismal ceremonies, each of the newly baptized is presented with an attractive certificate of baptism, together with a printed explanation of the significance of re-birth. A solo follows and a brief word of welcome from the reverend pastor. The program is concluded with solemn Benediction of the Blessed Sacrament. A class photograph is taken so that all may have a memorial of the occasion. The program from start to finish lasts one hour.

The newly baptized are invested with scapulars and enrolled in the Confraternity of the Immaculate Conception. This impressive ceremony may well be included in the public program, should it be judged that the time will not be prolonged unduly. Finally, those who have been baptized conditionally are given an opportunity to receive the sacrament of penance for the first time.

PLANNING FOR THE YEAR

The year's program is so planned that the baptisms following the close of the fall series are administered on the Sunday preceding Christmas. First Communion is received at Midnight Mass, with the front pews being reserved for the First Communicants, each of whom is permitted to bring a companion. These precede all others to the Communion rail.

The winter series is closed with baptism on the afternoon of Palm Sunday. First Communion is received on Easter Sunday at the nine o'clock solemn Mass. Members of the convert guild serve the Communion breakfast, after which there is a brief and appropriate program. The spring and summer series are closed in a similar manner.

DISPOSITION OF RECORDS

The dates of baptism and First Communion are duly recorded on the registration cards, which are then placed in a separate file of all the "graduates." As time goes on, this file is subdivided into two sets made up of the cards of those who have been confirmed and the cards of those who have not. An effort is made to keep contact with the convert at least until he has received the sacrament of confirmation.

Two "dead" files are preserved: one of non-Catholics who have not been received into the Church, the other of Catholics who have attended in the past. Should any of the "dead" come to life subsequently, their cards are pulled out and inserted in the current file.

TWO OR THREE LECTURERS

In a large city parish where two or three priests are available as instructors in the inquiry forum it is found desirable to have them rotate, each in turn giving two successive lectures. This arrangement provides variety for the audience, and allows each speaker a week or two in which to prepare for two talks. All the priests who are so associated attend each meeting, as far as possible, both for the purpose of becoming acquainted with the inquirers and to gather fresh viewpoints and inspiration from one another's presentation.

Professed candidates who express no preference regarding the personal counselor are apportioned among all the priests, in order that no individual instructor may be burdened needlessly with conferences.

When two priests are employed in the instructional work, they make a complete exchange of subjects in successive series. Thus, in the course of two series each treats all the topics in the entire course. An auditor may therefore repeat a complete series without hearing the same speaker twice on the same subject.

Where there are three lecturers the year's program similarly schedules each priest to handle each topic once in the course of three successive series. After the speakers have worked through a year in this system, substitution is easily arranged for in an emergency, and in case there happens at any time to be an overflow meeting, one of the priests who is not scheduled to speak can take part of the audience to another room and carry on the lecture of the evening.

THE CONVERT GUILD

In the system outlined above the director of the convert guild (an organization which encourages the "alumni" to stay together for further development in knowledge of the Church, in personal advancement in spirituality, and in works of zeal) has a splendid opportunity to build up his unit. He capitalizes on opportunities for meeting prospective members at regular meetings of the inquiry forum and at the Communion-breakfast gatherings. He is the heart and inspiration of the guild. But while taking interest in helping to plan the monthly or biweekly meetings, he aims to have the members themselves do the work of carrying out the programs, encouraging every individual to participate actively.

The director of the guild may not, and probably will not, succeed in enlisting a large percentage of the converts as enthusiastic members of the guild. But if he is himself deeply interested, and if he has the zeal of the Master, he will gather and hold together a precious nucleus of souls, men as well as women, who are ready and eager to develop themselves as intelligent and devout members of the Church Militant, zealous to do their generous bit for the spread of the Kingdom on earth.

This article has been written because the author was solicited to undertake it. He realizes that it will come to the attention of many priests who have had far more experience than he in convert work. He knows well that whatever measure of success has come to the inquiry forum of the Church of the Gesu has been brought about, under God's providence, through the unremitting encouragement of a zealous and generous pastor and the unqualified enthusiasm, support, and cooperation of fellow assistant pastors who have been associated in the same work. If this effort at putting our combined ideas on paper serves to help any others who are interested in this type of instruction, we shall be duly grateful.

19

Harvest in Harlem

Rev. H. B. FURAY, S.J.
Auriesville, New York

EDITOR'S FOREWORD: Raising the total of parishioners from 318 in 1933 to 6,500 in 1947 through conversions is indeed a remarkable achievement for the priests ministering at St. Charles Borromeo Church in the Harlem district of New York. Located in one of the most congested areas in the world, the parish appeared to be on its last legs in 1933, when nearly all the white parishioners had moved from that neighborhood. Father William J. McCann and his associates, however, had something to say about that. Pitching into the work of recruiting new parishioners among the colored people of the area, the priests labored with zeal, perseverance, and determination that would not brook defeat. The priests at St. Charles have given to us a stirring demonstration of what can be accomplished when an all-out effort is made to win converts for Christ.

❧

A STARTLING PROCESSION

EVEN FIFTEEN YEARS AGO the colored people of New York's uptown Manhattan lived in deepest Africa, so far as familiarity with things Catholic was concerned. In consequence they were considerably startled, one October afternoon in 1933, to observe at close hand a solemn and rather bizarre procession emerging from St. Charles Borromeo Church at 141st Street near Seventh Avenue.

The procession, which brought Sunday promenading to a halt on each of the several streets it traversed, was complete with altar-boys in cassocks and surplices and was climaxed by the resplendent vision of Father (now Monsignor) William McCann enveloped in a gold cape and gravely carrying a large missal. The missal was "just to be carrying something" and was strictly for effect, as indeed was the whole performance.

It was Father McCann's unargumentative but public announcement that, from here out, St. Charles Borromeo's intended to be an official and meaningful part of the life of the district. That the implied promise of the procession has been kept is proven by just two figures. In 1933 there were 318 parishioners in St. Charles and its subsidiary church, St. Aloysius. This year there were some 6,500 in the two. The difference represents an average, over all the years, of about 440 converts annually.

What is unknown is distrusted. Into such an atmosphere came Father William McCann and his brother, Father Walter McCann, when they took over old St. Charles, a magnificent, towering structure. The first years were years of patiently facing down a local attitude of resentment and even open hostility. There were, at first, some street incidents. Today anyone—Catholic or non-Catholic—who is anything but friendly to the priests and sisters of St. Charles is most likely a stranger or, if he is not, will be invited by the neighborhood to become a stranger.

The original procession of 1933 ended in the church, drawing numbers of the onlookers in with it. Questioned, many of these people revealed that they had been coming regularly to St. Charles Church, to attend services or to make visits, for as long as seven years. This was the hint to begin regular (and regularly advertised) convert classes.

Today, after years of planning and careful readjustment, the convert course is divided into twenty-eight sessions, the last three of which cover examinations, rehearsal for baptism, and baptism

✝

You are cordially invited to attend the Catholic Church anytime you may wish to come. Our Church is always open.

The Priests will do everything possible to make you feel at home and will gladly explain anything you may wish to know.

If you think you might be interested in becoming a Catholic you should give your name and address at the Church or Rectory.

The Priests will gladly tell you all you have to know about God and His Church.

You will find it most interesting—simple and enjoyable.

I am interested in becoming a Catholic

Miss
Mrs.
Mr. _____

Address_____ Apt._____

If under 16 years of age check here ☐

Invitation extended by the priests at St. Charles Church and St. Aloysius Church in New York's Harlem district.

itself. The other sessions are all hour-and-a-half classes held twice a week, Monday and Thursday nights. The entire course takes over three and a half months to complete and is given three times a year —right after Labor Day until just before Christmas, from the first of the year until around Easter, and from May until around August 15.

No new members are admitted to the course after lesson seven has been completed. The life of our Lord begins with lesson eight. Experience has shown that those who try to enroll toward the end are the "operators," the "something-for-nothing" folk, who simply must be taught that they cannot make smartness a substitute for sincerity.

Even those who have entered the course before lesson seven but after the first few classes must make up what has been missed in a special class held each Sunday afternoon at four o'clock. Also all instructions missed anywhere in the course, for sickness or any other reason, must be similarly made up.

DIRECT AND PERSONAL QUESTIONS

Catechumens come to Mass each Sunday, and their fulfillment of this duty is checked as carefully as their attendance at class. Regular notices to the home address serve as reminders to absentees. The sincerity of all, even those who have absented themselves, is evidenced by the fact that as many as forty at one time are in the make-up class, catching up.

Two priests give every class, each one taking half of the allotted time. It is a real class, but informal. Questions are in order at any time, and the set teacher policy is to give absolutely straight answers, no matter what the question—and sometimes the questions can be embarrassingly direct and personal. But a straight answer always is the only way to avoid effectually discouraging queries and is also the only way to keep the confidence of people who know no subterfuges when they are sincerely curious.

Stereoptical slides are used extensively in all the classes. The parish has over seven hundred of these on file, "begged, borrowed,

M_____

| FIRST | MIDDLE | LAST NAME |

Attendance 1 · 2 · 3 · 4 · 5 · 6 · 7 · 8 · 9 · 10 · 11 · 12 · 13 · 14 · 15

16 · 17 · 18 · 19 · 20 · 21 · 22 · 23 · 24 · 25 · 26 · 27 · 28 · 29 · 30

Address _____ **Zone** _____ **Apt** _____

Born _____ **Where** _____

Father _____ , **From** _____ **Religion** _____

**Mother's
Maiden Name** _____ **From** _____ **Religion** _____

Past Religion _____ **Baptized** _____ **What Faith** _____

Married 1st To Whom _____ **By Whom** _____

When _____ **Where** _____

Outcome _____

2nd To Whom _____ **By Whom** _____

When _____ **Where** _____

Outcome _____

Now Living Alone? _____ **Separated?** _____ **Divorced?** _____

===

Present Spouse His/Her Religion _____ **If Catholic,
Where Baptized** _____

When Baptized _____

Any Previous Marriage _____ **When** _____

Where _____ **To Whom** _____

Separated _____ **Divorced** _____

When _____ **Spouse Still Living?** _____

Children Name _____ **Age** ____ **Catholic Baptism?** _____

" _____ " ____ " _____

" _____ " ____ " _____

" _____ " ____ " _____

*Attendance record of person attending class of instruction at
St. Charles Church in New York's Harlem Area.*

and stolen over the years"—as Monsignor McCann puts it.

In every group undergoing instructions, spiritual, marital, and general family problems—of varying degrees of seriousness—are uncovered. These must be cleared up before the catechumen is received. It means yet more patient and painstaking work on the part of the priests.

THE FINAL EXAM

The final examination, which closes the formal instruction part of the course, is on the class text, a specially arranged and simplified version of the catechism. The pupils are normally nervous by the time the exams roll around, because these have been much talked up by the instructors and do, after all, mean a great deal in the life of the individual. Nevertheless the catechumens do quite well, a tribute to their attentiveness in class and to the fact that they do study seriously, insofar as their outside duties permit.

In all but one instance the examinations have thus far been oral. The one instance represents an occasion of smart carefulness on the part of one of the priests, which redounded to his confusion. The pupil was a young woman who, it was considered, was much too attractive and well-dressed to be serious about this matter. She was given a difficult, forty-question test, which had been used by Navy chaplains during the war with direly revealing results. She scored a handy thirty-eight out of a possible forty—and the priest slunk furtively from the scene in rich embarrassment.

The climax and reward of the long instructions are, of course, the mass baptisms. Normally, anywhere from thirty to forty visiting priests are present to assist, while a bishop presides. The large church is completely filled with those who are to be baptized, their godparents-to-be, their friends and acquaintances. Many outsiders are present, and invariably some of them are drawn to an interest in the next series of instructions.

What is the supply source of new members for the courses of instruction? The apostolic zeal of neo-converts is one answer. They feel that bringing a friend into the Church is a very concrete way

AN ACT OF CONTRITION

૪

Oh, my God! I am heartily sorry for having offended Thee, and I detest all my sins,

— WHY —

1—Because of Thy just punishments.
2—But most of all, because they offend Thee my God
Who art *all* good and worthy of all my love.

I firmly resolve
with the help of
Thy Grace:

1—To sin no more.
2—To avoid the near occasions of sin.
—*Amen.*

HOW TO GO TO CONFESSION

1. Examine your conscience—what sins did you commit since your last Confession? When was your last Confession?

2. Work up sorrow for your sins—it is only on condition that we are sorry for what we do to offend God that we are forgiven. (Look at a Crucifix.)

3. Promise God that you will try to avoid—not only your sins—but the people, places and things that make it easy for you to sin.

4. On coming into Confession, kneel down on both knees, and when the Priest is ready, bless yourself and say, "*Bless me Father, for I have sinned.*"

5. "This is my first Confession" or "It is a (week) (month) (year) since my last Confession."

6. "*These are my sins*................." (Tell number of TIMES as closely as you can remember.)

7. When you have finished telling your sins, say: "*For these and all my other sins which I can not now remember, I am heartily sorry and beg pardon and absolution of God and of you, Reverend Father.*"

8. Then listen to what the Priest tells you.

9. Listen for your penance—the prayers the Priest will tell you to say—if you do not hear the penance right, ask the Priest to repeat it.

10. The Priest will ask you to say your Act of Contrition.

11. When the Priest has finished giving you absolution, he says, "God bless you." This means that your Confession is over. Get up and leave the box.

12. Kneel down in Church and say your penance immediately. Thank God for His mercy to you.

Card used in preparing negro converts for their First Confession and Holy Communion at St. Charles Church, New York.

of showing their gratitude to our Lord for what has been given them. Another answer lies in the parish school, where about three hundred and fifty children are capably taught by the Sisters of the Blessed Sacrament. Of the first-graders in the school, only fifty percent are Catholic; but the graduating class is ordinarily a hundred percent Catholic. Yet the children, no matter what their insistence, are not allowed to receive baptism unless at least one parent is Catholic—so the children bring their mothers and fathers into the Church.

AN OASIS OF MORALITY AND FRIENDLINESS

How do the new converts stand up? Monsignor McCann's answer is: "Go and watch them." There is an average of five hundred at daily Mass during Lent. At the holy hour, eleven o'clock on New Year's Eve, the church is thronged. The people come armed with horns and clackers and are all set to go out, but first they come to spend the earliest and best time with our Lord.

In a district where overcrowded and underprivileged living conditions tend strongly to produce adult as well as juvenile delinquency, the priests of St. Charles have succeeded—through constant charity and constant hard work—in making the local Catholic Church an oasis of morality and friendliness.

The colored people, so used to being imposed upon, must be sure of a person before they will go on his word. They are sure now of the priests of St. Charles, and the harvest is very great. Of the total eleven hundred converts of all classes, races, and colors in New York in 1946, five hundred were in the parish of St. Charles Borromeo. The work is more than begun; it is well-established. The school problem, the question of vocations, improvement of housing conditions: These are next on the list.

20

The Ordinary Ways of Convert Making

Rev. JOHN T. McGINN, C.S.P.
New York

EDITOR'S FOREWORD: To achieve a definite goal, good intentions are not enough. A definite, practical, well-organized plan of procedure is necessary. Every priest is not only willing but also eager to win souls for Christ. But not every shepherd of souls has a practical and tested plan or method. Father McGinn meets the needs of thousands of clergy by supplying them with a careful, well-balanced, and proven modus operandi. No pastor can read it without being impressed by the thoroughness with which the whole problem has been thought out.

Teaching this subject to the Paulist seminarians, Father McGinn has saturated himself with the literature on the subject and with the accumulated experience of his great community, so singularly rich in traditions of convert work. In addition, he has conferred with many leaders in this field and has been quick to weave into his plan of action whatever techniques have proven fruitful. His article mirrors authentically the thirst for souls, the resourcefulness, and the flaming missionary zeal of the mighty patron of the Paulist Fathers, St. Paul, whose whole apostolate was a tireless, unremitting, ceaseless quest for converts for Christ.

Father McGinn is the director of the Paulist League, an organization of priests and lay people who cooperate with the Paulist Fathers by personal zeal, prayer, and the support of missionary enterprises in the systematic effort to win America for Christ. To offer detailed assistance to busy pastors, he has recently established the practice of issuing each month a release, Techniques for Convert-Makers. *It is a venture well calculated to enrich the labors of priests and to increase mightily the harvest of souls.*

In addition to many spiritual benefits, membership brings a copy of the monthly, The Paulist News, *and keeps the reader* au courant *with the numerous projects launched by the Paulists in spearheading the drive for the conversion of America. We ask all our readers, clerical and lay, to participate in the zealous and inspiring work of the Paulist League by joining it at once.*

THE ORDINARY WAYS OF CONVERT MAKING

THE WRITER takes the view that the American clergy are vividly aware of the necessity of a more systematic and energetic apostolate to the non-Catholics of our country. What they often seek (especially the younger clergy) is a handy outline of the rudimentary precepts which will effectively guide them in their daily ministry among our separated brethren. Convert making, like any other activity, has its simple basic principles. The following pages, therefore, are an attempt to sketch very briefly some of the indispensable requisites for success in the apostolate to Christ's "other sheep."

STEP NUMBER ONE

A PROPER POINT OF VIEW. Our frame of mind regarding any individual or group will profoundly affect our entire relations with them. The man who speaks of Catholics as "papists" betrays the presuppositions which forever act as a barrier to a proper understanding of Roman Catholics. While convert work can be one of the most consoling and fascinating of labors, it requires generous reserves of zeal, persevering patience, and unfailing kindness. And if a priest's primary assumptions regarding non-Catholics are awry, he will vitiate much of the good he hopes to accomplish even when he does not abandon the work as utterly hopeless.

Blessed Peter Favre, an outstanding apostle, considered this matter as of capital importance. "In the first place," he advised, "it is necessary that anyone who desires to be serviceable to heretics of the present age should hold them in great affection and love them very truly, putting out of his heart all thoughts and feelings that tend to their discredit."

The phrase "separated brethren" goes a long way toward indicating the manner in which we should regard the non-Catholics of our parishes. They are our brethren by various titles and in varying degrees. They were fashioned by the same Creator and stem from the same father, Adam. They are involved with us in original sin and in its consequences. They share with us the same destiny, and it was for them as for ourselves that Christ died and established his Church. Furthermore, many of them are validly baptized.

Unfortunately they are estranged brethren. Formerly they lived with us under the same spiritual roof, were nourished by the same Mother Church—and were one in faith, one in Christ, and one in obedience to Christ's Vicar. The tragic differences that cause them now to be outside the Church of Christ are many and far-reaching. But what should dominate our outlook is the fact that so many souls, once of the houses old of the faith, are now denied the fullness of Christ's grace and truth.

The story is told of a traveler who met a little girl, trudging along a dusty road, weighed down by a chubby baby. "Let me help you," he volunteered, "that child is too much for you." "He's not heavy," replied the tot, "he's my *brother*." Burdens become light when borne for those we love.

Regarding non-Catholics as our "separated brethren" cannot but stir us to sympathy and to a vigorous apostolate among them. It will prepare us to encourage any slight tendency on their part to look to their Father's house and to be alert for any small opportunity to facilitate their ultimate return. And it will purify the spirit in which we exercise our zeal. It will purge us of all unconscious meanness, of any attempt at a merely personal or factional victory, of a readiness to strike back for past bigotry. Instead of a warfare by which we seek to vanquish an enemy, we will strive tactfully to be reconciled with a beloved kinsman.

Loyalty to eternal truth and a sensitiveness to its rights should ever characterize our efforts. But if we must demolish error we can still sympathize with those who are enmeshed in error. We can be slow to attribute insincerity to them, patient at their sluggish progress, and jubilant at any minute gain we may achieve in their behalf. Seen in this light, convert work ceases to be a chore to which we go with reluctance and becomes a labor of love.

STEP NUMBER TWO

ENLISTING PRAYERS FOR CONVERSIONS. The longer we engage in convert work the more completely we realize the need of fervent and continuous prayer for conversions. Not many will forget that faith is a free gift of God, but actual experience among non-Catholics brings this truth home to us with ever increasing force and clarity.

The extent of religious ignorance, the plausibility of half-truth, the deep-rooted prejudices of many, the drag of human respect, the vitality of error, the inexplicable fear of the Church, the diabolical nature of bigotry, the weight of past habit, the costly sacrifices, and the painful journey required of many before they come to the light —these and deeper considerations soon persuade us of the paramount necessity of grace. We cannot do a divine work with merely human instruments.

The wise convert-maker will spare himself many unnecessary disappointments if he enlists a crusade of prayer that will precede, accompany, and fructify his own efforts. Unfortunately, the Catholic laity are not fully aware of this need. They do pray for sinners and for the poor souls, but they seldom pray for the conversion of their non-Catholic neighbors until some personal crisis brings this problem into their intimate circle. Indeed, the writer has known convents and seminaries where few, if any, prayers were said for the conversion of our nation. By frequent instructions and exhortations, however, the people can be easily led to widen their spiritual generosity to include the needs of non-Catholics.

All the customary parochial devotions offer opportunities to call this requirement to the attention of the faithful. The local novena services, the holy hour, evening devotions—no one of these should be without a few special prayers for the local convert apostolate. And this will inspire the people to do likewise in their private devotions. Then there are special groups and particular individuals whose cooperation may be easily captured: the teaching and nursing sisters, the local cloistered convent, the school children, the sick and shut-ins, and our devout penitents. To this ever swelling chorus of appeal the priest should add his own personal memento in Holy Mass and the Divine Office.

STEP NUMBER THREE

SOWING THE SEED OF TRUTH. There are many cases of instantaneous conversion but, ordinarily, it is a gradual process and a slow growth. "I have *planted*, Apollos *watered*, but God gave the *increase*" (1 Cor. 3:6). Missionaries from the beginning have recognized three separate stages in the spiritual history of their catechumens: the initial attraction to Catholicism, a growing interest in the Church and in her teachings, and the final decision to become a Catholic.

At these three stages, missionaries have corresponding duties: sowing the seed, nurturing the tender plant, and reaping the harvest. It is with the first of these that we are immediately concerned.

Much of the effort of a priest in reaching for converts must be devoted to the essential, preliminary task of making himself accessible to the non-Catholics of his locality and winning their esteem and good-will. No two parishes will offer precisely the same opportunities for this indispensable preparatory work.

Nevertheless, no locality will be so barren as not to offer numerous occasions to improve the dispositions of its non-Catholic citizens. Personal experience and observation of the methods of successful convert-makers indicate some fruitful approaches that prepare the way for implanting the first inklings of Catholic truth.

1. *Casual contacts.* Each day a priest meets a number of non-Catholics. He should regard every one of them as a potential friend, an influential ally, and a possible convert. If the priest is approachable, affable, and helpful, he will win their friendship, and they will speak well of him to their associates. Father Vieban, the beloved Sulpician, used to say that he never met a non-Catholic without trying to make him a little better disposed toward the Church.

2. *Mixed marriages.* They are often disastrous, but they can be the occasion of conversion. Many non-Catholics are more or less concerned about their lack of religion, and association with an exemplary Catholic often deepens their interest in the Church. Where the local priest keeps in touch with them and is generous with his time, they may often be persuaded to take a full course of instruction. This is one of our most fruitful sources of conversions.

3. *Cultivate community leaders.* Americans, for all their independence, are greatly influenced in their opinions and decisions by the molders of public opinion in their locality. Belloc used to say that before we make it fashionable to be Catholic we must first make it fashionable to sympathize with Catholicism. One of the best ways to accomplish this is to win the support of men of widespread prestige and influence. Some of the people whose good will or animosity greatly affect the local attitude toward the Church are officeholders, public officials, leading businessmen, professional men, editors, radio officials, educators, and other neighborhood notables.

4. *Use the mails.* Priests are notoriously poor at letter writing. Yet there are times when people are especially susceptible to the thoughtfulness of those who drop them only a few lines. A word of congratulation on an anniversary, or a note to one who is honored for some achievement, or the expression of condolence in bereavement has often helped to transform a bigot into a friend. I once knew a man whose son was kidnapped. He afterwards remarked, "I remember every solitary soul who spoke or wrote a kind

word to me that dreadful day."

5. *Cultivate community groups.* Numerous capable convert-makers take a page from the book of public relations experts. They work on the principle that one of the shortcuts to friendly contact with any community is through the organizations which are the rendezvous for large sections of the population. These include the Red Cross, Community Chest, luncheon and professional men's clubs, and associations that represent labor, veterans, farmers, co-operatives, and the like. Cooperation with them, on the part of a priest, is not to be recommended indiscriminately. But association with them is often the door to many private discussions on religion and wins invitations to address larger groups who never enter a Catholic church. Many an exemplary priest has broken the back of bigotry and paved the way for conversions largely through contact with these organizations.

6. *Preaching.* "Faith comes by hearing" (Rom. 10:17). At funerals, weddings, parish anniversaries, and at Easter and Christmas, there are usually some non-Catholics present at Catholic services. If a warm greeting is extended and an invitation to return, and if the sermon is one that gives immediate spiritual help and solid instruction, an immense amount of good can be accomplished. An effort should be made to bring non-Catholics to our missions, Forty Hours, novenas, and parish retreats. Many of them will come if we encourage the laity to invite and accompany them. Some priests arrange for a mission to non-Catholics, an open forum, an inquiry class, or even street preaching, and they either publicize Catholic radio programs or try to conduct one themselves.

7. *Catholic literature.* It is regrettable that only a small segment of Catholic printed matter ever reaches the hands of non-Catholics. Yet the channels of wide circulation are near at hand. The Narbeth Plan, the pamphlet rack in church and in public places, the parochial library, placing Catholic books and periodicals in public libraries, remailing Catholic periodicals, sending pamphlets, papers, or magazines to a selected list of good prospects—all are techniques that have abundantly proved their effectiveness.

No priest will be able to apply all these instruments, nor will any one of these suggestions prove infallibly successful in every case. But the cumulative effect of applying as many as seems feasible will usually produce beneficial results. Of course, no priest can be satisfied merely to create good will and to establish friendly contacts. He should aspire to win neophytes for instruction. But catechumens will come more readily and in greater numbers where the Church is respected and where the local pastor has cultivated cordial relations.

STEP NUMBER FOUR

ENLISTING THE LAITY. However energetic and resourceful a priest may be, there will be many non-Catholics who remain inaccessible to his immediate influence, but his Catholic parishioners are in daily contact with most of these souls. The Catholic laity are known, respected, and trusted. They are present when the non-Catholic asks questions concerning religion, gives voice to his spiritual perplexities, and discusses the problems of the day, most of which have moral or spiritual implications.

Much depends on the manner in which the laity conduct themselves in these discussions. If they are well-informed religiously, tactful, and zealous, they may remove prejudice, create interest in the Catholic outlook, and pave the way for formal instruction by a priest. On such occasions they should invite the non-Catholic to attend Catholic services or an inquiry class. Catholics engaged or married to non-Catholics, and Catholic relatives, friends, and neighbors of well-disposed non-Catholics, have exceptional opportunities to win candidates for instruction.

No matter how widely or continuously a priest announces his eagerness to welcome inquirers, many non-Catholics will not learn of his readiness to assist them, and many who do see one or another of his announcements will be more likely to accept his invitation if it is extended directly by a Catholic friend. Furthermore, it will relieve them of timidity and embarrassment if a Catholic offers to join them on their initial visit to a priest.

It is a mistake to rely exclusively on a few faithful "stand-bys" among the laity. The full momentum of the entire parish is required if best results are to be achieved. Even the lukewarm Catholic may be acquainted with non-Catholics who are ripe for conversion. Frequent instructions and announcements on the apostolic duties and opportunities of the laity, especially on the three Sundays preceding a new inquiry class, will awaken and strengthen their ardor. The measure of their interest and cooperation will often determine the number who come for instruction. The writer knows four laymen each of whom has been the means of directing twenty-five people to the Catholic Church!

STEP NUMBER FIVE

THE INQUIRY CLASS. It is becoming customary for the well-organized parish to include an inquiry class among its manifold activities. Some form of group instruction for converts was always practiced in the Church. The modern inquiry class is nothing more than an adaptation of the ancient catechumenate. It is winning increasing favor among the ablest of American priests because it results in mounting conversions with a relative economy of effort and time.

To begin with, the class creates the conditions under which moderately curious or interested non-Catholics may be successfully persuaded to study the Catholic religion. Despite widespread prejudice or indifference, increasing numbers of non-Catholics are more or less attracted to the Church. Their concern is not deep enough to induce them to assume the initiative and to apply for a formal course of individual instruction. Where there is no methodical technique designed to aid and encourage them, they remain friendly but seldom advance.

The group instruction plan, however, capitalizes on their good dispositions, removes their hesitations, and facilitates their instruction. It welcomes all comers, no matter what their motive or however slight their interest. It demands no previous intention of joining the Church. People are assured that they may come to one or to all the lessons as they choose. Since the class meets twice a week at a definite time and place, they are certain that our invitation is sincere and cordial and that every effort has been made to suit their convenience. Because it is continuous, they know they can begin the course at any time. These and other considerations combine to reduce to a minimum the difficulty of persuading them to consider the full case for Catholicism. Thus the class succeeds in bringing people to instruction who would not otherwise entertain the notion.

The second great merit of the class is that it is a time-saver for the clergy. It thus permits an ambitious parochial campaign for converts on a scale more commensurate with our obligations and opportunities. While the clergy recognize the necessity of a plan that will embrace large numbers of inquirers, they are deterred by the many other insistent duties they must fulfill. Yet most priests can arrange to devote two evenings a week to this activity. Where there is a class, they can multiply their neophytes without prohibitive demands on their time and energy. Priests who are not content with half-measures in making converts, yet are conscientious about their other duties, find that the most practical solution is class instruction for inquirers.

The priest who plans such a class studies his community and the character of its people. He selects two evenings a week, at a time and place that will best suit the convenience of his prospects. The size of his class will depend upon many factors, but much will hinge on how well he publicizes the course.

The writer has found the following devices most efficacious: Sunday Mass announcements; announcements in cooperating parishes; the parish bulletin; "ads" in the diocesan paper and in the daily press, along with occasional news items in both; handbills; a poster in the vestibule of the church and one placed on the lawn. Some of these attracted non-Catholics directly, and others reached Catholics who in turn invited non-Catholics to attend. The zealous Catholic laity are, unquestionably, the most fruitful source of catechumens.

Conducting the Class. The first meeting may not attract an overflow crowd, but persistent application will increase attendance gradually. The writer once began with a group of ten inquirers that later grew to one hundred. The initial gathering is of exceptional importance, since many will come with misgivings. But if the instructor is cordial and affable, he will soon establish a relationship of confidence and friendliness.

The director should explain that his purpose is to present, objectively, the teachings and practices of the Catholic Church, that there will be no charge for the course, and that no intention of joining the Church is required. He ought to stress the need of God's grace, to encourage prayer, and invite all to participate in the few prayers that open and conclude each class. He promises to explain one fundamental topic each evening and invites questions on that subject. Other questions he engages to answer before or after each class, at which time he is ready to provide books or pamphlets as supplementary reading. Each catechumen should receive a copy of the catechism and study it at leisure.

Early in the course, the priest should obtain pertinent information concerning the inquirers and record it on library cards: name, address, telephone; present religious affiliation; whether baptized or not, validly or invalidly; married or single, and any previous marriage. This card might also list the nature of the individual's difficulties, literature borrowed, any insight gained as to his dispositions and progress, and lectures attended or missed.

Some individual instruction will be required in every case. Each person will have his special problems which he may be reluctant to reveal or discuss in public. Some will miss lectures unavoidably, and these must be made up, while others will need special attention on matters that prove no problem to the remainder of the class. It is advisable for the priest to make it a practice to be in attendance a half-hour before and after each lecture. He can thus keep in close personal touch with his neophytes and may then arrange for longer, personal interviews when necessary or desirable.

It's the writer's experience that considerably over half of those who complete the instructions enter the Church immediately, even though many may not have foreseen this when they started. Others may delay for a while because of indecision or the opposition of their associates, but are received shortly after. Some may lack the gift of faith, but if the priest offers continued assistance, they may still be won. I know five priests who have each received one thousand converts into the Church; every one of them is an ardent advocate of the inquiry class.

STEP NUMBER SIX

INSTRUCTING CONVERTS. Two lessons a week for a period of three months is the ordinary practice. Any more would cause undue delay, excepting extraordinary cases; any less would be insufficient to assimilate the basic teachings of the Church. An excellent text is *A Catechism for Inquirers,* by Joseph I. Malloy, C.S.P. Additional reading in books and pamphlets should be provided according to the needs, leisure, and capacity of the catechumen. It hardly needs be added that the instructor should have a high regard for the teaching office and bring zeal, consecration, and enthusiasm to his task. A pattern to help the instructor to assemble and present his material ought to include the following elements:

1. *Doctrine.* Love and service of God depend upon accurate knowledge of God. If a man's convictions about God are wrong, as in the case of pagans and heretics, he cannot really love and serve God as he intended. Hence there should be a solid core of doctrine at the heart of every instruction. The widespread ignorance of the fundamental teachings of Christ makes this ever more imperative today. Humor, social amenities, individual difficulties, spiritual reflections, proof—all these have a legitimate place in the instructions. But they should not divert us from the essential task of telling the inquirer exactly what Catholics believe. The tragic penalties among converts for insufficient doctrinal instruction are superficiality, sentimentality, a religion of mere external practice, and, sometimes, defection from the Church.

2. *Clarity.* The catechism, like many of the world's great books, is small, but its simplicity is deceptive. It is a handy compendium of the fundamental dogmatic and moral teachings of Mother Church, but it deals in baffling mysteries, with the utmost brevity, and often in a highly technical language. In reality, it is a digest of

what the catechumen is expected to know at the completion of the course. Few books clamor so loudly for an accurate, lucid interpreter, who has learned how to make profound truths intelligible. Some aids to clarity that deserve special mention are explaining unfamiliar terms, concentrating on the essentials in each lesson rather than preoccupation with those problems which may well be left to the erudite, and the liberal use of stories, illustrations, and comparisons. Successful catechists preserve in a notebook or file anecdotes, proofs, and illustrations that they gather from reading, experience, or reflection.

3. *Relevancy*. Most inquirers share the secularist heresy which regards Catholic dogma as an academic matter that has little or no bearing on the insistent problems of the day. In our time it is not sufficient to say: "This is what Catholics believe." We must go on from there to explain: "And this is what the doctrine means to you, your family, your nation, and the world." To neglect this aspect of each lesson is frequently to leave unanswered the widest and most persistent of modern difficulties regarding the faith. In this section of the lesson we should try to put ourselves in the position of the inquirer. From that vantage point we might ask ourselves one of two questions: (1) What enduring question of mankind does this catechism chapter answer? (2) What help does it hold out to needy, troubled men? Thus, the chapter on the Trinity is the Catholic answer to the question, "What is God like?" The chapter on confession is the Catholic answer to the question, "Is there any sure release from the burden of sin?"

4. *Spirituality*. An inquirer must acquire facility in the "how" of Catholicism as well as in the "what" and "why" of it. While conversion is primarily a change of religious conviction, it is not complete until the moral and religious aspects of his personality undergo a similar transformation. It is a mistake to wait until actual reception before urging him to begin to lead the Catholic life. Most non-Catholics are unaccustomed to any regular religious practice and must be gradually habituated to the moral habits and devotional practices of Catholics. Consequently, no lesson is complete that does not assist the neophyte in the progressive readjustment

of his ideals and in adopting the religious devotions that follow upon awakening doctrinal convictions. This must be done tactfully, and no one should be pressed to undertake religious exercises that he cannot perform with sincerity. But most inquirers can be persuaded to pray, genuflect, and attend Mass and Benediction. A tour through the church, an explanation of the Mass, and an acquaintance with the prayer book and missal are essential. Suggested reading should include books or pamphlets on the spiritual life, the saints, and reading of the four Gospels.

5. *Review*. Each instruction should begin with a brief résumé of the chapters already covered. This will clarify matters insufficiently grasped, will aid the memory, and will show the context in which the new lesson will find its proper place. The instructor himself, after a lifetime of study and reflection, is constantly receiving new insights into the mysteries of the faith, so he can hardly expect the catechumen to grasp, at first hearing, more than a few of the implications of Christ's truth. Besides, the review will show the vital unity of Christian truth and will impart a balanced perspective so necessary in the formation of a truly Catholic mind.

STEP NUMBER SEVEN

THE FOLLOW-UP. It is obvious that the convert will be in need of aftercare following his actual reception into the Church. In many ways he will long remain a novice. No matter how skillfully the priest has imparted the instructions or how receptive the inquirer has been, it is impossible to convey in twenty lessons the abounding riches of Catholic truth and grace. The born Catholic has been blessed by exemplary parents, a Catholic home, and a Catholic education. He has known close association with good priests and nuns and has been surrounded by Catholic influences from infancy. Something akin to these inestimable advantages must be supplied for the convert after he makes his entrance into the Church. His grasp of Catholic dogma and morality must increase so that he will possess a truly Catholic outlook. His devotional and spiritual life should expand. His docility to his pastor, bishop, and to the pope should deepen. Yet the habits of a lifetime will often militate against this, his relatives and associates may throw obstacles in his path, and the secular atmosphere in which he lives will not be conducive to growth in the faith.

Priests, nuns, and the laity must all understand the needs of our newly converted brethren and be alert to come to their aid when opportunity or necessity arises. There will be a more or less awkward period of adjustment wherein the convert gradually grows accustomed to his new surroundings, becomes less and less uncomfortable and self-conscious, and comes to conduct himself as a Catholic "to the manner born." Then should follow a period of rich spiritual development wherein all the powers of his personality will expand, strengthen, and grow. If this does not continue, he may become a kind of associate member of the Church, censorious and only half-converted. Certainly, if he is to persevere until death, he must eventually learn self-reliance. He cannot be forever coddled. But his early days in the fold are critical, and he has a right to our understanding and support.

Where the convert remains in the parish in which he was instructed, the priest he has come to know may keep a watchful eye upon him. The nomadic conditions of modern life render this increasingly difficult, but if the instructor has kept a record of his inquirers, he may maintain contact by an occasional note. The writer has learned that even a Christmas card will encourage converts to reveal difficulties that have arisen and offers the opportunity to come to their aid.

Much can be accomplished if the laity are coached as to their duties and opportunities in this matter. Many former Protestants have been accustomed to a strong social bond among the members of a religious congregation. Other converts lack facility in making acquaintances. But if lay Catholics are quick to offer their friendship and to assist the convert with tact and generosity, many difficulties will be surmounted.

The writer has nothing but praise for those convert clubs that are everywhere multiplying. They offer perhaps the best solution to the problem of the convert who might otherwise remain isolated, lonely, or alien within the fold. These clubs usually project a yearly program which is a happy balance of social and educational activities. They bring together people who have similar interests and needs. They serve to channel the talents of our new converts in advancing the apostolate to non-Catholics; indeed, converts often become the best convert-makers.

It would be fantastic, humanly speaking, to say that America can be easily or swiftly converted, but a wide mission experience convinces me that every parish has a surprisingly large number of non-Catholics who are extremely close to Catholicism. If the clergy were to apply themselves, prayerfully and perseveringly, to the ordinary ways of convert-making, we would soon multiply the number of converts now received. Once convert work becomes one of the ordinary, customary activities of each of our priests, the conversion of our country will be well under way.

21

Summing Up

Rev. JOHN A. O'BRIEN, Ph.D.

CAREFUL PERUSAL of the preceding chapters drives home to the reader the fact that there are certain significant developments in convert work which are worthy of being singled out for special stress. Accordingly, we undertake in this closing chapter to enumerate a few of the outstanding means and methods by which both priests and laymen can win souls for Christ.

GROUP INSTRUCTION PLAN

Perhaps the most significant fact brought out in the whole study is the remarkable fruitfulness resulting from the use of the group instruction plan. Virtually every parish reporting an unusually high total of converts is using that method. In parishes where the instructions had been given individually, it was found that the adoption of the class plan doubled or tripled the average annual total previously received. Priests who had been skeptical about the plan became enthusiastic after using it and perceiving the economy of effort and the vastly greater results achieved.

Moreover, the people being instructed usually prefer the class method, where they can relax and be more at ease than when the individual is the soul target of the priest's oratorical efforts. Furthermore, they profit by the questions occasionally asked by others and frequently derive added courage to take the step which they see many others likewise preparing to take.

The class method should always be supplemented, of course, by abundant individual contact and instruction. By coming to the room a half-hour or so before the instruction begins, the priest—better still if several are available—will be able to meet each individual and to have a little chat with each one and thus find out how the individual is progressing and ascertain whether or not he needs some individual attention. By remaining for a little while after the class, the priest will be able to have additional private conferences with similar good results. In addition, there should be definite appointments for conferences with each individual to make sure that the person has no obstacles to his entrance into the Church and to give him some advice, instruction, and encouragement suited to his needs. The discerning priest will be quick to size up the amount of time and help to be given to each individual after the first or second talk with the person.

So impressive have been the results from the group instruction plan that some bishops have already requested all their pastors to institute the inquiry class and to conduct it two or three times a year. The class of instruction usually is held twice a week, for about three months. Particularly during the last month, all the members are given individual conferences and are provided all the help and encouragement to make an affirmative decision in the matter.

ENLIST LAITY

The study brings out clearly that the enlistment of our laity in convert work is urgently needed if we are to win constantly increasing numbers of converts. That achievement will require the joint efforts of all the priests and all our Catholic laity. The strange and disturbing fact to all students of the convert movement is the failure to educate the laity concerning their duty of assisting in the work of winning souls.

"Why, the idea of trying to win a convert," a lay friend said to us recently, "never even occurred to me. Like practically all other Catholic acquaintances of mine, I have always assumed that the proper thing to do was to avoid discussion of religion with non-Catholics. Hence, in all my life I have never tried to bring a non-Catholic to Mass with me or to loan him a Catholic book, or to suggest that he come with me to a priest to receive a good course of instruction in the Catholic religion." In that utterance there was mirrored, we think, the attitude of probably ninety-nine per cent of the Catholic lay men and women of our land.

Is it not evident that we must launch a vigorous and determined crusade on a national scale to dissipate such apathy and to make clear to all our laity the divinely appointed duty of striving to win souls for Christ? Obviously, sermons must be preached frequently on this subject. Articles, pamphlets, and books must be written on this general theme and be widely circulated among our people.

We must point out to our people the spectacular growth of the Witnesses of Jehovah—a growth of more than a thousand percent in six years—due to the crusading missionary zeal of all their members. How deeply stirred our Catholic laity will be when they learn that if we registered the same proportionate gains as the Witnesses of Jehovah, the people of America would be won for Christ and for the Church founded directly and immediately by him. That tremendous achievement would have been effected in less than the six years taken by the Witnesses to achieve their growth.

COURSES IN SEMINARIES

Our seminaries hold the key to the solution of the convert problem in America. In their hallowed halls our future priests are trained. It is evident that training in the technique of recruiting prospects and instructing them must be given in the seminary. In addition, there must be imparted to them that quenchless thirst for souls which will drive them in all their priestly years to search, in season and out of season, for the sheep that are lost, strayed, or stolen.

If convert work is presented as an integral part of the priestly ministry, they will not wait after their ordination for prospects to ring the rectory doorbell. They will go out after them. They will spend two or three hours each day in looking up prospects and in arranging for their instruction. Recall the observation, of the Chicago pastor who won 1,300 converts in 21 years, that a minimum of two hours a day should be spent by every priest in convert work.

At Kenrick Seminary, as at other major seminaries, definite instruction in convert work was given to the seminarians, particularly to the members of the Brownson Club organized for this purpose. The results which those members have achieved since their ordination have been striking indeed.

Flinging themselves with all their youthful energy and determination into the apostolate for the strayed sheep, they have succeeded in winning thousands back into the fold. They have given a stirring demonstration of what our seminarians can achieve on a nationwide scale when definite training in convert work is given for at least the four years preceding ordination.

The long summer vacation offers an excellent opportunity for the seminarians to put into practice the training they are receiving in the seminary. They can assist their respective pastors by looking up prospects and fallen-aways and by selling the young men on the idea of joining the Convert Makers of America and becoming faithful and zealous workers in that organization.

Making a house-to-house canvass, the seminarian will acquire a world of experience in the important art of "selling" the religion of Christ to the non-church-going people who fill most of the homes in every city block. In this way seminarians will supplement their theoretical training in the seminary with field work in the parish so that they will be experienced in all the techniques of convert work, including that of class instruction, by the time of their ordination.

If every seminary in our country would stress convert making and, like the Paulist seminary at Washington, institute a four-year course in it and give its students the opportunity for field work, we would have an army of 40,000 expert leaders to direct the labors of our 25,000,000 laity along efficient and fruitful lines. There is no doubt that in this way our seminaries would play the role of quarterback in calling the signals that would lead to the gathering of the great white harvest in America for the divine Master.

RECLAIMING FALLEN-AWAYS

In our zeal in searching for converts, we must not forget our fallen-aways and those who are in the process of lapsing. Recent studies disclose that the number of fallen-aways is far greater than most of us have imagined. Let us offer an illustration. In a community where we had just completed a public course of lectures for non-Catholics and had secured the assurance of twenty-five members of the class that they were going to embrace the faith, we got the jolt of our life. At just about that time a house-to-house canvass of the entire city had been completed by the Victory Noll catechists.

The cards of people living within the limits of that particular parish and claiming to be Catholics were turned over to the pastor. Imagine his surprise when, in going through the cards, he discovered not less that 885 souls registered as Catholics, of whom he had no trace in the parish register. The total souls listed in that parish amounted to 2,325. This meant that a number equal to one-third of his listed parishioners were lax in the practice of the faith, maintained no definite practical affiliation, offered no regular financial support, or were entirely out of the Church.

The incident we have cited has occurred in substantially the same form in hundreds of communities where a careful house-to-house canvass has been made. "For years," remarked a pastor recently, "I have prided myself upon knowing my people. I have made it a practice to take a daily walk in the parish. I have instructed my parishioners to notify me when a new family moves into the parish so I can affiliate such a family at once.

"A short time ago the ministerial association and the YMCA sponsored a house-to-house canvass. When the cards of people who registered as Catholics, and as residing within my parish limits, were turned over to me, I got the shock of my life. Hundreds of people of whom I had never even heard had registered as baptized Catholics. I'm convinced now that this is typical of what would be found in most of our city parishes."

Many similar investigations compel us to concur with the conclusion of that zealous shepherd of souls. The winning of America for Christ involves two important plans of campaign. One is to win those who have not been born in the faith; the other is to hold all those who have inherited at birth the precious patrimony of the true faith. Priests and people need to launch a vigorous and well-organized campaign to discover any Catholics who are lapsing or who have already fallen away and reclaim them to the active and fervent practice of the faith of Christ.

In that important campaign, our seminarians can play a key role by conducting the house-to-house canvass during their summer vacation and by helping the pastor in instructing and in reclaiming these members of the household of the faith, who stand in urgent need of remedial treatment.

OPEN FORUM

Some forty years ago we visited the cathedral in Denver, where Father Hugh L. McMenamin was conducting an open forum each Sunday evening. He used it as a feeder for his convert classes, which enabled himself and his priestly associates to achieve an average of about 64 converts, year after year. This device has proven effective along these lines in many places. In visiting the Farm Street Church in London we found that a variation of it in the form of a pulpit dialogue was being employed with success. A priest in one pulpit proposed questions and difficulties which were answered by a priest in another pulpit. We followed this plan on Sunday evenings during Lent at St. John's Church at the University of Illinois with profitable results.

Recently we visited Grand Rapids, where we found the pulpit dialogues conducted by the two Paulist Fathers in charge of the newly established Catholic information center attracting large crowds of people, both Catholic and non-Catholic. We present the program of such pulpit dialogues, along with the information concerning the same given on the back of the program, as we feel pastors of parishes where there are two or more priests will be interested in making greater use of this device of attracting larger numbers of non-Catholics to an exposition of Catholic faith and practice. Since the crucial problem in winning converts is that of recruiting prospects, we think that the open forum or the pulpit dialogues will prove of increasing usefulness along these lines.

USE OF THE RADIO

Because it reaches so many people, the radio has become an important instrument for the dissemination of Catholic truth. A number of splendid Catholic programs are now being broadcast. The more the better. In some of the programs we are considerably limited in the presentation of distinctive doctrines and practices of the Catholic religion. It is to be hoped that we will find increasing opportunity to present in a friendly, expositional manner the principal doctrines and practices of our faith. Monsignor J. A. Gabriels informs us that he uses his broadcast each Sunday to interest hearers in the classes of instruction which he and his assistants are constantly conducting at the Church of the Resurrection in Lansing, Michigan.

His experience indicates how helpful it would be if pastors could arrange to speak over local radio stations each week and thus interest many more non-Catholics in the investigation of the religion of Jesus Christ. We feel that we have just scratched the surface as far as the use of the radio is concerned for the winning of souls for Christ. It will richly repay us to study carefully how we can make greater use of this marvel of the air for the advancement of the truths of Christ.

NEWSPAPER PUBLICITY

The contributors to this work have pointed out the rich returns they have derived from the use of newspaper publicity. In some instances, the story can be put across in the form of a news item. In other cases, a paid advertisement is inserted. Because the newspaper goes into thousands of homes in which no Catholic priest would ordinarily enter, it is worthwhile to have our invitation to classes of instruction printed in the daily newspaper. Every priest

The Catholic Information Center

Presents

Nine Wednesday Evening

PULPIT DIALOGUES

Given by

The Paulist Fathers

Cathedral of Saint Andrew

Wednesdays at Eight O'Clock

October 15

RELIGION: So Stuffy!

October 22

COMMANDMENTS: No Fun!

October 29

CHRIST: A Good Man!

November 5

CHURCH: Don't Need It!

November 12

WORSHIP: My Own Way!

November 19

SIN: Can Priests Forgive It?

November 26

DEATH: That's All!

December 3

MARRIAGE: A Private Affair!

December 10

CATHOLIC LIFE: Superstitious!

Hear Catholic Truth Defended
Against Modern Indifference

Interesting   Informative   Challenging

All Cordially Invited

The Pulpit Dialogues

In 1946 more than 100,000 Americans asked to be received into the Catholic Church For the first time they saw that all the Catholic Church taught was true.

Most of them had some help from the Catholic laity — an invitation to Mass, or to a lecture, a pamphlet, or a book, an introduction to a priest, and, of course, prayers

In arranging these Pulpit Dialogues we feel sure that our Catholic people will welcome this opportunity of inviting their non-Catholic friends to hear an exposition of Catholic teachings For those who are not of our faith are often eager to test the soundness of the arguments underlying the doctrines of the Catholic Church

Many have been reluctant to investigate the Church because they fear embarrassment or because they fear to intrude upon Catholic services. These fears should have no substance now These Pulpit Dialogues have been arranged for the purpose of eliminating all grounds for timidity or apprehension They will be given primarily to enlighten our non-Catholic brethren in regard to the doctrines which the Catholic Church teaches and pratcices.

We the Paulist Fathers, of the Catholic Information Center, welcome you, therefore, and hope you will take advantage of this opportunity to hear Catholic truth explained. In your family circle, or, certainly, among your friends, there are many who will appreciate your invitation to hear these Pulpit Dialogues. Their chance to learn Catholic' truth may depend no you

If this invitation should come to any who by birth, heritage or training should be practical Catholics, and who are not such now, let it be a reminder to them that now is the acceptable time to return to the Sacraments and enjoy the peace which they impart.

Any of the priests of your parish will be happy to facilitate your return to the Church

The Question Box

Anyone may ask any questions about the Catholic Church Questions should be written and placed in the box at the door of the church. No name or address need be used, unless a reply is desired by mail

Class of Instruction

We hope that many who attend these Pulpit Dialogues will wish to continue their investigation of the Catholic Religion For these there will be a Class of Instruction Opportunity to join this class will be announced during the series of Pulpit Dialogues

Pamphlets

A pamphlet dealing with the subjects discussed during Pulpit Dialogues can be secured in the vestibule of the church

Father John F Ritzius, CSP
Father Paul V Maloney, CSP

who has thus used the newspaper will testify to the appearance at his class of people of whose existence he was previously completely unaware.

The Religious Information Bureau, under the direction of Father Lester J. Fallon, C.M., and under the sponsorship of the Knights of Columbus of Missouri, is doing an outstanding job in bringing to the people of that state a knowledge of many of the teachings and practices of the Catholic faith through carefully prepared advertisements.

Many persons whose interest is thus aroused are provided with pamphlets and, if the interest warrants it, are offered the complete course of instruction by mail provided by the Confraternity Home Study Service. Father Fallon informs us that a considerable number of converts, instructed through his correspondence course, owe their initial interest to these carefully worded advertisements.

If the Knights of Columbus and other Catholic organizations in other states could be enlisted to sponsor similar campaigns of paid advertisements, we would go a long way toward removing the veil now hiding so much of the Catholic faith from the minds of our fellow countrymen. Think of reaching our non-Catholic compatriots through weekly advertisements, giving to them important insights into many of the doctrines and practices of the Catholic faith which are so often misunderstood!

DISTRIBUTION OF PAMPHLETS

Because of its small and compact character, the pamphlet fits into the hurried, staccato tempo of our day. It is an admirable medium of getting across a knowledge of the basic teachings of our holy faith to the non-Catholic population. The Witnesses of Jehovah are doing an outstanding job in the distribution of such literature. Their phenomenal growth testifies eloquently to the efficacy of such efforts. We make an earnest plea for the installation of pamphlet racks displaying fifty to a hundred titles in the vestibule of every Catholic church in our land.

We urge likewise our Catholic laity to form the habit of taking home with them each Sunday a pamphlet, reading it carefully themselves, and then loaning it to a dozen or more non-Catholic friends. In this way we shall blanket America with pamphlets and shall use them as a means of recruiting millions of prospects for courses of systematic instruction in the Catholic faith. We have but scratched the surface of the usefulness of the pamphlet for convert work; we recommend the use of this pocket-sized literature to every Catholic man and woman as a helpful means of enabling them to win each year several converts for Christ.

THE PAULIST MAGAZINE

The Paulist Fathers have established a monthly magazine, *Information*, designed particularly for convert work. It is of the digest size and is brimful of helpful suggestions for the winning of converts. It features the conversions of many leading persons and shows the line of reasoning which has appealed to each. We recommend every Catholic family subscribe to this magazine so that it may receive abundant help and guidance in the fulfillment of its divinely appointed task of winning converts for Christ.

THE PAULIST LEAGUE

The Paulist League has been formed by the Paulist Fathers for the specific purpose of winning America for Christ. Its members receive a monthly release, *The Paulist News*, which keeps them informed of developments in the convert field. The members are asked to cooperate with the Paulist Fathers by works of personal zeal, by prayer and by the support of missionary enterprises. Holy Mass is offered daily for the welfare of all members. They share in all the Masses, prayers, and good works of all the Paulist Fathers and in the prayers and Communions of all Paulist candidates for the priesthood. Additional spiritual privileges are granted by the Holy See. Membership is as follows: individual, $1.00; associate, $2.00; family, $5.00; life, $100.00. We encourage all our readers to join the Paulist League and thus supply reinforcements to the zealous and tireless workers who are spearheading the Church's drive for the winning of America for Christ.

CONVERSIONS AMONG NEGROES

The national survey we conducted brings out clearly the unusually fruitful field that is to be found for convert work among our Negro brethren. The largest number of converts are being won today in those parishes which are ministering to our colored countrymen. They stand in need of the help, comfort, and strength provided by the religion of Jesus Christ. They respond with appreciation to the priests and people who strive to bring to them the knowledge of Christ's saving truths. By redoubling our efforts to win these souls for Christ, we shall render a great service to the Church.

The communists are working overtime in their feverish efforts to indoctrinate these good people with the teachings of Marx and Engels. We have at the present a very small percentage of the Negroes of the United States in the Catholic fold. The work of the pastors in colored parishes, who are winning 200 and more converts annually, shows us clearly that we all must roll up our sleeves and pitch wholeheartedly into the divinely appointed task of bringing the full gospel of Christ to enrich and emancipate and beautify the lives of our colored brethren.

INSTRUCTION BY MAIL

The study shows that there are thousands of people who are hesitant about ringing a rectory doorbell and asking for a course of instruction. We can meet the need of that vast multitude by making known to them the availability of instruction by mail. Not only in country districts where no Catholic church exists, but also in large cities there are many people who would prefer to receive the first information about the Catholic faith through the mail. Hence, we suggest that priests and people make more widely known the availability of such correspondence courses free of charge. Doubtless if we could get across this information to millions of non-Catholics, the Confraternity Home Study Service would be ministering to a far greater clientele than it is now reaching.

While sooner or later a priest must come personally into the picture, evidence clearly indicates that in the initial stages the mailman is a more acceptable caller at the door. We hope that this splendid service will grow by leaps and bounds and that, as the misunderstandings and prejudices of our non-Catholic neighbors are dissipated, they will welcome as among their dearest and best friends the priest of Jesus Christ.

A HOLY CRUSADE

If this symposium brings out any one truth clearly, it is that the conversion of America will demand more than the efforts of 40,000 priests. We must make our lay people convert-minded. We must preach to them in season and out of season the duty of winning souls for Christ. We must fill them with a flaming zeal for the propagation of the faith of Christ. We must fill them with a divine discontent until each individual has formed the habit of winning several souls for Christ annually. What the Witnesses of Jehovah have done, we, too, can do—and more.

Peter the Hermit went through the countries of Europe preaching the need of a crusade to rescue the Holy Land from the hands of the Mohammedans. His cry was, "God wills it!" We, too, must sound that crusading cry in every parish and outmission of our land. We must echo and re-echo the words of Christ addressed to all his disciples: "Going therefore teach ye all nations . . . teaching them to observe all things whatsoever I have commanded you" (Matt. 28:19–20).

We can be sure of the assistance promised us by the divine Master when he said: "And behold I am with you all days, even to the consummation of the world" (Matt. 28:19–20). With that divine assistance we cannot fail. St. John sounds the keynote of our ultimate success in those prophetic words: "This is the victory which overcometh the world—our faith" (1 John 5:4).